Praise for This Book

"A solid text on autoethnography that balances epistemological and methoc this text addresses that gap."

—Kenneth Fasching-Varner, Louisiana State University

"This text proposes activities that aim to teach self-reflexivity and explicate how to engage in autoethnographic inquiry. Such a hands-on, applied approach is key for learning this mode of inquiry."

—Amy Heuman, Texas Tech University

"Impressive in its scope, the text is intuitively sequenced, incorporates a tremendous amount of relevant information, as well as examples that leave the reader craving more."

—Lois McFadyen Christensen, University of Alabama at Birmingham

"The material in this book is well researched and offers a wide array of specific theories and methods with which to ground your work."

—Jeanne L Surface, University of Nebraska Omaha

"This exhaustively-researched text is the most comprehensive work on the subject that I have encountered."

—Peter H. Khost, Stony Brook University-SUNY

"This book provides not only a particularly clear overview and historical framing of the methodology; it invites readers into a meaningful and critical enactment and experience with autoethnography."

—Angela C. Coffee, Century College

"This book has the potential to open up the concept of autoethnography in many creative and inspiring ways."

—Mirka Koro-Ljungberg, Arizona State University

"As practitioners, visionaries, scholars, and researchers we have access to a text that wonderfully examines the complexities and nuances of autoethnography in a way that can be useful both inside and outside the classroom."

—Joquina Reed, Texas A&M International University

"A very thorough and thoughtful introduction to and explanation of autoethnography. This text explores the historical foundations, theoretical frameworks, and future directions of autoethnography as both process and product."

—Xyanthe Neider, Washington State University

"I am much more informed about autoethnography because of this text; while there was much I knew, I learned so many things reading through this book."

—Nicholas E. Husbye, University of Missouri, St. Louis

SAGE was founded in 1965 by Sara Miller McCune to support the dissemination of usable knowledge by publishing innovative and high-quality research and teaching content. Today, we publish over 900 journals, including those of more than 400 learned societies, more than 800 new books per year, and a growing range of library products including archives, data, case studies, reports, and video. SAGE remains majority-owned by our founder, and after Sara's lifetime will become owned by a charitable trust that secures our continued independence.

Los Angeles | London | New Delhi | Singapore | Washington DC | Melbourne

AUTOETHNOGRAPHY

PROCESS, PRODUCT, AND POSSIBILITY FOR CRITICAL SOCIAL RESEARCH

SHERICK A. HUGHES
University of North Carolina at Chapel Hill

JULIE L. PENNINGTON
University of Nevada, Reno

Los Angeles | London | New Delhi
Singapore | Washington DC | Melbourne

FOR INFORMATION:

SAGE Publications, Inc.
2455 Teller Road
Thousand Oaks, California 91320
E-mail: order@sagepub.com

SAGE Publications Ltd.
1 Oliver's Yard
55 City Road
London EC1Y 1SP
United Kingdom

SAGE Publications India Pvt. Ltd.
B 1/I 1 Mohan Cooperative Industrial Area
Mathura Road, New Delhi 110 044
India

SAGE Publications Asia-Pacific Pte. Ltd.
3 Church Street
#10-04 Samsung Hub
Singapore 049483

Acquisitions Editor: Helen Salmon
Development Editor: Eve Oettinger
Editorial Assistant: Chelsea Pearson
Production Editor: Veronica Stapleton Hooper
Copy Editor: Judy Selhorst
Typesetter: C&M Digitals (P) Ltd.
Proofreader: Sally Jaskold
Indexer: Jean Casalegno
Cover Designer: Karine Hovsepian
Marketing Manager: Susannah Goldes

Names: Hughes, Sherick A., author. | Pennington, Julie L., author.

Title: Autoethnography : process, product, and possibility for critical social research / Sherick Hughes, University of North Carolina at Chapel Hill, Julie Pennington, University of Nevada, Reno.

Description: Thousand Oaks : SAGE, [2017] | Includes bibliographical references and index.

Identifiers: LCCN 2016027363 | ISBN 9781483306766 (pbk.)

Subjects: LCSH: Ethnology—Authorship. | Ethnology—Research.

Classification: LCC GN307.7 H84 2017 | DDC 305.42—dc23
LC record available at https://lccn.loc.gov/2016027363

16 17 18 19 20 10 9 8 7 6 5 4 3 2 1

• Brief Contents •

• Detailed Contents •

PART II • DOING AUTOETHNOGRAPHY: FROM BRAINSTORMING TO GUIDING PROCESS   55

Chapter 5. Third Guiding Process: Synthesizing New-Self Insights With MICA   110

With George Noblit

PART III • THE FUTURE OF AUTOETHNOGRAPHY: A PRISM OF POSSIBILITY   143

Chapter 6. The Possibility of Autoethnography as Critically Reflexive Action Research   144

Chapter 7. Anticipating the Future of Autoethnography as Critical Social Research   168

Appendixes   195

• Preface •

At campus events, it is not unusual to find me singing the fight song of my alma mater, the University of North Carolina at Chapel Hill. With the first thunderous clap, I join the rhythm and singing of the refrain, "I'm a Tarheel born, I'm a Tarheel bred and when I die, I'm a Tarheel dead. . . ." Unlike many of the fellow alumni with whom I sing at the state's public flagship, I am quite literally a Tarheel born and whose family was enslaved and bred in the Tarheel state in the 1800s. Having that little nugget of knowledge about the particular history of my family in the state brings pain and pride, progress and push-back; sending electrical signals of struggle and tiny ripples of hope up and down my spine each time I sing that refrain. (Hughes, 2013)

When Sherick A. Hughes initiated the proposal for a SAGE textbook on autoethnography that centered its applications in critical social research, his spouse commented in jest, "When professors have a midlife crisis, they write a textbook." While professors today who were born in 1975 tend *not* to be associated with the midlife crisis debate (Freund & Ritter, 2009), she inadvertently identified the impetus for this text. First, Hughes's midlife crisis, as illustrated in the opening quotation, is inextricably linked to a sort of dual citizenship that affords both privilege (as a professor and a doctor of philosophy) and penalty (as a political and numerical minority in the United States) (Alexander, 2010; Collins, 2000). Part of the crisis that he experiences as a Black male Tarheel is in the lived contradictions, in the frequent struggle to find ways to position himself outside the academy in order to illuminate and learn from his own contradictions at the intersections of romanticism and resistance; nostalgia and ignorance; and law, tradition, and transition.

Second, while writing the proposal for the first edition of this text at 40 years old, Hughes was living technically in midlife, considering the most recent life expectancy data available to him at that time. Black males in the United States (like him) had an estimated life expectancy of 71.8 years, lower than that for White males (76.5 years), Black females (78 years), and White females (81.3 years) (Kochanek, Arias, & Anderson, 2013). Third, he was experiencing the midlife crisis of structural inequity and inequality in the United States (Alexander, 2010; Hughes, 2006) within the wake of misguided education reforms (Berliner, 2014) and an unrealized American dream including racism, sexism, heterosexism, classism, ethnocentrism, religious discrimination, and xenophobia. Furthermore, his initial proposal for this textbook was developed during an international "crisis of confidence" in the academy (Ellis, Adams, & Bochner, 2011, p. 1). Inspired by postmodernity, the crisis of confidence introduced "new and abundant opportunities to reform social science and reconceive the objectives and forms of social science inquiry" in ways that exposed how the "'facts' and 'truths' scientists 'found' were inextricably tied to the vocabularies and paradigms the scientists used to represent them" (Ellis et al., 2011, pp. 1–2). Moreover, the crisis of confidence continues to involve the challenge for critical social scientists to resist "impulses of authoritatively entering a culture, exploiting cultural members, and then recklessly leaving to write about the culture for monetary and/or professional gain, while disregarding relational ties to cultural members" (Ellis et al., 2011, p. 2; see also Denzin & Lincoln, 2008b).

Hughes's frustrations with the crisis of inequity and inequality alongside the crisis of confidence moved him to seek an alternative route in the academy toward "producing meaningful, accessible, . . . evocative [and analytic] research grounded in personal experience . . . issues of identity politics . . . experiences shrouded in silence" (Ellis et al., 2011, p. 2). Autoethnography emerged as an invaluable alternative for him, just as it has for many other scholars of color in education (e.g., Berry, 2005; Chavez, 2012; Hairston & Strickland, 2011) as well as those conducting educational research in a wide array of social science disciplines (e.g., Banks & Banks, 2000; Laubscher & Powell, 2003; Peterson, 1990). The autoethnography genre offers critically reflexive self-storytelling that can illuminate (a) the internalized counternarratives that might disrupt the dominant cultural claims of neutrality, objectivity, color blindness, and meritocracy (Flores Carmona & Luschen, 2014; Richardson, 2000); and (b) the effective knowledge, skills, and dispositions that are not learned in the classroom and that are not privileged in most U.S. educational settings.

Hughes has shared more than a decade of overwhelmingly positive experiences through autoethnography with students, peers, colleagues, and audiences of national academic associations, including the American Educational Studies Association (AESA) and the American Educational Research Association (AERA). The consistency of the transformative educational outcomes of (a) applying autoethnography as a process for addressing crises of inequity and confidence and (b) observing and sharing the initial costs and ultimate benefits of autoethnography as a product convinced him that there may be some useful possibilities from the methodology that could be transferable to others via text. Some of his autoethnography work has been published in peer-reviewed journals such as *Educational Researcher, Urban Education, Educational Studies,* and *Educational Foundations* and in university textbooks including Diem and Helfenbein's *Unsettling Beliefs: Teaching Theory to Teachers* (2008), Hughes and Berry's (2012) *The Evolving Significance of Race: Living, Learning and Teaching* (2012), Flores Carmona and Luschen's *Crafting Critical Stories: Toward Pedagogies and Methodologies of Collaboration, Inclusion, and Voice* (2014), and Hancock, Allen, and Lewis's *Autoethnography as a Lighthouse: Illuminating Race, Research, and the Politics of Schooling* (2015).

With hopes of building on previous work, we intend this autoethnography textbook to serve as a guide for students, teachers, teacher educators, and educational researchers throughout the social sciences as they move toward a *critical and reflexive way of writing or representing* (graphy) inherent *personal complications and possibilities* (auto) in relation to larger *cultural contexts* (ethno). While revising the manuscript following a rigorous set of blind peer reviews initiated by SAGE, Hughes realized the need for an additional voice of clarity and inclusivity for the project, and he found that voice in his previous writing partner and fellow ethnographer/autoethnographer, Julie L. Pennington. Fortunately, Pennington agreed to coauthor the book, bringing an invaluable and accessible lens to the vision that we, Hughes and Pennington, share for autoethnography as critical social research. In the following sections, we provide our individual first-person accounts of the personal paths we followed into autoethnography. We then present information about the purpose, structure, and scope of our textbook.

Hughes's Journey Into Autoethnography

My journey into autoethnography began with a sincere search for ways to improve my craft more than a decade ago, when I was a newly hired tenure-track assistant professor of color teaching and working at a historically predominantly White institution (PWI) of higher education. I remember my parents' initial confusion and concerns about my first contract: "How do you like it?" "You know, you are a doctor now, and they still have you as an assistant to the professor?" After I explained the tenure-track process—with its academic charges to maintain exemplary teaching, research, and service, alongside its promise and the opportunities afforded an assistant professor (as opposed to an assistant *to* the professor)—to my parents, they seemed more confident that my new title and position reflected the degree that I had been granted. Like most parents within my sphere of influence, my mom and dad are always more confident than anyone else about their child's ability to find ways to improve and thrive in the face of complex academic challenges and possibilities. In fact, it is not unusual for them to remind me that my track record from grade school to grad school provides more evidence to support their confidence in my academic trajectory.

Logically, my mom and dad seemed as hurt and frustrated as I was when I shared with them the anonymous student course evaluations from the first course I taught in diversity, equity, and social justice. I realized that the course didn't meet my high expectations. However, I hadn't expected course evaluation scores that were more than one standard deviation below the mean, coupled with paragraph-long diatribes from several students. Some of the comments would be familiar to anyone who has experienced low scores on course evaluations, such as (and I paraphrase) "This is the worst course that I have taken" and "Dr. Hughes should not be allowed to teach here." Other anonymous evaluations, however, took a particularly racial turn, with phrases like "Dr. Hughes is a racist" and "All I learned in this class is that he is Black." Initially, I couldn't fathom how someone could be in a course for 15 weeks while having such strong negative emotions about the course and me without saying anything publicly, giving me no hint of these negative emotions that were expressed anonymously.

At the end of that first academic year, I began to meet other scholars of color from around the globe who had had similar experiences, as we learned through our dialogues at the annual meetings of two major national associations (i.e., AERA and AESA). Those faculty members continue to serve as critical friends with whom I share interpretations and translations of my experiences at PWIs in the challenging position of teaching *as* other, and teaching *to* others, while teaching *against* othering. These co-reflexive critical dialogues (Hughes & Willink, 2014) led me to consider how I may be part of the problem that I was experiencing. Of course, structural racism is an important culprit to name. It gets into our skin, our hair, our hats, our coats, and our hearts, and it informs our experiences across the color line. Still, I longed for a method to study myself as an ethnographic case for a full year of teaching and how any of my pedagogical changes might either improve or undermine the course from the perspective of the students and me. Moreover, I was moving closer to understanding that the influence of any of the changes that I initiated in the course would, in essence, highlight possibilities and unveil spaces where I was complicit in some of the problems that I initially perceived. This longing and searching for a framework toward critical self-study marked an invaluable moment in my trajectory, when I became more critically conscious than ever before of the particular intersection of the crisis of inequity, the crisis of inequality, and the crisis of confidence in my roles as an educator and educational researcher of color at PWIs. "I've got it. I'll develop my own method for an in-depth, critical long-term study of the self, of teaching as other against othering at PWIs," I thought. "I'll call it auto-ethnography," I said aloud and alone in my office at the end of spring semester of 2004. At the time, I had already received a contract to transform my dissertation into what later became an award-winning book based on an ethnography on school desegregation in North Carolina, *Black Hands in the Biscuits Not in the Classrooms: Unveiling Hope in a Struggle for Brown's Promise* (Hughes, 2006). Surely, I was on a roll! The only next step was to Google search the term "auto-ethnography." It was just a formality in my mind—certainly no one had already introduced such a methodology. Clearly, I was wrong, very wrong.

Many publications emerged from this search, as you might imagine; however, the first autoethnography article from a peer-reviewed journal that I recall reading was Laubscher and Powell's (2003) piece in the *Harvard Educational Review*. I was drawn to the piece because it not only spoke truth to power but also spoke to the experience of co-teaching as other, against othering, and it alluded to the possibilities of critical reflexive autoethnography for self-exploration en route to pedagogical improvement. With autoethnography, my students and I began pursuing self-critical and reflexive inquiries such as "How might I be part of the 'midlife' crisis of inequity and crisis of confidence that I perceive?" Autoethnography is not a magical savior, but when I apply autoethnography thoughtfully and carefully with the aid of rigorous formal and informal peer review, it offers a blueprint from which I can begin to construct responses to such inquiries as I seek to improve my own research, teaching, and service. It also enables me to offer intellectual substance through publications like this one that may be meaningful and useful for readers like you.

Pennington's Journey Into Autoethnography

In 2000, as I prepared for my dissertation proposal, I found myself questioning the changing views of literacy education in the elementary school where I had both learned to become a teacher as an intern in 1987 and taught as a teacher for more than a decade. Autoethnography became a way for me to acknowledge, examine, and critique my experiences as a classroom teacher during my transition to teacher educator and researcher in a highly politicized context. At the time, the state of Texas was undergoing significant policy changes in relation to literacy and language instruction. George W. Bush was governor, and my elementary school, three miles from the state capitol building, was moving from a dual-language Spanish/English model and multiage configuration to a test-focused segmented curriculum driven by high-stakes testing. Witnessing the substantial changes swiftly overtaking the school, I was drawn to ethnographic notions of data collection. I respected the long-term immersion in the field and the commitment to developing relationships with the community; these elements of ethnography were aligned with aspects of my relationship with my school and its surrounding community. Two faculty members in my program encouraged a critical ethnographic perspective. Enrique "Henry" T. Trueba was an encouraging member of my committee and shared his work and knowledge of ethnography with me through courses, his own work, and many mentoring conversations. Angela Valenzuela was also a significant influence; her book *Subtractive Schooling* (1999) was the type of work that inspired me. Douglas E. Foley introduced me to autoethnography, suggesting it as a way to encase the story of my school within my own experiences. His reflexive ethnographic work demonstrated the importance of researchers' relationships with the communities they study. With the encouragement of these ethnographers, I went on to complete my dissertation using autoethnography and was able to publish my dissertation as a book. Autoethnography has continued to influence my work, and I have completed several additional autoethnographies related to my own development as a teacher, a teacher educator, and a researcher. Racism has played a prominent role in my work, and autoethnography has been a means to critique my own White privilege in ways that studying others does not afford. I have seen autoethnographic work change not only my understanding of myself and the contexts I inhabit but also how teachers learn about themselves and the children they teach.

Purpose and Central Questions of This Textbook

Our aim in this book is to describe the epistemological and methodological processes involved in the history of legitimizing autoethnography in the academy, including recent efforts to explore autoethnography's evocative (e.g., Ellis, 2008), analytic (e.g., Anderson, 2006), and hybrid empirical evocative/analytic (e.g., Hughes, Pennington, & Makris, 2012) possibilities. We discuss how critics and authors of autoethnography products work at problematizing the narcissistic "self" in relation to others (Holman Jones, 2005). We provide guidance for synthesizing one's own autoethnography as well as the autoethnographies of others that share central phenomena of interest. In line with these aims, we address three central questions:

1. What evidence from autoethnography in educational research indicates *legitimizing processes* (translating autoethnography as a legitimate educational research standard, method, and methodology), *problematizing processes* (translating autoethnography as a critical condition of traditional educational research standards and methods), and *synthesizing processes* (translating autoethnography as a candidate for meta-synthesis)? With regard to synthesizing processes, what can we learn from autoethnographic cases of the past in the present for imagining a future of meta-synthesizing autoethnography?

2. How do these processes work to help autoethnographers engage cultural and familial sources of knowledge to use in their classrooms that necessarily (a) disrupt pedagogical practices that often focus on deficit thinking and (b) transfer and translate silenced/ignored/excluded history into publishable empirical research? (See, e.g., Hughes, 2008a; Laubscher & Powell, 2003.)

3. How does one begin to do an autoethnography? To answer this question, we discuss (a) autoethnography preactivities (including descriptions and web links to simulation and implicit association tasks); (b) steps toward "good enough" autoethnography methods for undergraduate and graduate students (Hughes, 2008c); (c) exemplary autoethnographic articles published in high-impact factor journals (e.g., Hughes et al., 2012; Pennington, 2007; Pennington & Brock, 2012; Winograd, 2002); (d) exemplary undergraduate- and graduate-level autoethnographies; and (e) exemplary syllabi from autoethnography undergraduate and graduate coursework (Ellis, 2004; Hughes, 2008a).

As is evident in the three central questions above, our purpose in this book is to offer readers an introduction to the methodological tools and concepts of autoethnography. We describe how autoethnographers go about collecting, analyzing, and reporting data, and we discuss some of the ethical and political elements that surround the genre. Ultimately, we conceptualize the book as a cogent summary for novice and experienced educational researchers in the social sciences both within and outside the field of education. Our aim is to communicate with a minimum of jargon, so that the book is accessible to and practical for faculty, students, and others not familiar with autoethnography.

In this textbook we treat ancillary topics and possible futures for the genre in a succinct manner, but we aim primarily to offer an expansive description beyond the "how-to" of the methodology. This book is both conceptual and practical, as it focuses on autoethnography as process and product through the framework of elements that animate the genre (i.e., legitimizing, problematizing, and synthesizing). The book is at the cutting edge of autoethnography methods with its inclusion of (a) the dual foci of a critical reflexive lens with theoretical and practical applications, (b) the potential of assemblage (Denshire & Lee, 2013) in relation to autoethnography, and (c) the consideration of a future with Noblit and Hare's (1988) *meta-ethnography* (synthesizing existing qualitative studies for the purpose of unveiling untapped perspectives, interpretations, reflections, and implications) and Ellis's (2009) *meta-autoethnography* (synthesizing new autoethnographic interpretations, reflections, and vignettes with old autoethnographic work). In addition, we introduce a defensible way to engage the *meta-synthesis of individualized and coauthored autoethnography (MICA)* method.

Structure of the Textbook

This book is divided into three parts. This approach is intended to give readers a sense of autoethnography as critical social research and how it is evolving by focusing on it with a product lens (Part I), a process lens (Part II), and a lens of possibility (Part III). Part I, "Histories and Applications of Autoethnography as Critical Social Research," begins with a comprehensive account from the origins of autoethnography to its various contemporary iterations and applications, which is intended to provide a view of autoethnography's past in the present for the future. Many, if not most, readers of this book have undoubtedly heard *something* about autoethnography, and they may find themselves feeling indifferent about it, attracted to it, or repulsed by it. By clarifying confusing information, dispelling misinformation, and unveiling disinformation in a way that blends the discussion of standards, traditions, and transitions, we hope to offer a framework through which readers can begin to see both the forest and the trees of autoethnography. Each chapter opens with a "Focus Your Reading" section, features various text boxes containing interesting facts and definitions, and concludes with suggested individual and group activities.

Chapter 1, "Autoethnography: Introduction and Overview," discusses (a) iterations, definitions, and illustrative sample applications; (b) multiple histories of autoethnography—including its ontological, epistemological, paradigmatic, axiological, and methodological moorings, including where it fits in the larger context of self-study (Bullough & Pinnegar, 2001) and action research (Weil, 1998); (c) contemporary autoethnography in relation to other qualitative genres; and (d) the analytic versus evocative autoethnography debate as well as other critiques of autoethnography, such as Chang (2008) and Anderson (2006) versus Ellis (2008, 2009). Chapter 2, "Mining and Priming Critical Social Theory for Autoethnography," discusses autoethnography's connections to critical theory. The chapter highlights only published, peer-reviewed, and named connections of autoethnography to critical social theorizing, like the Hughes (2008a) link of critical race theory to autoethnography. Moreover, Chapter 2 addresses judgment calls and trade-offs with critical theorizing. It includes pedagogical questions that are intended to prompt further dialogues. By the end of Part I, readers should know about the origins of autoethnography and its influence on educational research.

Part II, "Doing Autoethnography: From Brainstorming to Guiding Process," provides readers with critical theory-into-practice information on doing autoethnography as educational research in the social sciences, including understanding and addressing the genre's most common critiques (e.g., Delamont, 2007, 2009). The chapters of Part II connect critical theory to practice for readers by centering three guiding processes of autoethnography: problematizing, legitimizing, and synthesizing. By the end of this part of the book, readers should understand how the dynamic processes of problematizing and legitimizing guide the evolution of autoethnography as process and product of educational research. Readers should also become familiar with the prewriting exercises, activities, prompts, and rubrics that are essential resources for developing the types of autoethnographies that are published by peer-reviewed journals of social science. Drawn from high–impact factor journals that adhere to the blind peer-review process, these resources include such things as web links to autoethnography preactivities. Chapter 3, "First Guiding Process: Problematizing What You Know for New-Self Insight," discusses (a) finding the relevant problem to pursue, (b) finding your purpose/your phenomenon of interest, and (c) linking the phenomenon of interest to the central autoethnographic question. Chapter 4, "Second Guiding Process: Legitimizing Autoethnography With Three Approaches," addresses the processes of legitimizing autoethnography for the larger social scientific audience, including (a) establishing the relevant literature to review and critique, (b) applying ethics in relation to autoethnography (Sieber & Tolich, 2013), (c) confirming/disconfirming the criticisms of autoethnography, (d) collecting personal memory data, (e) collecting self-observational and self-reflective data, and (f) collecting external data and member checking. This chapter would be incomplete at best without a discussion of the final element of legitimizing autoethnography: evaluation. We explore various published criteria for evaluating the merit and worth of autoethnography in the academy and consider the most current promising practices in the evaluation of autoethnography for educational research. Chapter 5, "Third Guiding Process: Synthesizing New-Self Insights With MICA," discusses the art and science of synthesizing in autoethnography. It highlights traditional data synthesis processes engaged in autoethnography, including the development of concepts into codes, codes into categories, and categories into themes; and the synthesizing of understandings across one's own body of autoethnographic work. The chapter also moves readers toward constructing a method for synthesizing autoethnography written by other authors, also known as qualitative meta-synthesis for individualized and coauthored autoethnography, or MICA. This method presents three possibilities for meta-synthesizing autoethnographies, a process introduced in this textbook as an alternative way to begin synthesizing information across the autoethnographies of multiple authors. Autoethnography's focus on a central phenomenon of interest and research questions tends to animate three possibilities for synthesis: (a) refutational synthesis, (b) lines-of-argument synthesis, and (c) the creation of analogies. By the end of Part II, readers should be able to articulate the challenges and possibilities of constructing a method for meta-synthesizing autoethnography and should be able to understand how this process differs from the meta-ethnography work of Ellis (2004).

Part III, "The Future of Autoethnography: A Prism of Possibility," anticipates the future of autoethnography based on past and current trends related to this qualitative genre in educational research. Chapter 6, "The Possibility of Autoethnography as Critically Reflexive Action Research," discusses the potential for moving from theory into practice through the application of autoethnography as critically reflexive action research, or CRAR, using an "epistemologies of practice approach" (Weil, 1998, p. 37). This move may not only attract quantitative educational researchers but also necessitate their becoming autoethnographers each time they initiate social science educational research on marginalized populations. Promising examples of autoethnography as CRAR are referenced in this chapter. The final chapter of the book, Chapter 7, "Anticipating the Future of Autoethnography as Critical Social Research," discusses the continued growth of autoethnography in education and in the educational research of other social sciences. Technological advancements such as social media provide some rich possibilities for conducting autoethnographies and disseminating autoethnographic findings. In light of these advancements, Chapter 7 also discusses (a) taking risks in autoethnography, (b) exploring qualitative theses and dissertations, (c) determining "good enough" autoethnography, (d) access to and availability of data, (e) politics and autoethnography, (f) the sustained growth of autoethnography as well as continued skepticism toward the genre, (g) social media and autoethnography, (h) new syntheses of ideas, and (i) the increasing acceptance of autoethnography. The chapter includes a list of highly selective peer-reviewed journals with a qualitative focus that publish autoethnographies as well as a list of scholarly publishers that publish autoethnographic work. It concludes with a call for an evolving online reading list for autoethnography. Part III is followed by appendixes that include a sample autoethnography assignment, a sample syllabus, and sample autoethnographic research from students.

Scope of the Textbook

This textbook may be useful in courses emphasizing qualitative research methodology at the undergraduate and graduate levels. It can serve both advanced undergraduate and graduate student populations and scholars in fields related to psychology, education, language and literature, sociology, anthropology, ethnic studies, communication studies, and other fields that utilize qualitative research, like public health sciences, nursing, and medical education. For instructors who are interested in introducing this method to their students but don't feel confident in using it, the book presents conceptual and practical resources toward creating autoethnographies (e.g., Muncey, 2010). The book covers both epistemological and methodological information, along with sample preactivities, vignettes, writing prompts, concept mapping, coding and narrative translation tools, and techniques that will prepare students for immediate applications in the "real" world. We anticipate this volume being used and adopted by a diverse array of professors for their courses. In addition to the field of education, this book will be useful in courses throughout the university informed by qualitative and critical cultural studies perspectives, including courses in sociology, anthropology, nursing and allied health, ethnic studies, and communication and cultural studies.

Engaging Autoethnography: Toward Savvy Teaching and Learning

Ultimately, our goals and objectives for this book are to facilitate your teaching, learning, and application of autoethnography's processes, products, and possibilities. We offer you the following suggestions for using this book as you engage in learning about and teaching autoethnography. First, you would be well served by reading each chapter through quickly before you attempt to study its contents, in order to gain an overview of the text before you engage it more deeply. The individual and group activities that we provide at the ends of chapters have proven useful for university and national professional development courses that we have conducted during the past decade. We hope that you find some of them useful as you work toward writing your own private autoethnography and/or autoethnography that you can share with the public through print media, television, film, radio, and/or the Internet. Second, in today's high-stakes testing accountability world, some of you may long for someone to tell you what to memorize for quick recall. We suggest that you begin thinking about autoethnography less as a set of alternatives to memorize than as a tool kit you can use in weighing, considering, and challenging your taken-for-granted "good" self.

A sort of David Letterman "top 10" list of the best ways to begin writing an autoethnography does not appear in this textbook. Instead, the guidelines and resources presented here are intended to support what Noblit and Hare (1988) call *communicative competence*, whereby readers compare and contrast information provided in the book with their own reality and decide for themselves which concepts and practices are important and useful to them. Finally, when you finish reading this text, we suggest that you commence a lifelong journey of thinking critically and reflexively about what autoethnography can be in your professional and personal life, how you might reach your highest professional and personal potential with it, and what contributions you might make to your program of studies, your program of research, your field, and the social sciences in general with this additional methodological tool in your intellectual tool kit.

• Acknowledgments •

Sherick A. Hughes

To my spiritual support: United Church of Chapel Hill (Pastors Rick and Jill Edens, Pastor Susan Steinberg, Pastor Jenny Shultz, and Pastor David Mateo), Tacoma Park Presbyterian Church (Pastor Mark Greiner and Kolya Braun-Greiner), Philadelphia Baptist Church (Pastor Wade Staten Sr.), New Sawyer's Creek Missionary Baptist Church (Pastor Sam "Kenny" Shaw). My faith in a higher power has been sustained by your humble, but powerful, work. Thank you.

To my family: My inspiration, my daughter, Micah Hughes, who accepted my proposal to name the particular form of qualitative meta-synthesis introduced in Chapter 5 after her; my wife, Megan Hughes, who held down the home fort for many a fortnight while I was writing; my parents, Maise and Jessie Hughes Sr.; my siblings, Theresa, Jessie Jr., Elvese, Janifer, Kent, and Shelia, and the descendants of Edmond and Amie Hughes and Papa and Ida Walston of Camden, North Carolina; my siblings-in-law, Dora and Charles, and descendants of Clara and James Sykes, who built me and who sustain me; my parents-in-law, Trish and Don Hoert, and the descendants of Clarence and Isabelle Hoert and Polly Thompson of Ohio, who welcomed me into their family and provided a home away from home across the color line.

To my surrogate family of North Carolina: Marion, Lenora, and Joelle Clark; Ms. Lyles Betts, Lewis Betts, and John Plymale; Pam Sanderson Hinson, Marilee Sanderson, and Stacey Pinney of the Triangle area of North Carolina; Janine McClellan, Vasana Hemvong, and Holly Henderson of Wilmington, North Carolina; Derek and April Harrison of Chapel Hill, North Carolina; the Osmundson family of Currituck, North Carolina (and Harrisonburg, Virginia); the Blakeslee and Groves families of the Triangle area of North Carolina; the Dunn family of Sneads Ferry, North Carolina; George Noblit (coauthor of Chapter 5) and the Noblit family of Snow Camp, North Carolina; and my former Fendal band members, Jason Marks, Eric Blakeslee, and Courtney Coble. The fact that I consider you my surrogate family members is enough said. Thank you for influencing my trajectory more than you may ever know.

To my surrogate family out of state: Aaron and Tayaka Daniels; Melissa Ramirez Kilmer and Mark Kilmer; Martha Kransdorf, Ms. Anne Donnellan, and Betsy; Lore Rosenthal and Michael Hartman; Jeannette Holman and Laura Holman; Angelica and John Butte; Elizabeth Mitchell, Daniel Littleton and Storey Littleton, Mrs. Hermie Littleton, Uncle Miggy Littleton, Penny and the Good Ms. Padgett; Maria Joie and Ron Austria; pioneers of the United Opt Out and Save Our Schools movements, including Jesse "The Walking Man" Turner, Bob George and Betsy, Becky Smith, and the "Fab 5," Ceresta Smith, Morna McDermott, Bess Altwerger, Ruth Rodriguez, and Peggy

Robertson. The fact that I consider all of you surrogate family members living outside my home state of North Carolina is enough said.

To my students 2003–2013: University of Toledo students Albert Wiggins, Sammy and Melissa Spann, and Dave Ragland; University of Maryland–College Park (UMD) students Dawn Jacobs, Angela Lawrence, Tamyka Morant, and Dawn Smith; Maria "Joie" Austria, Xiao Liu, Khambrel Ward, Erica McKinney, Maggie Corfield-Adams, Rod Carey, Laura Yee, Wyletta Gamle, and Meg Austin-Smith. You are my first children of the academy, and I continue to learn from you.

To my students 2013–present: University of North Carolina at Chapel Hill (UNC) doctoral students Nitasha Clark, Sharon Shofer, Meghan Harter, and Esmeralda Rodriguez (coauthors of Chapter 3); Alicia Smith, Matt Green, Dani Parker, Shelby Dawkins-Law, Terrell Morton, Kym Butler, Helen Avis, Jeremy Godwin, Derrick Drakeford, Omar Simpson, and Michael Thornburg; Emily Freeman, Tommy Ender, Torrie Edwards, Elizabeth "Liz" Allen, Hana Baskin, and Andrews University student (visiting doctoral student at UMD) Charity Garcia; Gallaudet University student (reciprocal doctoral course student at UMD) Sarah Schatz; UNC Moore Undergraduate Research Apprenticeship Program 2013 and 2014 students Christopher Robinson, Uriel Rafael, and Alicia Smith; the approximately 90 students from the 2012 and 2014 American Educational Research Association professional development course on autoethnography. You are my second children of the academy, and I continue to learn with you and from you.

To my inaugural UNC class of PhD students for the Interpretive Research Suite & Carter Qualitative Thought Laboratory and new graduate certificate in qualitative studies (2012–present): lab research assistants Jeremy Godwin, Cherish Williams, and Wenyang Sun; graduate certificate students Allison LaGarry, Susan Hedges, Meghan Harter, Tara Pressley, Nitasha Clark, Joseph Hooper, Tim Conder, Summer Pennell, Hillary Parkhouse, and Jeremy Godwin. You have made my life as a researcher enriched and sustainable.

To my senior faculty colleagues: at UNC, George Noblit (coauthor of Chapter 5), Mary Stone Hanley, Deb Eaker Rich, Linda Tillman, Frank Brown, Henry Frierson, Bill Malloy (retired) and the late Carol Malloy, Charles Thompson, and Bill McDiarmid; at Washington State University, the late Elson Floyd (also a UNC alumnus); at UMD, Randy McGinnis, David Imig, Peter Leone, Bob Croninger, Patricia Hill Collins, Bonnie Thornton Dill, Ruth Zambrana, Steve Koziol, and Carol Parham; at University of Virginia, Robert Q. Berry III; at Indiana University–South Bend, Dean Marvin Lynn; at University of Texas–San Antonio, Theodorea Berry and Michael Jennings; at University of Illinois–Chicago, Dave Stovall, Bill Ayers (retired), Steve Tozer, and the late Bill Watkins; at University of California, Berkeley, Zeus Leonardo; at University of Texas–Austin, Angela Valenzuela and Luis Urrieta; at Miami of Ohio, Denise Taliaferro Baszile; at University of Pittsburgh, H. Rich Milner IV; at University of Miami, Josh Diem and Beth Harry; at Cornell University, Sofia Villenas and Troy Richardson; at University of Toledo, Dale Snauwaert, Martha Kransdorf, Lynn Hamer, Mary Ellen

Edwards, and Lisa Kovach; at New York University, Pedro Noguera; at Michigan State University, Chris Dunbar; at Southhampton University, Kalwant Bhopal; at University of Illinois, James Anderson; at University of Arizona, Luis Moll; at Emory University, Vanessa Siddle Walker; at University of Nevada, Reno, Julie L. Pennington; at California State University–Monterey Bay, Christine Sleeter; at University of Wisconsin, Carl Grant; at North Carolina State University, Amy Halberstadt; at University of San Francisco, Kevin Kumashiro; at Washington University of St. Louis, Odis Johnson; at Duke University, Ben Reese, William "Sandy" Darity, and Ahmad Hariri; at NIH/NINDs, Kris Knutson; at Northwestern University, Jordan Grafman; at UNC Center for Developmental Science, Andrea Hussong and Amy Briceno. You are my elders, my teachers, and I continue to learn from you.

To my junior faculty colleagues: James Martinez, Valdosta State University; Muhammad Khalifa, Michigan State University; Juan Carrillo, Dana Thompson-Dorsey, and Claudia Cervantes-Soon, UNC; Aimee Papola-Ellis, Loyola University of Chicago. I am honored to have you in my professional life, and you continue to open my eyes to new possibilities within the struggle for equity and social justice.

To my AERA PD Course Committee: George Wimberly and Maurice Brown.

To my editors, Helen and Eve, and reviewers at SAGE: You are brilliant and patient. Helen Salmon, you are not only one of the best editors in the academy worldwide, but you are also a world-class woman and mentor. This textbook would not exist without you. Thank you, Helen.

To my blind peer reviewers: Your comments and critiques were invaluable to making this book reader- and user-friendly.

To my coauthor: Julie Pennington, you are one of the most exciting, bold, and brilliant writers I have the pleasure to know. Your contributions to this textbook are more invaluable to me than you may ever realize. You are one of the first autoethnographers whose work I read, and it's hard to believe that a decade later, we are friends. What is not hard to believe is that my graduate students have said to me, "You actually know Pennington, wow!" "Wow," is right, as I continue to learn from your writing and your thirst for equity and social justice, as well as your kindness and humility.

This book is offered in memory of my aunt *Margaret Walston,* who went from being a school "secretary" to completing college and having an illustrious career of teaching and mentoring across the color line in elementary school for 30 years and who taught music and played organ for the church choir for 50 years. Aunt Margaret was instrumental as a key informant, linking me to participants for the ethnographic study that went on to produce both a Phi Delta Kappa dissertation award and a Critics' Choice Book Award from the American Educational Studies Association. The book is also offered in memory of *Glen Sanderson,* a humble, middle-class White man in the printing profession, who alongside his wife, Marilee, and daughter, Pam (one of my best friends since I was 18), always treated me as Claude Steele describes, like a *valuable person with good prospects,* by coming eagerly to my presentations on equity, race, and education, even when my biological family members could not attend, and happily providing numerous days and nights of food, fellowship, and shelter before and after my wife and I moved away from the state. I would be remiss to close my portion of these acknowledgments without offering memories and gratitude to *our first family dog of nearly 12 years, Raleigh Franklin Hughes,* who kept us exercising with long, fun neighborhood walks, provided companionship on long trips together and at home when one of us was either ill or had to be out of town for work, and did his designated family jobs—sanitation and border security—quite diligently. Helping my wife raise and train Raleigh, a black Lab mix, from a 2½-year-old rescue to the adult dog he became challenged me to consider how providing the best care is crucial, often in the moments when I have the least left to give.

Julie L. Pennington

To my parents, Edward and Mary, who both supported me throughout all of my endless years of education and from whom I learned the most important lessons: caring, honesty, and resilience. They provided me with a strong foundation and the recognition that learning never ends.

To my teaching colleagues, Carmen, Lynn, Lupe, Minerva, and Rosalinda, who in my first years of teaching constantly and lovingly pressed me to critique my positioning as a White teacher in a Latino/a school. I still hear them as I teach teachers today.

To my university colleagues, Cindy Brock and Kathy Obenchain, who have supported my autoethnographic efforts when autoethnography was unheard of and unknown in education.

To previous autoethnographer Patrick Slattery, who as a guest speaker in one of my graduate courses shared his art installation and altered how I saw research.

To my coauthor, Sherick, who so graciously engaged me in ways that pushed my thinking and always placed the need for autoethnography as a means of justice in the forefront of our work together.

To the SAGE Publishing family and Helen and Eve, who welcomed me with open arms and supported my contributions with wonderful feedback and care.

Publisher's Acknowledgments

SAGE wishes to acknowledge the valuable contributions of the following reviewers.

Ricia Anna Chansky, University of Puerto Rico at Mayagüez

Lois McFayden Christensen, University of Alabama at Birmingham

Angela C. Coffee, Century College

Judith Davidson, University of Massachusetts Lowell

Maricela DeMirjyn, Colorado State University

Kenneth J. Fasching-Varner, Louisiana State University

Diane Gavin, University of Phoenix, School of Advanced Studies

Mary Louise Gomez, University of Wisconsin–Madison

Amy N. Heuman, Texas Tech University

Nicholas E. Husbye, University of Missouri, St. Louis

Peter H. Khost, Stony Brook University

Mirka Koro-Ljungberg, Arizona State University

Xyanthe N. Neider, Washington State University

K. Reed, Texas A&M International University

Jeanne L. Surface, University of Nebraska Omaha

Gresilda A. Tilley-Lubbs, Virgina Tech

Faith Wambura Ngunjiri, Eastern University

• About the Authors •

Sherick A. Hughes, MA, MPA, PhD, is associate professor in the School of Education at the University of North Carolina at Chapel Hill. He is the founder/director of the Interpretive Research Suite and Bruce A. Carter Qualitative Thought Lab as well as founder/codirector of the Graduate Certificate in Qualitative Studies. His research, teaching, and service involve, broadly, critical race studies and Black education, the social context of urban and rural schooling, interdisciplinary foundations of education, and qualitative methodology in education. He has authored or coauthored more than 50 manuscripts accepted for publication, and his books on nuanced Black family pedagogy since *Brown v. Board of Education* and the evolving significance of race earned 2007 and 2014 Critics' Choice Book Awards from the American Educational Studies Association. He was also the 2016 recipient of the prestigious Distinguished Scholar Award from the American Educational Research Association.

Julie L. Pennington, PhD, is professor of literacy studies in the College of Education at the University of Nevada, Reno, and director of the Center for Learning and Literacy. She has focused on the areas of literacy and diversity throughout her career as a classroom teacher and literacy intervention teacher for 14 years and currently as a teacher educator and researcher. Her research interests include the use of autoethnography in teacher education and the pursuit of questions related to how teachers approach literacy instruction in linguistically and culturally diverse settings.

Histories and Applications of Autoethnography as Critical Social Research

PART I

*For it is impossible for [me] to begin to learn what
[I] have a conceit that [I] already know.*

—Epictetus, *Discourses*, 108 A.D./1920

Autoethnography represents a process, product, and possibility for learning more about a subject that you presumably know quite well—yourself. Centering yourself as the subject of interrogation, analysis, and critique rests on the Epictetian notion that you must come to this type of research with questions. You must come realizing that you do not already know yourself as well as you might think. You must come with questions about your identity and your role(s) in society. The goal of this book is to provide you with a process for pursuing critical questions about yourself in ways that challenge your knowledge. Our intent is to help you recognize that engaging in autoethnography means welcoming the opportunity to learn more about your participation in one or more cultural groups, communities, and contexts while contributing to critical social research. We have organized this book into three parts. In Part I, we introduce you to the multiple histories and applications of autoethnography as *critical social research* (Harvey, 1990). The two chapters of Part I provide a comprehensive account of autoethnography's origins and then extend the discussion to include its various applications and forms.

Autoethnography is a complex form of research. Many voices have shaped the genre, from postpositivist to postmodern viewpoints. As such, many, if not most, readers of this book have undoubtedly heard *something* about autoethnography, and they may find themselves feeling indifferent about it, attracted to it, or repulsed by it. Our agenda is to provide a balance of practical experience and knowledge about the past and the present for the future of autoethnographic scholarship. We believe that active participation will help you internalize some of the more abstract ideas you will encounter. Therefore, most chapters conclude with group and individual activities, followed by lists of a few web links to relevant pieces and other resources for you to consider in the future. By the end of Part I, you should be able to define autoethnography, describe its origins, name different forms of autoethnography that are prominent in the literature, name arguments against autoethnography, and articulate five key ideas to consider when applying autoethnography as critical social research.

Chapter 1, "Autoethnography: Introduction and Overview," provides a comprehensive introduction and overview of the genre that is grounded in peer-reviewed research and Hughes's experiences in engaging autoethnography with students at a highly selective and highly ranked research-driven university (the university, with an acceptance rate of 28% of more than 30,000 first-year applicants, has been ranked by *U.S. News & World Report* in the top 30 in the United States and the top 45 of 1,000 ranked in the world). The chapter includes discussion of the following:

- The histories of autoethnography
- The various iterations and applications of autoethnography
- Five key ideas to consider when applying autoethnography
- Debates and critiques pertaining to autoethnography

Chapter 2, "Mining and Priming Critical Social Theory for Autoethnography," discusses autoethnography's connections to critical social theory. The chapter focuses on the following:

- Theories related to the history of autoethnography
- Evidence of specific critical social theories linked to autoethnography from published, contemporary peer-reviewed research

Moreover, Chapter 2 discusses judgment calls and trade-offs with critical theorizing for autoethnography. If you are new to autoethnography, then you probably have limited knowledge or experience with it. As coauthors of this volume, we aim to share our experience: Hughes is an educational researcher who has engaged in critical social research on education-related topics for nearly two decades, and Pennington has used autoethnographic work in educational research for more than 15 years. While there are many ways to develop autoethnography, we focus on a critical reflexive stance. We reference autoethnography publications that center reflexivity, or critical self-reflection and self-critique, as the critical means for improving one's own approach to educational theory, policy, practice, praxis, and leadership. With these intentions, the research highlighted in Chapter 2 includes scholarship from the critical social research wings of the discipline of education as well as educational research from the critical social research wings of nursing and allied health, medicine, English, psychology, sociology, anthropology, communication, and cultural studies. Applications and iterations of autoethnography in critical social research have grown rapidly in the past 20 years, and while they are all related, they can be quite diverse. Ultimately, we hope to offer a framework through which you can begin to see both the forest and the trees of autoethnography as you prepare to include this method in your qualitative research tool kit.

1

Autoethnography

Introduction and Overview

●

Focus Your Reading

- What is the history of autoethnography as it relates to traditional qualitative research approaches?

- How does autoethnography function as a broad methodology as well as a specific method of data collection and analysis?

- How is autoethnography debated and critiqued because of its focus on the self?

- What are five key ideas to consider when applying autoethnography as critical social research?

Histories of Autoethnography

Prior to discussing the functions and forms that define autoethnography as contemporary critical social research, we need to address the histories of autoethnography and how the genre has evolved. We begin this introductory chapter by delving into the historical evolution of the naming of autoethnography. **Autoethnography** in its most simplified definition is the study of the self (Reed-Danahay, 1997, p. 9). While related to autobiography, narrative, and ethnography, it is unique from a research perspective in that the researcher is the subject of study. We view autoethnography as part of the broader family of qualitative approaches that includes ethnography, self-study, and narrative inquiry. By using the phrases *histories of autoethnography* and *historical evolution,* we intend to highlight evidence from multiple published perspectives on the historical lineage of autoethnography. The histories of the genre detailed here are drawn primarily from five academic sources: Hayano (1979); Reed-Danahay (1997); Anderson (2006); Elder, Bremser, and Sheridan (2007); and Ellis, Adams, and Bochner (2011). One might think of each publication as adding a piece to a larger puzzle that provides a more complex historical picture of how autoethnography evolved to become what it is today.

When each of the histories is examined in isolation, it can appear to be unique, but the histories of autoethnography are connected. Various names and ideas may be used to describe the basic ideas behind autoethnography, but they are all related to autoethnographic work. Many research traditions inform autoethnography. Just as in the story about the six blind men describing an elephant—one touching the trunk and saying the animal was like a snake, another touching a leg and saying it was like a tree, yet another touching the elephant's side and saying it was like a wall, until a passerby told them they were all touching an elephant—it is only when we stand back and see the big picture and understand the relationships between the research traditions that we can understand the breadth and scope of autoethnography. Therefore, it is necessary to consider the histories of autoethnography in tandem in order to gain the most comprehensive view of its origins.

Autoethnography is similar to approaches such as ethnography, narrative inquiry, self-study, and hermeneutics. Each examines how people understand relationships between humans and their sociocultural contexts. The differences among them lie in the approaches' disciplinary roots, roots that shape their questions and their focus on specific research data collection and analysis methods. While **ethnography** rests on studying individuals within their communities, narrative inquiry also focuses on the stories of individuals in various contexts. Self-study highlights how tasks such as teaching are undertaken and examined, whereas hermeneutics focuses on the meanings of products and ideas from the past. All of these approaches, encased within their disciplines, target how we understand ourselves in relation to larger social structures and communities. Table 1.1 compares and contrasts traditional qualitative approaches with autoethnography.

While all of these approaches are related to autoethnography, we will focus on autoethnography's relationship to ethnography. Most of the histories of autoethnography describe the genre as a relatively new social science born in the discipline of anthropology a little more than 50 years ago (Reed-Danahay, 1997). Anthropology, which focuses on the study of people, has its roots in the 1800 founding of the Society of Observers of Man in Paris, and discussions between anthropology and ethnology date back to 1840 (Tax, 1964). Although written nearly 30 years afterward, the work of Anderson (2006) takes us back in time to view the social sciences before Hayano (1979), thereby providing additional context for the beginnings of autoethnography. There has always been an autoethnographic element in qualitative sociological research (Anderson, 2006). Researchers often noted their role in the research process, attempting to explain, justify, or understand it, as evidenced by details from the early years of sociology in the United States after World War I:

What Is Ethnography?

The term *ethnography* is derived from two Greek words: *graphein*, meaning "to write," and *ethnoi*, meaning "the nations" or "the others."

(Erickson, 2011, p. 45)

> Robert Park's interest in the biographical backgrounds of his University of Chicago graduate students encouraged many of his students to pursue sociological involvement in settings close to their personal lives, arenas with which they had a significant degree of self-identification. Nels Anderson's *The Hobo* (1923), for instance, drew heavily on his personal experience with the lifestyle of homeless men. . . . But while Park's students often had enduring personal connections with the social settings and groups that they studied, they seldom, if ever, took up the banner of explicit and reflexive self-observation. . . . The only examples of self-narrative from these scholars came in the form of occasional methodological notes and/or what Van Maanen (1988) has referred to as "confessional tales" of fieldwork experiences. (Anderson, 2006, pp. 375–376)

TABLE 1.1 ● Traditional Qualitative Approaches Compared/Contrasted with Autoethnography

Approach	Disciplinary Roots	Possible Questions
Autoethnography	Literary arts Anthropology Communication studies	What am I learning by examining my identities, power, privileges, and penalties within one or more cultural contexts?
Ethnography	Anthropology Sociology	What are the cultural characteristics of "others"? What can be learned from the cultural contexts of "others"?
Narrative inquiry: autobiography (life history)	Literary arts Sociology Theology Anthropology History	What story or stories should I write about myself (or others) that can serve to document, justify, and/or atone for my (or their) experiences?
Self-study	Education Sociology Psychology	How can a formal systematic approach to studying my teaching and learning inform my practice?
Hermeneutics	Linguistics Literary criticism Theology	What are the conditions under which a human action occurred or a human-made product was produced in the past that makes it possible to interpret its meaning in the present?

Focused as they were on observing and analyzing others in the settings studied, even the social scientists of the legendary Chicago School had no qualitative language that assigned particular merit to self-observation (Anderson, 2006). While ethnographers of both the first generation (1930s) and the second generation (1960s and 1970s) of the Chicago School often had autobiographical connections to their research, they were neither particularly self-observational in their method nor self-visible in their texts (Anderson, 2006). An anthropologist in the 1960s at the University of Chicago stated, "We pursue scientific problems, not practical or political or social problems" (Tax, 1964, p. 249). Still, Anderson (2006) mentions some notable examples of social scientists experimenting more explicitly with self-observation and analysis in the 1960s and 1970s, including but not limited to anthropologist Anthony Wallace and sociologist David Sudnow. The self-observational study by Wallace (1965) of the cognitive "mazeway" he constructed and used for driving to work is one example. Sudnow's (1978) description of the detailed processes and stages of skill acquisition he experienced as he learned to play improvisational piano jazz represents another.

Historical puzzle pieces shared by Anderson (2006) provide some insight into the context surrounding the coining of the term *autoethnography* by Raymond Firth in 1956. Firth was discussing an argument that took place between Jomo Kenyatta (first president of the independent Kenya) and Louis Leakey (acclaimed 20th-century archaeologist/anthropologist) during a public lecture in London in 1928 (Elder et al., 2007; Reed-Danahay, 1997). Both men claimed "insider" knowledge of Kikuyu customs. Born in Kenya and educated abroad, both Kenyatta (a Kikuyu tribal man) and Leakey (the son of Christian missionaries who worked with the Kikuyu) earned doctoral degrees in anthropology. Elder et al. (2007) aptly describe the center of their argument as "Who has the right to represent a society and through what methodological means?" Is it Leakey, with his traditional hypothesis-driven anthropology, or Kenyatta, whose work seemed to introduce to the West a combination of autobiography and anthropologic ethnography to represent the Kikuyu people? Fellow anthropologist David Hayano recognized Kenyatta's book *Facing Mount Kenya* (1938/1965) as the first published autoethnography in his article "Auto-Ethnography: Paradigms, Problems, and Prospects," which appeared in the high–impact factor journal *Human Organization* in 1979.

Related to the specific turn to autoethnography, some anthropologists began actively questioning their ways of knowing about others. Ruth Behar demonstrates a critical view of the historical rooting of social science research in relation to the representation and supposed understanding of the other. Schooled in the traditional approach to anthropology, she raises the question in ways similar to the Kenyatta and Leakey argument. In her collection of essays *The Vulnerable Observer: Anthropology That Breaks Your Heart* (1996), she details her questioning of her role as an anthropologist:

> In anthropology, which historically exists to "give voice" to others, there is no greater taboo than self-revelation. The impetus of our discipline, with its roots in Western fantasies about barbaric others, has been to focus primarily on "cultural" rather than "individual" realities. The irony is that anthropology has always been rooted in an "I"—understood as having a complex psychology and history—observing a "we" that, until recently, was viewed as plural, ahistorical, and nonindividuated. (p. 26)

Questioning and unveiling the self is at the heart of critical autoethnographic work. While Hayano (1979) credits Raymond Firth with coining the term *autoethnography,* Ellis (2008) links the two men by crediting Hayano with moving autoethnography beyond the debate in Firth's London seminar to the academic mainstream. Describing the potential of autoethnography, Hayano anticipated its capacity to create an alternative venue for marginalized voices. The significance of his contributions to the genre cannot be overstated. As Anderson (2006) notes:

> Hayano argued that as anthropologists moved out of the colonial era of ethnography, they would come more and more to study the social worlds and subcultures of which they were a part. In contrast to the detached-outsider characteristic of colonial anthropologists, contemporary anthropologists would frequently be full of members of the cultures they studied. (p. 376)

By 1979, Hayano's questioning of who has the right to represent the lives of others was a foundational idea related to autoethnography. Once the question was asked and researchers begin to explore answers, there was a "crisis of confidence," not exclusively related to autoethnography but in relation to all types of research methods and areas of inquiry. This historical period has been described as "the fourth moment . . . crisis of representation" (Denzin & Lincoln, 2008a, p. 24) in qualitative work in general. Adding another layer to the historical context, Ellis et al. (2011) describe this "crisis of confidence" (para. 2) in the research community as emerging from the 1980s and inspired by the movement away from **postpositivism** toward **postmodernism**.

What Is Autoethnography?

Autoethnography involves a critical study of yourself in relation to one or more cultural context(s).

(Reed-Danahay, 1997, p. 9)

Researchers questioned their ability to be completely objective when studying others, noting the tendency for researchers from powerful dominant groups to use oppressed groups for their own purposes, with little regard for the populations studied. The moral and ethical aspects of research were brought to light and critiqued. Scholars in the 1980s and 1990s began illustrating how the so-called facts and truths of social scientists' findings were inextricably tied to the very vocabularies and **paradigms** that were used to represent them (e.g., Kuhn, 1996; Rorty, 1982). Furthermore, many social scientists began recognizing that different kinds of people view the world through different lenses, and thereby make different assumptions about the world. Scholars like Anzaldúa (1987) and Valenzuela (1999) began rejecting conventional ways of thinking about research and ways of doing research. This movement of a critical mass of social scientists supported the recognition of the myriad ways that personal experience can influence the research process. It also opened the door for autoethnography as "one of the approaches that acknowledges and accommodates subjectivity, emotionality, and the researcher's influence on research, rather than hiding from these matters or assuming they don't exist" (Ellis et al., 2011, para. 3).

During this time, Harold "Bud" Goodall became known as one of the pioneers of autoethnography, building on the work of Thomas Benson at Penn State University. In 1981, Benson is said to have authored the first published autoethnography in the field of communication studies, titled "Another Shootout in Cowtown." In 1988, Michael E. Pacanowski's publication "Slouching Towards Chicago" was the second published autoethnography in communication studies. Goodall's *Casing a Promised Land* (1989) was the third autoethnographic contribution to the field and the first book-length study that employed autoethnographic methods. The popularity of Carolyn Ellis's autoethnographic work in the field that followed in the 1990s and 2000s ultimately extended the genre within and beyond communication studies. While anthropologist Ruth Behar's *Translated Woman* (1993) included an autobiographical chapter she described as "the biography in the shadow" (p. xvi), Behar worried about including herself in her work, a strong indication of the field of anthropology's view of researcher placement in the 1990s. Scholars today tend to embrace how autoethnography enlists a rewriting of the subjective self and the cultural context replete with hidden and explicit rules and norms for sustained participation. Autoethnography appears to be gaining particular credibility and influence in top-tier research articles of the social sciences (e.g., Dalton, 2003; Laubscher & Powell, 2003; Romo, 2005; Sparkes, 2000; Winograd, 2002). Autoethnography has also expanded to educational contexts in the wake of high-stakes accountability testing in the United States, posing questions such as "How might my experiences of race, class, and/or gender and sexuality offer insights about my ability to address these issues in a given cultural event/situation?"

Rather than seeking to escape **subjectivity**, teachers and teacher education researchers of the new millennium are considering autoethnographic techniques precisely because of the qualitative genre's capacity to engage first-person voice and to embrace the conflict of writing against oneself as one finds oneself entrenched in the complications of one's positions (e.g., Pennington, 2004; Romo, 2005; Winograd, 2002). For example, as a teacher working in a school where high-stakes testing altered not only the teachers' methods of teaching but also their views of the students and their community, Pennington (2004) used autoethnography as a way to position herself within her research study. Writing in the first person throughout the book, Pennington reveals the history of the school and the teachers' experiences reflected in her own seeking to "contextualize the literacy views of the teachers through comparisons to the views of administrators in the school district and the policies of the state" (p. 1). The study illuminates the teachers' and the researcher's critiques of the ways in which high-stakes accountability testing limited the students' literacy. Autoethnography has become more than a response to researcher positioning in relation to those studied—it has developed into a specific methodology relying on distinct research methods.

Defined Functions of Autoethnography Applied as Critical Social Research

Research methodology is viewed as the overall combination of beliefs that ground a study. It involves recognizing the ontological, epistemological, and methodological aspects of research. It also involves paying attention to the *"paradigm* (Guba, 1990a, p. 17) or interpretive framework, a 'basic set of beliefs that guides action' (Guba, 1990a, p. 17)" (Denzin & Lincoln, 2011, p. 13). The autoethnographic work described in this section exists within the complexity of the qualitative tradition; authors bring a variety of interpretive frameworks to their study of themselves in relation to particular cultural contexts and conditions.

Autoethnography Defined as Methodology

When citing autoethnography as **empirical** research methodology, we refer to the larger notion of paradigmatic purposes and constructions of a study rather than simply the method of doing research, as in the type of data collected or a specific means of analysis. Autoethnography as a genre—or, as some prefer, a subgenre—"includes an array of descriptors (e.g., critical autobiography, ethnobiography, ethnographic poetics, emotionalism, evocative narratives, first-person accounts—to name a few)" (Rossman & Rallis, 2012, p. 94). Still, the term *autoethnography* appears (at least for now) to be the descriptor of choice for this hybrid qualitative genre. In contrast to the term's *auto* (which refers to the author's presentation of critical reflections and interpretations of personal experience), *ethnography* is commonly used to refer to a key qualitative approach to studying the rules, norms, and acts of resistance associated with cultural groups. Consequently, the hybrid term *autoethnography* has come to be the favored name for a form of critical reflexive narrative inquiry, critical reflexive self-study, or critical reflexive action research in which the researcher takes an active, scientific, and systematic view of personal experience in relation to cultural groups identified by the researcher as similar to the self (i.e., us) or as others who differ from the self (i.e., them). It is precisely the hybridity of the genre that allows it to be applied as a stand-alone **methodology** as well as a complementary **method** for assembling data from the five traditional empirical approaches to **qualitative research**: phenomenology, ethnography, narrative inquiry, case study, and grounded theory.

Although connected to those five approaches because of the way it draws on personal narrative, autoethnography can be distinguished by how it affords authors the flexibility to position themselves in relation to the social, cultural, or political in ways that are otherwise off-limits to traditional empirical approaches to qualitative

Methodology and Methods

Methodology is the established and evolving approach to and foundation of a research study.

Methods are the actual techniques, tools, or means used for data collection and analysis.

research. Our analysis of autoethnography as critical social research reveals various levels of explanation and usage of notions related to autoethnography. We begin by differentiating between the framing of autoethnography as a methodology and as a method. From a broad perspective, there is a clear delineation between researchers who utilize autoethnography as a larger ontological and epistemological foundation for their work and others who rely on autoethnography's focus on the self to bring themselves into research inquiries based on various qualitative methods. In other words, some autoethnographers conceptualize their studies in ways that align with our depiction of autoethnography as a methodology—that is, they understand that the foundation of their work is reliant on their studying themselves. For example, many authors who are seeking to bring previously silenced perspectives to the forefront consciously use their identities as epistemologies, or as ways of knowing. Hermann-Wilmarth and Bills (2010) demonstrated an in-depth use of autoethnography as a means to address the study they conducted with their students. Adapting to the ongoing data collection, they responded to their students' resistance to discussing their LGBT experiences by being "at once researchers, participants, informants, and subjects" (p. 260). Their autoethnographic study utilized queer theory, grounded theory, and comparative analysis and allowed them to study their students and their identities. This work illustrates how some scholars situate autoethnographic work in existing research strategies and contribute to the field under study. Teacher education typically addresses preservice and inservice teacher learning, and Hermann-Wilmarth and Bills (2010) transformed their teacher education focus to include the role of the teacher educator.

Autoethnography is also used both to study the self and to present alternative perspectives. DeLeon (2010) pressed autoethnography to the forefront in critically examining his own identity. His autoethnography was detailed and situated in research traditions of narrative inquiry with a message of "challenging privileged academic discourses" (p. 408) encased within personal narratives of DeLeon's experiences. Authors such as DeLeon have used autoethnography to counter colonizing voices by creating spaces for previously sequestered narratives. Houston (2007) also applied autoethnography to address the crisis of representation and situated autoethnography as a form of resistance. Due to the intimate nature of identity and contextualized experiences, autoethnography's centering of the author allows intimate aspects of understandings and experiences, often inaccessible to researchers, to become a part of narratives and contribute to the field. Several studies have brought autoethnography into the study of others. Camangian (2010) clearly explicates autoethnography in his study examining the use of autoethnography as a tool for high school students to understand their identities within larger social contexts. Building theoretically from a caring (Noddings, 1992) and critical literacy foundation (Freire, 1968/1972), Camangian constructed a conceptualization of autoethnography that was essential to his research query, stating, "To foster a critical literacy of caring, I taught autoethnography as a strategic pedagogical tool for students to examine the ways they experience, exist, and explain their identities" (p. 183). Methodologically, Camangian sustains the use of autoethnography throughout the article, continually integrating its use into the research focus, analysis, and interpretation. Hughes (2008a) also has brought autoethnography into the classroom as a means for critical race pedagogy, noting, "Our narratives also speak to the internal and external pursuit of specific pedagogical help for overcoming the educational impediments of race, class, and gender oppression" (p. 88).

Overall, studies that concentrate on the ontological, epistemological, and methodological representation of autoethnography are characterized by the consistent portrayal of autoethnography's relationship to the inquiry, paradigmatic affiliations, and how autoethnography contributes to the standing knowledge in educational research. Although we have attempted to detail the histories and definitions of autoethnography, this is still a very novel and sometimes impossible task as viewed by certain schools of thought, owing to the positioning of the researcher as the focus of study. Therefore, making clear connections to preexisting research perspectives is crucial, and many scholars situate autoethnography as methodology in relation to specific areas of critical social research. Table 1.2 illustrates how particular researchers have related their autoethnographic work to the larger research schools of thought or paradigms.

Other studies rely on autoethnography to center the self as subject and then move on to use a variety of established research methods to collect, analyze, and represent data. Representation of the self in most studies has utilized first-person narrative descriptions and rationales from introduction to conclusion, while Theoharis (2008) and Tsumagari (2010) demonstrate the use of third person. Autoethnography is also applied as a methodology to explicate the role of the researcher in relation to research participants, at times making the researcher a participant in the study as well. These uses of autoethnography, while deliberate, are unique in their adoption of autoethnography during the study to illuminate the researcher's methodological and paradigmatic shift to include the self (e.g., McClellan, 2012; Spenceley, 2011). At the other end of the spectrum, autoethnographies are deliberately conceptualized before a study in order to examine a personal experience within a particular context (e.g., Tsumagari, 2010; Wright, 2006), to illuminate gaps in particular domains (e.g., Jones, 2009; Quicke, 2010), to demonstrate transformative experiences (e.g., Long, 2008; Tour, 2012), or to engage in self-critique (e.g., Preston, 2011; Schulz, 2007).

When autoethnography is the foundation for any type of published inquiry, the negative assumptions about situating such a critical form of self-guided inquiry must be addressed from conception to dissemination. The centering of the self as a research subject is clear and supported by rationales that address more than research methods; the researcher positions the self in ways that are epistemological. For example, Henning (2012) completed a study of her own learning in which autoethnography was epistemologically and methodologically the foundation for her inquiry into her

TABLE 1.2 ● Authors Seeking/Making a Link from Autoethnography Methodology to Tradition	
Connections of Autoethnography Methodology to Traditional Tools	**Authors Seeking/Making the Connection**
Autoethnography and critical social theory	Camangian, 2010; Chavez, 2012; DeLeon, 2010; Garza, 2008; Houston, 2007; Hughes, 2008a; Kahl, 2010; Mayuzumi, 2009; Pennington, 2007; Quicke, 2010; Reta, 2010; Schulz, 2007; Woods, 2010, Wright; 2006
Autoethnography as self-study	Attard & Armour, 2005; Pennington, 2006; Pennington & Brock, 2012; Wright, 2006
Autoethnography as narrative inquiry	Camangian, 2010; Carless, 2012; Chavez, 2012; DeLeon, 2010; Garza, 2008; Hamilton, Smith, & Worthington, 2008; Jones, 2009; Long, 2008; Nutbrown, 2011; Pennington, 2007; Quicke, 2010; Smagorinsky, 2011
Autoethnography with counternarrative, *testimonios*, and identity	Camangian, 2010; Chavez, 2012; Correa & Lovegrove, 2012; DeLeon, 2010; Hughes, 2008c; Mayuzumi, 2009; Pearson, 2010; Quicke, 2010; Reta, 2010; Tour, 2012
Autoethnography and ethnography	Henning, 2012
Autoethnography and phenomenology	Rossman & Rallis, 2012; Tsumagari, 2010
Autoethnography and grounded theory	Hermann-Wilmarth & Bills, 2010; Theoharis, 2008
Symbolic interactionism	Anderson, 2006

experiences, beginning with the research question, "What can a seasoned, face-to-face teacher and occasional online teacher learn by taking an online course?" (p. 13). She utilized "memories, self-observations and reflections and textual artifacts" (p. 14) and found that she sought to stay in control of her learning, had concerns about interacting with others, and also had emotional concerns. Her recommendations connect to her findings about her own learning and add to the field's knowledge base.

Autoethnography can help us think about the researcher and the researched as equally open to change (Hermann-Wilmarth & Bills, 2010, p. 270). One example of such an in-depth use of autoethnography is Hermann-Wilmarth and Bills's (2010) work noted above, in which they applied the genre as a means to address a study conducted with students. Autoethnography is also used to study the self and to present alternative perspectives precisely because of the way it involves "reflexively writing the self into the ethnographic text; isolating that space where memory, history, performance, and meaning intersect" (Denzin, 2014, p. 22). Slattery (2001) uses Foucault and the artist Jackson Pollock to examine the regulation of the human body and sexuality as they relate to his experiences as a student in a Roman Catholic school in the 1960s. His work illuminates not only his experiences but also how they connect to notions of schooling in what he refers to as the "hidden curriculum of the body" (p. 394). Such insights and analysis would not be easily gathered through interviews and observations of research participants. It is Slattery's voice and intimate representation that bring the findings to the surface and help us to understand the regulatory nature of schooling (see Appendix A for more detailed discussion of Slattery's work).

Researchers who use autoethnography as a means to justify their inclusion in their studies vary in their depictions of autoethnography as either empirical research methodology or empirical research method. In the next section we detail how researchers use autoethnographic methods as a means of actually doing data collection and analysis.

Autoethnography Defined as Method(s)

Autoethnography is frequently used as a research method, technique, tool, or means for self-examination and relied upon for specific techniques of data collection, data analysis, and representation. Autoethnographic methods of data collection and analysis are inclusive of many types of qualitative methods, such as reflective journaling, videotaping, interviewing, and fieldwork. The distinction between more common qualitative studies and autoethnographic studies that focus on the self lies in the subject under study. Data collection and analysis methods are unique to autoethnography in these types of studies. Researchers within the ethnographic tradition often use traditional ethnographic methods to focus on culture and fieldwork while highlighting the researcher as subject (Henning, 2012; Houston, 2007; Martin, 2011; Nutbrown, 2011; Pennington, 2007; Quicke, 2010). Others adopt a more evocative approach, relying on notions of autoethnography as critical reflections (Attard & Armour, 2005; Woods, 2010), performative presentations (Correa & Lovegrove, 2012), *testimonios* as counternarratives (see Camangian, 2010; Chavez, 2012; Correa & Lovegrove, 2012; DeLeon, 2010; Hughes & Berry, 2012; Mayuzumi, 2009; Pearson, 2010; Reta, 2010), emotional recall (McMahon & Dinan-Thompson, 2011; Nutbrown, 2011; Sander & Williamson, 2010), and narrative constructions (Carless, 2012).

Centering the story of the self and focusing exclusively on narrations and descriptions of personal experience are the hallmark of autoethnographic studies, yet the studies vary widely in their level of description of the methods used. Correa and Lovegrove (2012) present their *testimonio* as a performance (as a play); these researchers relied on their "meetings, as we discussed our childhood memories and a shared sense of dis/connection with our different Latina/o cultures" (p. 350). For example, Garza (2008) relies on autoethnography in using his personal journals from his first year as a school superintendent as his primary data sources. He defines autoethnography and then moves to presenting journal excerpts directly and chronologically.

Titled "autoethnographic moments," these are dated but otherwise presented without categorization or analysis; they read like a peek into his personal journals organized by date. Garza constructs his conclusions as lessons learned from his journal entries. Long (2008) utilizes a continuous first-person description of her spiritual experiences, integrating theory and related scholarship to her illness. She describes her research methods as follows: "During [my illness] I kept a notebook, I scribbled on scraps of paper and I annotated novels. . . . I felt compelled to write" (p. 190). She then ties her writing to learning experiences in the classroom and makes clear recommendations based on her analysis. Preston (2011) combines personal reflections and transcripts of data interactions with participants. She relies on recordings of her work with her counseling clients. Her focus on herself is clearly articulated as she reflects on her data: "I have not yet understood the meaning of countertransference through my training. . . . I am preoccupied with my own problem, and have not fully understood the true meaning of the counselor's role" (p. 118). Autoethnographic methods are integrated into all of the studies described above in unique ways, yet all of the methods used rely on data collected and analyzed in specific ways.

The application of autoethnography as method(s) in some of the most current scholarship illustrates various degrees and means of describing and defining autoethnography. Most of the observed studies mention the term *autoethnography,* while some of them use the term only in the abstract (Sander & Williamson, 2010; Tobin, 2011). Autoethnographic work is employed primarily as a method to study the self as an educator (Attard & Armour, 2005; Hamilton, Smith, & Worthington, 2008; Henning, 2012; Hermann-Wilmarth & Bills, 2010; Hughes, 2008a; Kahl, 2010; Woods, 2010). Within the field of teacher education, Hamilton et al. (2008) compare and contrast autoethnography with self-study and narrative inquiry, describing the value of centering the self within teacher education. In some cases, autoethnography has been used as a method along with notions of caring to bring students and self-reflection into the research and learning process (Camangian, 2010; Hughes, 2008a; Jones, 2009; Pennington, 2007). Autoethnography has also been used as a method to provide alternative viewpoints in particular disciplines (Carless, 2012; Fox, 2008; Jones, 2009; Martin, 2011) or contexts (Clough, 2009; Garza, 2008; Houston, 2007; Long, 2008). The permutations of autoethnography vary across disciplines and according to the depth and breadth of how autoethnography is described and used as a method.

Iterations and Examples of Autoethnography Applied as Critical Social Research

Autoethnography takes more than 20 different forms, and that is only counting those that have appeared in the published social science forms of autoethnography. Remember, autoethnography outside the confines of social science can take on additional hybrid forms of poetry, performance, art, and audiovisual media beyond those listed here. As Ellis et al. (2011) note, "The forms of autoethnography differ in how much emphasis is placed on the study of others, the researcher's self and interaction with others, traditional analysis, and the interview context, as well as on power relationships" (para. 15). In this section we name and define those forms of autoethnography and offer illustrative examples and/or relevant references. The work of Ellis et al. (2011), Hughes and Willink (2015), and Denzin (2014) is particularly useful for locating and defining these various iterations and for providing examples of them in alphabetical order (see Table 1.3).

Applying Autoethnography as Critical Social Research: Key Considerations

Autoethnography involves locating a meaningful phenomenon of interest and considering a *critical reflexive* approach to thinking and writing. These elements of autoethnography tend to be quite a bit more challenging to engage mentally than initially anticipated by most of our students, for several reasons. First, it is difficult to locate and focus on meaningful, personalized central questions and to engage productive diverse groups that challenge us to see and resist the matrix through those questions, all the while trying "not to separate [our] personal and professional philosophies" (Milner, 2003, p. 205). Reflection alone seems to take an author to one necessary, but insufficient, place. Conversely, a reflexive complicit lens challenges an author to question taken-for-granted knowledge and how the matrix can adversely influence one's pedagogy, teaching, learning, policy, and practice. Milner (2003) challenges preservice and inservice teachers, as well as teacher educators, to revisit whether they truly believe "oppression is wrong" and how they may or may not "display this belief at school" (p. 205).

Milner's (2003) work is instructive here because it also challenges autoethnographers to pursue inquiry and writing that motivates them to reconsider how best to portray their anti-oppressive selves through "discourse and actions outside of school resulting in a form of social justice" (p. 205). Dropping the editorial "we" of the public transcript (Scott, 1990) is a critical component of autoethnography, particularly in the U.S. context, where writers and speakers in public venues enlist unsolicited representation to articulate given points they are trying to make. Autoethnographers engage reflexivity during this element by confronting the reality of being critically conscious while considering how they might be complicit in problems of teaching, learning, and living that they perceive. On a practical note, although we and most of our students have engaged resistance (Giroux, 1983) in the matrix of domination before, it has too often been not a transformative resistance or the form that people act out to begin "resisting domination in myriad ways" (Jennings & Lynn, 2005, p. 20).

By now you have seen that autoethnography is not a simple one-size-fits-all study of the self, because it can vary according to the broad methodology used, the actual methods of research

What Is Critical Social Research?

Critical social research encompasses a broad range of social science studies that purposefully challenge existing understandings and foundations of knowledge, while also embracing various research approaches across multiple disciplines.

(Jupp, 1993)

TABLE 1.3 ● Types of Autoethnography: Descriptions and Citations	
Types of Autoethnography	**Descriptions and Citations**
Analytic autoethnography	Ethnographic work in which "the researcher is (1) a full member in the research group or setting, (2) visible as such a member in the researcher's published texts, and (3) committed to an analytic research agenda focused on improving theoretical understandings of broader social phenomena" (Anderson, 2006, p. 375).
Co-constructed narratives	Narratives that "illustrate the meanings of relational experiences, particularly how people collaboratively cope with the ambiguities, uncertainties, and contradictions of being friends, family, and/or intimate partners. Co-constructed narratives view relationships as jointly-authored, incomplete, and historically situated affairs. Joint activity structures co-constructed research projects. Often told about or around an epiphany, each person first writes her or his experience, and then shares and reacts to the story the other wrote at the same time (see Bochner & Ellis, 1995; Toyosaki & Pensoneau, 2005; Vande Berg & Trujillo, 2008)" (Ellis, Adams, & Bochner, 2011, para. 23).
Collaborative autoethnography	Autoethnography that involves "the coproduction of an autoethnographic (duoethnography) text by two or more writers, often separated by time and distance" (Denzin, 2014, p. 23, citing Diversi & Moreira, 2009; Gale & Wyatt, 2009; Wyatt, Gale, Gannon, & Davies, 2011).
Community autoethnographies	"Similar to interactive interviews, *community autoethnographies* use the personal experience of researchers-in-collaboration to illustrate how a community manifests particular social/cultural issues (e.g., whiteness; Toyosaki, Pensoneau-Conway, Wendt, & Leathers, 2009). Community autoethnographies thus not only facilitate 'community-building' research practices but also make opportunities for 'cultural and social intervention' possible" (Ellis et al., 2011, para. 22).
Critical co-constructed autoethnography	A relatively new method from Cann and DeMeulenaere (2012) that is informed by "critical theory, critical pedagogy and critical race theory" (p. 146). It is intended to provide "a way for collaborating activist researchers to reflect on the tempo, uncertainty and complexity of research relationships that cross boundaries into more personal spaces such as friendships" (p. 146). The method as a product was also developed to name and "create spaces for collaborating researchers to work across differences" (p. 146). Moreover, the method was developed as a defensible "process of collectively reflecting together about our work . . . as a means to avoid a false consciousness and examine the transformative work we attempt to do as researchers, authors, college teachers" (p. 153). One example of critical co-constructed autoethnography is the work of Hughes and Willink (2015), who applied the method as a systematic approach to learning from their co-reflexive critical dialogues in their ethnographic work on school desegregation in the coastal Albemarle area of North Carolina. The researchers sometimes participated in different interviews with the same informants—Hughes as a self-identified Black male doctoral student from the Albemarle area and Willink as a self-identified White female doctoral student from the North.

Types of Autoethnography	Descriptions and Citations
Critical performance autoethnography	Autoethnography that involves critical reflexive writing, rehearsal, and performance that engages "Conquergood's triad of triads: (1) the I's: imagination, inquiry, intervention; (2) the A's: artistry, analysis, activism; (3) the C's: creativity, citizenship, civic struggles for social justice" (Denzin, 2014, p. 25, citing Madison, 2005, p. 171, and Madison, 2012, pp. 189–190; Pennington & Prater, 2014).
Deconstructive autoethnography	Autoethnography that "shifts attention from the narrative I to the performative I, contesting the meanings given to voice, presence, experience, and subjectivity" (Denzin, 2014, p. 25, citing Jackson & Mazzei, 2009, pp. 307–313).
Duoethnography	Collaborative research methodology in which two or more researchers juxtapose their life histories in order to provide multiple understandings of a social phenomenon (Norris & Sawyer, 2012, pp. 9–10). "Duoethnographers use their own biographies as sites of inquiry and engage in dialogic narrative, often realized in collaborative writing and collaborative autoethnography" (Denzin, 2014, p. 23, citing Gale, Pelias, Russell, Spry, & Wyatt, 2013; Norris & Sawyer, 2012).
Estrangement autoethnography	Autoethnography in which the researcher purposefully performs in countercultural ways, thinking and acting in ways that are counter to the status quo, the norms and rules of the dominant culture. In this way, the autoethnographic researcher can critically and reflexively examine responses of self and others while in an estranged state and respond to the theoretical body of knowledge on the area being studied (Keenan & Evans, 2014b). In short, estrangement autoethnography can reveal and thus lead to a challenge of taken-for-granted knowledge. For example, Keenan and Evans (2014a) contribute evidence of the effectiveness of estrangement autoethnography in enhancing university student learning and provide a model for undertaking the performance of estrangement. Their work explores the use of estrangement autoethnography as a means to encourage student autonomy, enhance learning to challenge student perspectives of normal environments, and problematize perspectives on consumer culture to support learners' experiential knowledge on which to base their use of theory.
Indigenous/native ethnographies	Ethnographies developed "from colonized or economically subordinated people, and . . . used to address and disrupt power in research, particularly a (outside) researcher's right and authority to study (exotic) others. Once at the service of the (White, masculine, heterosexual, middle/upper-classed, Christian, able-bodied) ethnographer, indigenous/native ethnographers now work to construct their own personal and cultural stories; they no longer find (forced) subjugation excusable (Denzin, Lincoln, & Smith, 2008)" (Ellis et al., 2011, para. 16).
Interactive interviews	Interviews that provide "an in-depth and intimate understanding of people's experiences with emotionally charged and sensitive topics" (Ellis, Kiesinger, & Tillmann-Healy, 1997, p. 121). Interactive interviews are collaborative endeavors between researchers and participants, research activities in which researchers and participants—one and the same—probe together about issues that transpire, in

(Continued)

TABLE 1.3 ● (Continued)

Types of Autoethnography	Descriptions and Citations
	conversation, about particular topics (e.g., eating disorders). Interactive interviews usually consist of multiple interview sessions, and, unlike traditional one-on-one interviews with strangers, are situated within the context of emerging and well-established relationships among participants and interviewers (Adams, 2008). "The emphasis in these research contexts is on what can be learned from interaction within the interview setting as well as on the stories that each person brings to the research encounter" (Ellis et al., 2011, para. 21).
Interpretive autoethnography	"A critical performative practice, a practice that begins with the biography of the writer and moves outward to culture, discourse, history, and ideology" (Denzin, 2014, p. x).
Interpretive performance autoethnography	Autoethnography that "allows the researcher to take up each person's life in its immediate particularity and to ground the life in its historical moment. . . . Interpretation works forward to the conclusion of a set of acts taken up by the subject while working back in time, interrogating the historical, cultural, and biographical conditions that moved the person to experience the events being studied (Denzin, 2001, p. 41). These events occur in those sites where structure, history, and autobiography intersect" (Denzin, 2014, p. x).
Layered accounts	Accounts that "focus on the author's experience alongside data, abstract analysis, and relevant literature. This form emphasizes the procedural nature of research. Similar to grounded theory, layered accounts illustrate how 'data collection and analysis proceed simultaneously' (Charmaz, 1983, p. 110) and frame existing research as a 'source of *questions and comparisons*' rather than a 'measure of truth' (p.117). But unlike grounded theory, layered accounts use vignettes, reflexivity, multiple voices, and introspection (Ellis, 1991) to 'invoke' readers to enter into the 'emergent experience' of doing and writing research (Ronai, 1992, p. 123), conceive of identity as an 'emergent process' (Rambo, 2005, p. 583), and consider evocative, concrete texts to be as important as abstract analyses (Ronai, 1995, 1996)" (Ellis et al., 2011, para. 20).
Meta-autoethnography	Autoethnography that involves the researcher's layering of new interpretations, reflections, and vignettes onto his or her older autoethnographic work. Developed by Carol Ellis (2008), who introduces as an example of meta-autoethnography a process in which she collects a dozen of her stories about loss in her family and her childhood and then translates across those stories in search of new epiphanies, revelations, and understandings. In short, Ellis (2008) describes meta-autoethnography as a systematic process of critical reflexive thinking and synthesis of one's own previous autoethnography work in order to learn from it and through it.
Mini-autoethnography	A shortened version of autoethnography that sacrifices the breadth and depth of critical reflexive study for a clear and sustained focused on three salient experiences, episodes, moments, or events from one's life. As represented in Appendixes B and C of this textbook, mini-autoethnography can be a useful assignment for learners who

Types of Autoethnography	Descriptions and Citations
	are undergraduate students or researchers new to the genre; it is also useful for learners in large groups and those under relatively short time constraints (Wallace, 2002). For example, Wallace (2002) conducted a mini-autoethnography of three institutional moments in which he saw a set of conditions that invited him to speak or write as a gay academic to make political interventions in dominant culture.
Narrative ethnographies	"Texts presented in the form of stories that incorporate the ethnographer's experiences into the ethnographic descriptions and analysis of others. Here the emphasis is on the ethnographic study of others, which is accomplished partly by attending to encounters between the narrator and members of the groups being studied (Tedlock, 1991), and the narrative often intersects with analyses of patterns and processes" (Ellis et al., 2011, para. 17).
Performance autoethnography	"The merger of critical pedagogy, performance ethnography, and cultural politics; the creation of texts that move from epiphanies to the sting of memory, the personal to the political, the autobiographical to the cultural, the local to the historical. A response to the successive crises of democracy and capitalism that shape daily life; showing how these formations repressively enter into and shape the stories and performances persons share with one another. It shows how persons bring dignity and meaning to their lives in and through these performances; it offers kernels of utopian hope of how things might be different, better" (Denzin, 2014, p. 25, citing Denzin, 2003; Pelias, 2011).
Personal narratives	"Stories about authors who view themselves as the phenomenon and write evocative narratives specifically focused on their academic, research, and personal lives (e.g., Berry 2007; Goodall, 2006; Poulos, 2008; Tillmann, 2009). These often are the most controversial forms of autoethnography for traditional social scientists, especially if they are not accompanied by more traditional analysis and/or connections to scholarly literature. Personal narratives propose to understand a self or some aspect of a life as it intersects with a cultural context, connect to other participants as co-researchers, and invite readers to enter the author's world and to use what they learn there to reflect on, understand, and cope with their own lives (Ellis, 2004, p. 46)" (Ellis et al., 2011, para. 24).
Racial autoethnography	Autoethnography that combines racial autobiography, ethnography, and critical reflexive self-narratives to begin learning "about the idea of race, [as] . . . underutilized as a tool to familiarize and orient students in the process of critical inquiry for nursing research. The aims of racial autoethnography is to: (1) reposition students to effect an epistemological change, (2) challenge dominant ideology, and (3) function as a link between the student and critical theories for use in nursing research. Students [are encouraged to engage] in and share reflective narrative about a variety of instructional materials. . . . Reflective narratives are presented in a framework that addresses . . . racial identity development" (Taylor, Mackin, & Oldenberg, 2008, p. 342).

(Continued)

TABLE 1.3 ● (Continued)

Types of Autoethnography	Descriptions and Citations
Reflexive, dyadic interviews	Interviews that "focus on the interactively produced meanings and emotional dynamics of the interview itself. Though the focus is on the participant and her or his story, the words, thoughts, and feelings of the researcher also are considered, e.g., personal motivation for doing a project, knowledge of the topics discussed, emotional responses to an interview, and ways in which the interviewer may have been changed by the process of interviewing. Although the researcher's experience isn't the main focus, personal reflection adds context and layers to the story being told about participants (Ellis, 2004)" (Ellis et al., 2011, para. 18).
Reflexive ethnographies	Ethnographies that "document ways a researcher changes as a result of doing fieldwork. Reflexive/narrative ethnographies exist on a continuum ranging from starting research from the ethnographer's biography, to the ethnographer studying her or his life alongside cultural members' lives, to ethnographic memoirs (Ellis, 2004, p. 50) or 'confessional tales' (Van Maanen, 1988) where the ethnographer's backstage research endeavors become the focus of investigation (Ellis, 2004)" Ellis et al., 2011, para. 19).

used, and how it can be represented. We propose that despite all of these variations, some basic ideas can be used to delineate autoethnography. We have identified five of them: critical reflexivity, educative experiences, privilege-penalty experiences, ethical concerns, and salient experiences assembled and shared. Moreover, while working in qualitative research as a doctoral candidate, Hughes's former doctoral advisee Nitasha Clark developed the acronym CREPES as a mnemonic tool for easier recall of these five key ideas: *c*ritical *r*eflexivity, *e*ducative experiences, *p*rivilege-penalty experiences, *e*thics, and *s*upported-salient narratives. Each idea is described below in more detail.

Idea 1: Autoethnography considers *critical reflexivity.*

In applying autoethnography as **critical social research**, it is key for autoethnographers to consider their own roles with critical reflexivity, whereby they come to view themselves as complicit (at least partially) in the problems they perceive. Discussing such complicity can place scholars in quite a vulnerable position. It is the crucial consideration of unveiling the vulnerable self that can free the mind of self-deception without self-deprecation. In addition, it is imperative for autoethnographers to anticipate a complicit and vulnerable self with regard to sharing sensitive information with others as they grapple with the complications of their educational positions. After engaging this process, autoethnographers may return to it as part of the lifelong journey of improving their craft. Hughes's students often lamented when engaging this crucial element, as he initially did, stating, "Before I knew about how all of this domination stuff creeps into my classroom, I didn't have to worry about what to do about it." Our blissful, naive selves in this way, without a reflexive, complicit lens on our perceptions of problems, ultimately limit our ability to optimize the potential of our educational research endeavors.

Idea 2: Autoethnography considers *educative* experiences.

A second key idea of autoethnography involves an in-depth view of one's educative experiences along the lifelong spectrum. Educative experiences inside and outside schools and classrooms are crucial for autoethnographers to consider as they engage in critical reflexive thought processes. Bullough and Pinnegar (2001) concur with the need to approach studies of the self from multiple levels of a lifelong educational experience and with a reflexive lens: "The connection between autobiography and history must be apparent, the issues attended to need to be central to teaching and teacher education" (p. 20). Patricia Hill Collins (1990) describes the matrix also as being experienced and resisted, taught and learned on three levels: "personal biography; group or community level of the cultural context created by race, class, and gender; and the systemic level of social institutions" (pp. 226–227). The group or community level of the cultural educational context is particularly important to consider as it seems to be a major social site for reproducing biased responses (including the *hits, misses,* and *false alarms* discussed by Swim & Stangor, 1998; see Appendix D for discussion of these concepts).

Idea 3: Autoethnography considers *privilege-penalty* experiences.

A third key idea of autoethnography concerns the deception, contradiction, ignorance, and denial of interlocking systems of oppression (including race, class, and gender as particularly dominant and oppressive). These constitute what Collins (1990) names "the matrix of domination" (i.e., the matrix). She criticizes any scholarly position that identifies as fundamental only the oppression with which it feels most comfortable while classifying all others as less important in the matrix. For her, the matrix presents "few pure victims or oppressors" because an "individual derives varying amounts of penalty and privilege from the multiple systems of oppression in which everyone lives" (p. 230). For example, from Collins's Black feminist standpoint, "white women are penalized by their gender, but privileged by their race," and "depending on the context, an individual may be an oppressor, a member of an oppressed group, or simultaneously oppressor and oppressed" (p. 224). It is crucial for autoethnographers to consider privilege and penalty alongside the social forces they perceive, identify, and study in relation to themselves.

Cleveland's (2005) work can be instructive here for autoethnography teachers and learners as he builds on Collins's (1990) work by having his students "unpack" or identify privileges on their own. As a self-identified Black male, often teaching as "other," in his teacher education classroom, Cleveland addresses ability privilege, class privilege, heterosexual privilege, male privilege, and White privilege. He links three primary reasons to the success of this approach: avoiding "shame or blame"; identifying that everyone is privileged in one way or another and, as a result, some are more privileged than others; and informing students that, as a result of these privileges, we are all capable of oppressing others (p. 67).

Idea 4: Autoethnography considers relational *ethics*.

A fourth key idea that can be crucial to developing autoethnography involves the critical self-examination of relational ethics. Ellis et al. (2011) assert that autoethnographers "consider 'relational concerns' as a crucial dimension of inquiry . . . that must be kept uppermost in their minds throughout the research and writing process" (para. 31). Most of the time, it is a necessity for autoethnographers to be able to "continue to live in the world of relationships in which their research is embedded after the research is completed" (para. 31). In light of this necessity, at least three logical obligations for autoethnographers can be drawn from the evidence provided by the autoethnographies reviewed here: (a) autoethnographers must be cognizant of the promise and the potential problems of showing their work to others implicated in or by their texts, and must take extreme care in considering whether and how to encourage others to engage in *member checking* (i.e., the opportunity to "check" and respond to how they are represented in the autoethnographic text); (b) autoethnographers must protect the privacy and safety of others by altering identifying characteristics in their publications, such as "circumstance, topics discussed, or characteristics like race, gender name, place, or appearance"; and (c) autoethnographers must stay aware of how their work is interpreted and understood, because, as Ellis et al. (2011) explain, "the essence and meaningfulness of the research story is more important than the precise recounting of [socially constructed] detail" (para. 31).

Indeed, autoethnography presents particular ethics concerns due to the need for researchers not just to protect the identities of others mentioned in their studies but also to ensure that their own agendas and identities do not sacrifice the credibility of their studies. When the researcher includes a great deal of his or her own identity in an autoethnography, greater danger exists for that researcher stance to influence the questions and direction of interviews with participants. Yet, to date, relatively few peer-reviewed journal articles have discussed the role of ethics when autoethnography is applied as empirical educational research. Similar to other qualitative researchers, autoethnographers have an obligation to address ethical decisions shaping research design, methodology, and analysis and to report on consent and confidentiality agreements (Duran et al., 2006). In addition to these obligations, it is incumbent on all qualitative researchers in the academy, including autoethnographers, to determine the necessity and parameters of approval from an institutional review board (IRB) (Duran et al., 2006). Although autoethnography can be translated across the other standard obligations quite seamlessly, obtaining IRB approval is complex when this method is applied.

Conventional qualitative research methods require consent forms for each adult and child observed (during focused observation) and/or interviewed during the course of the research. However, if autoethnography is to continue offering a venue for unveiling and critiquing underrepresentation, marginalization, and oppression, how might autoethnographers go about obtaining informed consent from individuals, groups, and institutions that subject the **subaltern** (i.e., the excluded, oppressed, or marginalized person) to underrepresentation, marginalization, and oppression? Would we be remiss to ignore the unique ethical dilemmas, risks, and social costs to be considered by subaltern autoethnographers, who may act to protect themselves and their families in ways that challenge ethical reporting as interpreted by some of the more powerful and privileged members of the academy? There are no simple responses to this line of inquiry; however, it may be sufficient to say here that autoethnographers have traditionally considered relational ethics concerns "as a crucial dimension of inquiry that must be kept uppermost in their minds throughout the research and writing process" (Ellis et al., 2011, para. 31).

There is some promise for addressing the ethics gap in autoethnographic educational research, as some autoethnographers have presented research and findings in ways that honor site access agreements and consent from participants in pursuit of ethical reporting. They have also been aware of potential conflicts of interest and researcher perspectives that may influence how the empirical research is reported. However, even with identifying information seemingly omitted by the researcher, direct and indirect disclosure of participant identities can occur. In response to this type of ethical threat, some autoethnography has evolved into a method(ology) that can allow participants "to talk back to how they have been represented in the text" (Ellis et al., 2011, para. 31). Autoethnographies highlighted by Hughes, Pennington, and Makris (2012) implemented one or more of the following processes that respond to Ellis et al.'s (2011) relational ethics concerns:

1. Application of pseudonyms for all proper nouns and pronouns (e.g., Berry, 2005)

2. Member checking (e.g., Hughes, 2008a, 2008c)

3. Coauthorship with key informant (e.g., Laubscher & Powell, 2003)

For example, Berry (2005) specifically illustrates the ethical care that autoethnographers can engage when reporting potentially volatile information about a student:

> "School is like a jail, the students are like prisoners, the teachers are prison guards and the principal is the warden," said one student I'll call D. Students were assigned to read a chapter of the text entitled *Metaphors of Schooling* and I was in the midst of facilitating a discussion based on an in-class small group assignment to develop metaphors and similes of school. When D provided his response, the class responded in thunderous applause, some students standing while clapping. (p. 40)

Samples like Berry's suggest that, similar to those of ethnography researchers, the methodological concern for ethical reporting obligates autoethnographers to protect the privacy of the people described in their self-study research.

Through verbal and written confidentiality agreements, the autoethnographic process can involve member checking, as mentioned previously. Such member checking led Hughes (2008a) to completely rewrite a manuscript after receiving feedback from the student centered in the piece, whom he identified by the pseudonym Maggie. She described his original draft essentially as inaccurate and self-aggrandizing. Moreover, the need to maintain the privacy of those in everything from autoethnographers' monographs to their photographs is paramount (Sieber & Tolich, 2013). Adherence to the ethics of autoethnography is demonstrated by the great care and self-critical discretion applied by the researchers highlighted above, and more research is needed that specifically speaks to ethics in educational research that applies autoethnography as method and methodology. One way autoethnographers can respond to confidentiality issues is to consider coauthorship with one or more others mentioned in their work. In another example, we learn from Laubscher and Powell (2003) about the promise and problems of co-teaching a diversity- and equity-based psychology course across color, class, and cultural lines.

Idea 5: Autoethnography considers *supported-salient* narratives.

A fifth and final key idea to consider when applying autoethnography as critical social research involves the selection of supported-salient narratives for exploration and in-depth critique. We interpret the idea of supported-salient life narratives as *memorable personal stories from one's life that can be supported by evidence from related critical social research literature*. This is an important idea that separates autoethnography from traditional storytelling. One anonymous reviewer of this text when it was in manuscript form reminded us that we should note here the distinction between thinking *about* a story and thinking *with* a story. As Frank (1995) explains, thinking "about a story is to reduce it to content and then analyze that content. Thinking with stories takes the story as already complete; there is no going beyond it" (p. 23). Moreover, one might surmise that "stories are a unified whole, and rather than dismantling and deconstructing them for the [sole] purposes of research or treating them as another set of data, we want to experience the stories *as stories* and the effect they have on the storyteller, the audience, and our own lives" (Herrmann & DiFate, 2014, p. 300). We find evidence in autoethnographic scholarship that autoethnographers exist somewhere along a continuum that ranges from leaning toward thinking about stories (e.g., Anderson, 2006; Chang, 2008) to leaning toward thinking with stories (e.g., Ellis, 2004; Ellis & Bochner, 2000), with some falling somewhere in between (e.g., Hughes, 2008c; Pennington, 2007). Whether thinking about a story, thinking with a story, or both, autoethnographers are expected to support the story with evidence to be garnered, so "readers will have no difficulty recognizing the authority of the scholarly voice, not just its authenticity" (Bullough & Pinnegar, 2001, p. 20).

Initially, autoethnographers supported the postpositivist goal of **triangulation** of narrative sources of evidence, which essentially involves gaining evidence from at least three sources addressing the same issue (Hughes, 2008c). For example, an autoethnographer may examine him- or herself critically after a salient cross-cultural experience by providing narratives from his or her own experience and narratives from at least two other people who shared that experience. Through the supported-salient narrative idea, multiple "themes should be[come] evident and identifiable across the conversation represented or the narrative represented" (Bullough & Pinnegar, 2001, p. 20). Because autoethnography narratives (like all other narratives) are inherently flawed with subjectivity and implicit bias, supportive evidence from peer-reviewed publications can help readers become less concerned about whether autoethnographers are lying and more concerned about finding "gaps and inconsistencies and associations" (Luttrell, 2000, p. 512).

> ## Assemblage
>
> Assemblage is a data collection method designed to represent a multilayered moment. It relies on literature, items, and accounts assembled in a unique form.

The advent of **assemblage** in autoethnography encourages autoethnographers to consider purposefully exposing the type of gaps, inconsistencies, and associations (Gurin & Nagda, 2006) that may emerge when they compare the stories of others to the stories they tell themselves. Assemblage, translated as a data collection strategy, involves the gathering of a collection of items, including relevant literature, that fit together to provide multiple perspectives and rich, multilayered accounts of a particular time, place, or moment in the life of the autoethnographer. Assemblage is steps beyond traditional qualitative triangulation; Denshire and Lee (2014) "liken it to the assembling of artifacts from an archaeological site . . . made up of different forms and modes of representation" (slide 7). The ultimate goal of assemblage is "to foreground, through juxtaposing multiple accounts, one against the other, an uneasy, unstable relationship between the writer and the self" (slide 7). For example, assembled audio and reading transcripts, coupled with aesthetically magnetic cultural artifacts and journaling notes, could force a sort of constant comparison that requires the autoethnographer to rethink and reconstruct his or her own autoethnography to share with interested audiences. Similarly, member checking may produce yet another piece of the assembled evidence, as the autoethnographer seeks feedback from others who are quoted or implicated in the research. The assemblage concept can also be added to member checking in order to challenge the autoethnographer to compare/contrast her or his interpretations and analyses against additional sources from assenting and/or dissonant narratives.

Irrespective of the data collection strategy chosen (i.e., triangulation or assemblage), at the end of the day the autoethnographer must decide what story components to share, as well as when and how to share them. Additional details about assemblage are provided in Chapter 2, which focuses specifically on doing autoethnography.

Debates and Critiques of Autoethnography

As noted earlier in the chapter, autoethnographic-type work was critiqued from the very beginning by Louis Leakey and other social scientists who essentially rejected Jomo Kenyatta's hybrid autobiography/ethnography methodology as too subjective to meet the scrutiny of rigorous research. The growth of the multiple applications and iterations of autoethnography in the observed scholarship has not come without scholarly criticism of the genre. One traditional ethnographer initially even called for the removal of autoethnography from the lexicons of empirical research (Delamont, 2009). Other scholars restrict the application of autoethnography as an empirical endeavor by endorsing its usage only on some occasions and under limited conditions (e.g., Anderson, 2006; Walford, 2009). For these scholars, autoethnography falls short of the rigorous academic standards applied to ethnography. Delamont (2009) argues that ethnographic research is "hard, physically tiring, intellectually taxing and demanding of a high level of engagement, where at every stage crises can arise" (p. 61). The obvious message and assumptions underlying these critiques of autoethnography are that the method lacks the substance to withstand the standard scrutiny of the academy and that autoethnographers simply devalue the academy's standards. An appreciation of the "insights that can be drawn from reflexive writing about ethnography" should not then "retreat into autoethnography," which Delamont describes as "an abrogation of the honourable trade of the scholar" (p. 61). Instead, opponents suggest that an alternative to the autoethnographic turn is "reflexive autobiographical writing" (Delamont, 2009, p. 61). Delamont proposes this alternative as a route to improve "the empirical research of others" because "it has analytic and pedagogic power" and the "potential to improve research," unlike "the domestic guilt episode" that opponents equate with autoethnography (p. 61). These rejections of autoethnography are centered on the perceived weaknesses of the researcher as subject.

A relatively small group of established qualitative scholars in the United States and the United Kingdom are seeking to protect and preserve the integrity of ethnography by applying autoethnography through a traditional realist empirical lens that denies the deliberately evocative and performative applications of autoethnography toward change or social justice. Walford (2009) considers the nuances of autoethnographic applications and questions whether the usage of evocative autoethnography even "warrants the name ethnography as it has been traditionally understood" (p. 271). These ethnography-protection scholars contend that important divisions can and should be drawn between autoethnographers such as Denzin (2014) and Ellis and Bochner (2000), who are champions of a much more evocative, subjective, and emotionally engaging autoethnography, and those who challenge their position. Among the latter group of autoethnographers, Leon Anderson and Heewon Chang tend to be seen as champions, because they are read as defending a form of autoethnography more closely linked to traditional ethnography and to formal research practices (Walford, 2009, p. 276). Ethnographic reports should be distinguished by the need to be "logically constructed and be clear about what empirical claims (factual and explanatory) are being made and what empirical data have been generated that support those claims," according to Walford (2009, p. 272). Tradition calls for attempts to reduce ambiguity and to exhibit precision in ways that analytic autoethnographers argue are absent from the autoethnographic work of their evocative counterparts. As previously noted, Chang's (2008) work is often mentioned by the keepers of ethnographic tradition as a model for the type of autoethnography that might warrant an association with the terms *empirical* and *ethnography*. As Walford (2009) writes:

Chang (2008) restricts her consideration to a form of autoethnography that "shares the storytelling features with other genres of self-narrative but transcends mere narration of self to engage in cultural analysis and interpretation" (p. 43). Chang sees autoethnography as being centrally focused on the concerns of anthropology and argues that it should not be seen as a form of therapy. Her recent book (Chang, 2008) has four chapters out of 10 devoted to generating autoethnographic data, starting with the importance of the research focus, then going through personal memory data, self-observation, self-reflective data and external data. (p. 279).

In support of the return of the "simple empiricist," Walford concedes that storytelling (as applied in autoethnography) is "central to educational ethnography," but he argues that autoethnographers often forget "that the traditional purpose has been to communicate something about others" (p. 280). Much to the chagrin of those who favor analytic autoethnography, Anderson (2006) asserts, *"autoethnography* has become almost exclusively identified with those advocating the descriptive literary approach of evocative autoethnography" (p. 377). Those in the analytic autoethnography camp interpret evocative or emotional autoethnography as moving too far away from traditional empirical scholarship. For example, Anderson states:

> I am concerned that the impressive success of advocacy for what Ellis, Kiesinger, & Tillmann-Healy (1997) and Ellis (2004) refer to as "evocative or emotional autoethnography" may have the unintended consequence of eclipsing other visions of what autoethnography can be and of obscuring the ways in which it may fit productively in other traditions of social inquiry. (p. 374)

Similar to Walford, Anderson seeks to legitimize autoethnography by embedding it in **realist ontology**, **symbolic interactionist** epistemology, and traditional ethnographic qualitative research. He complicates the notion that empirical evidence can be gathered from evocative autoethnography.

According to Anderson (2006), analytic autoethnography is "ethnographic work in which the researcher is (1) a full member in the research group or setting, (2) visible as such a member in the researcher's published texts, and (3) committed to an analytic research agenda focused on improving theoretical understandings of broader social phenomena" (p. 375). From this perspective, only analytic (not evocative) autoethnography can elicit the type of empirical evidence (or data) that will withstand the tradition of rigor and scrutiny in the academy. The goal and, indeed, the "hope" of the pioneer of analytic autoethnography is "that other scholars will join [him] in reclaiming and refining autoethnography as part of the analytic ethnographic tradition" (Anderson, 2006, p. 392).

In their scholarship, Delamont (2009), Walford (2009), Anderson (2006), and Chang (2008) provide arguments for either removing or beginning to reclaim autoethnography as an empirical endeavor because of what they perceive to be epistemological and/or methodological gaps. After more than a decade of deliberation, we find neither more knowledge and more gaps nor more truth and more beauty when we compare and contrast evocative autoethnography and analytic autoethnography. We find them serving different purposes for different research audiences. We find weaker and stronger examples of them in the critical social research literature, but not in any disproportionate sense. One anonymous reviewer of the manuscript for this textbook even argued that the "evocative versus analytic" argument is now being downplayed, citing as evidence what he or she interprets as limited attention to the debate in the relatively recent *Handbook of Autoethnography* (Holman Jones, Adams, & Ellis, 2013a). Therefore, we posit that both analytic and evocative autoethnography are worth learning for the sake of having options for responding to the phenomenon of interest and the autoethnographic inquiry that drives the research.

Concluding Thoughts

Autoethnography resides within the qualitative tradition and is interpretive and subject to wide ranges of expression and methods. It provides opportunities for close examination, understanding, and dissemination of the inner worlds of those engaged in critical self-reflexive inquiries. In this chapter we have introduced five key ideas for you to consider when applying autoethnography as critical social research. Researcher voices have long been absent from the educational field, where the study of teaching is often integrated into the profession of teaching. Understanding how educators comprehend and recognize themselves and their educational histories and contexts allows another perspective, the missing piece of the multifaceted existing standpoints in critical social research. The research discussed in this chapter illustrates both the promise and the potential perils of autoethnography, including some of the major critiques of the genre with regard to relational ethics, legitimacy, rigor, and utility. Moreover, this chapter has addressed the differences between using autoethnography as a methodology and using it as a method. While there are many applications and iterations of autoethnography, we do not advocate prescribing or constraining the presentations of it down to one privileged type.

Group Activity

Purpose: Involve students in thinking about autoethnography and recording their ideas.

Activity: Journaling (see Table 1.4).

Evaluation: Determine whether students are thinking about autoethnography and how they may use journaling, with check-ins throughout the semester.

TABLE 1.4 ● Autoethnography Writing Prompt Worksheet		
This worksheet is structured to help you initiate the data collection for your autoethnography. An early step of the methodological process is to identify your past or present positions and the values of your background. Then you can analyze the complexity of patterns, establish theoretical frameworks, and compare/contrast your data with those of other ethnographies or autoethnographies.		
Background	**Autoethnography Position (i.e., narrative represents your distant past, near past, present, or projected future)**	**Values of Your Background: How important was it to you (in the past), is it to you (in the present), and/or will it be to you (in the future)?**
Cultural/ethnic background		
Religious background		
Country background		
Family rituals or traditions		
Cultural or social group		
Political leanings		
Values in the community		
Your lifestyle		
Interests and hobbies		
Likes and dislikes		
Special Topics (examples)	**Write down words and phrases related to the special topic that immediately come to mind**	**Experience (including vicarious experiences as through media, movies, and books, and your own personal experience)**
Selected cultural group		
Selected country or nation		
Selected continent		

Source: Adapted from Nice (2007).

Individual Activity

Purpose: Expose students to a viewpoint suggesting that we all have privileges and penalties in our society.

Activity: Think-pair-share in which students first work alone to "unpack" and identify relevant privileges and penalties in their lives and then meet in groups to share and extend what they have identified.

Evaluation: Determine whether students understand privilege and penalty.

Sites for Students to Consider

Duncan, M. (2004). Autoethnography: Critical appreciation of an emerging art. *International Journal of Qualitative Methods, 3*(4). http://www.ualberta.ca/~iiqm/backissues/3_4/pdf/duncan.pdf

Holt, N. L. (2003). Representation, legitimation, and autoethnography: An autoethnographic writing story. *International Journal of Qualitative Methods, 2*(1). http://www.ualberta.ca/~iiqm/backissues/2_1/html/holt.html

2

Mining and Priming Critical Social Theory for Autoethnography

Focus Your Reading

- What is a theory? What is social theory? What is critical social theory?

- What components of theory and theoretical frameworks might autoethnographers consider?

- How do many autoethnographers engage theory in a manner that resembles Paulo Freire's approach to mining and priming knowledge?

- What exemplars of critical social theory emerge from contemporary autoethnography in highly selective peer-reviewed publications?

- What guidelines might autoethnographers consider when infusing theory into their work?

As we have noted previously, autoethnography is similar to all research in that it is driven by theory. Even though the autoethnographic focus is on the self, there are various theoretical frames through which autoethnographers view themselves and their work. Everyone has theories about how the world works. They may or may not know the academic names for their theories, but they have theories. All scholarly disciplines rely on particular theories to explain processes and phenomena. As a researcher, it is your responsibility to name and explain your theoretical view for your readers. Therefore, this chapter is designed to help you consider or reconsider the application of critical social theory in autoethnography research. This chapter further informs autoethnographers more broadly about the application of theory.

Critical social theory and the theories that fall under that umbrella are the concepts that tend to inform the work of autoethnographers. Therefore, in this chapter we offer further insight into the concept of critical social theory, particularly with reference to how it is influenced by the work of the late scholar-activist Paulo Freire. We propose Freire's approach to "mining and priming" knowledge through critical pedagogy as one way to describe how critical social theory is often framed within prominent autoethnography research. We then present exemplars of emergent critical social theories in autoethnography research to demonstrate how such theory has been and can be applied to enhance such research. We conclude the chapter with discussion of some important steps you should consider when infusing theory into your autoethnography research and some ideas for you to consider as you imagine relationships and connections at the intersection of theory and autoethnography for your future projects.

What Is Theory?

World history suggests that our ancestors generated theories based on evidence collected from their lived experiences. They formulated theories as they attempted to explore,

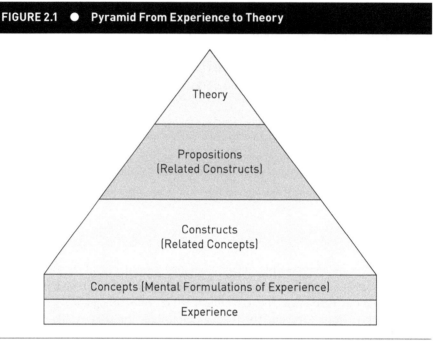

FIGURE 2.1 ● Pyramid From Experience to Theory

Source: Adapted from Anfara and Mertz (2006).

describe, and explain how the world worked and how they worked in relation to it. When our ancestors developed what they considered to be a useful theory, they measured its utility with evidence of the extent to which the theory improved their ability to anticipate, predict, explain, and plan. The ability to generate a theory, albeit not named as such by our early human ancestors, was crucial to the survival and advancement of our species. Today, theory continues to be an integral part of human survival and advancement, particularly as it applies to the evidence-based models, frameworks, and lenses that we develop to view, anticipate, predict, explain, and plan to address our social world.

All theories are grounded in the experiences of individuals and shaped by their disciplines. For example, in the teaching and learning experiences (i.e., the events, encounters, and episodes) of students, educational practitioners, school leaders, administrators, and policy makers lie the concrete foundation of theories. Such experiences are differentiated through their categorization into *concepts*. A concept can be thought of as a complex mental formulation of experience (Chinn & Kramer, 1999). Examples of concepts in education include pedagogy, disability, collaboration, engagement, management, support, achievement, curriculum, peers, and instructional. Compatible concepts can be aggregated to become *constructs*, such as instructional support and peer collaboration. (Milner & Tenore, 2010). *Propositions* describe relationships among two or more constructs. For example, researchers may notice connections between instructional support and the application of peer collaboration strategies in low-re-sourced schools. *Theories* comprise related propositions. Theories are at the top of the pyramid, and as such, they are the furthest from experience. Thus, for your own autoethnography, it will be important for you to consider the hierarchy of abstraction (i.e., from the actual experience to the theory developed about that experience) illus-trated in Figure 2.1 (Anfara & Mertz, 2006).

What Is Social Theory?

Social theory has been described as being like pottery—it cracks, it breaks down, only to be rehydrated and replaced by an innovative version of it to explain a new time (Noblit, 1999). This analogy is intended not as an argument against the idea of gener-ative knowledge but instead as an argument against grand theories. In the typical line of autoethnographic thinking, theory is not fact, but historicism—an explanation of lived experiences told in its own relative present time about the past for the future. It is in this light that we view our predecessors and our own autoethnographies, with any working transferable knowledge and theorizing that arises for them and from them. The historicism argument engenders a particular focus on basic paradigms and the nature of related habits of thought. Table 2.1 lists some of those perspectives and habits of thought that can inform and be informed by autoethnography.

Assimilationist Social Theory

Assimilationist theoretical perspectives such as genetic inferiority theory promote the axiology of assimilating "inferior" people versus gifted and talented people into their appropriate roles as ethical behavior. Assimilationist theories may involve an **ontology** that is supportive of either a single social reality or multiple social realities as constructed by human beings; however, these theories, including cultural deficit/inferiority theory, are tied closely the need for non–dominant cultural members of the social world to assimilate into and be judged by the reality of the rules and norms of the dominant cultural practices of the privileged. Furthermore, assimilationist the-ories like genetic inferiority theory and cultural deficit/inferiority theory support an **epistemology** that offers no interactive links between researchers and participants and proclaims that for one's knowledge to gain social acceptance and mobility, it must be assimilated into the dominant culture. The methodology accompanying assimila-tionist theorizing is chiefly quantitative. Theorizing for qualitative genres, including autoethnography, exists in opposition to assimilationist theorizing. In fact, the the-oretical perspectives and habits of thought of autoethnography lean toward the plu-ralist theories, often with specific language that critiques assimilationist perspectives. One example of these perspectives, discussed in detail later in this chapter, comes from an autoethnographer who critiques Dabrowski theory as assimilationist after spending more than two decades engaged in a program of research that centered the theory as a promising explanation for gifted and talented personality attributes (Piirto, 2010).

Theoretical Perspectives and Habits of Thought	Assimilationist Social Theory (e.g., genetic inferiority theory, Dabrowski theory, cultural deficit theory)	Pluralist Social Theory (e.g., cultural difference theory, critical theory, Freirean critical theory; feminist theory; Black feminist theory; queer theory; critical race theory; social justice leadership theory; transformative learning theory)
Axiology (habits of thought on values and ethical behavior)	Values suggest that assimilating "inferior" versus gifted and talented people into their appropriate roles is ethical behavior.	Respect for cultural norms; beneficence is defined in terms of the promotion of human rights, social justice, and social reciprocity.
Ontology (habits of thought on reality)	Multiple, social realities, but to survive and thrive in life, one must assimilate into the reality proposed by the dominant culture.	Rejects cultural relativism; recognizes that various versions of reality are based on social positioning; conscious recognition of consequences of privileging versions of reality.
Epistemology (habits of thought on knowledge, relation between knower and known)	Few interactive links between researcher and participants; proclaims that to be successful, knowledge needs to be assimilated and judged by dominant cultural norms.	Encourages interactive links between researcher and participants; knowledge is socially and historically situated; need to address issues of power and trust.
Methodology (habits of thought on one's approach to systematic inquiry)	Quantitative (chiefly)	Qualitative (dialectic/dialogic), but quantitative and mixed methods can be used; contextual and historical factors are described, especially as related to oppression.

TABLE 2.1 ● Theoretical Perspectives and Habits of Thought (Dis)Connected to Autoethnography

Pluralist Social Theory

Pluralist theoretical perspectives, like cultural difference theories, promote an axiology that supports respect for cultural norms and defines beneficence in terms of the promotion of human rights, social justice, and social reciprocity. Pluralist ontology rejects cultural relativism and yet recognizes that various versions of reality are based on social positioning, with a conscious recognition of consequences of privileging some versions of reality above others. Pluralist epistemology promotes knowledge production that can be critiqued and an understanding of the inextricable ties between researchers and participants. Moreover, knowledge production from this perspective is understood as socially and historically situated, thereby necessitating attention to issues of power and trust, as with critical theory. The methodology of pluralist perspectives is characterized by qualitative means (i.e., dialectic/dialogic). Quantitative methodology and mixed methodologies can be applied, however, only when in-depth contextual and historical factors are described, especially as they relate to oppression. It is important to note here that the latter methodologies do not have a track record of publications that adhere to the axiology, ontology, and epistemology standards of the pluralist theoretical perspectives.

Cultural difference theory submits that there are differences across cultures in home and school practices that can sometimes make it challenging for students to reach their highest potential in school. The major prediction of this theory is that respecting and working with and from cultural differences will help teachers and students optimize educational experiences and outcomes. Although the two are related as pluralist theories, critical theory stands in contrast to cultural difference theory with its contention that the dominant cultural group has gained too much power, enforced partially through schooling, and this power is oppressive to many non–dominant cultural groups. Instead of assuming the greater legitimacy of one cultural group over another, critical theory asks about the power relationships among the cultural groups (Tozer, Violas, & Senese, 2008).

Critical theory drives social research down a path that reveals common struggles for equity and justice throughout the world by assessing the power/privilege relationship(s) within cultural contexts and searching for related/relevant problems and solutions. Before we began writing this textbook, we reviewed social theory in published autoethnographies of critical social research from 2003 to the present. The review revealed many articles conveying processes for infusing theory into autoethnography in a manner that closely resembles the *mining and priming* of critical social theory, a phrase inspired by the work of the late critical social theorist and scholar-activist Paulo Freire (1974). This review also supported the rationale for our emphasis on critical social theory.

What Is Critical Social Theory?

A major source of **critical social theory** is associated most often with Western thought, specifically the thought of the sociopolitical analysts of the late 19th and early 20th centuries affiliated with the Frankfurt School, a school of thought in social theory and philosophy that originated at the Institute for Social Research (Institut für Sozialforschung) in Frankfurt, Germany. The influence of the Frankfurt School on critical social research is acknowledged worldwide. The Institute for Social Research was founded in 1923 with the aim of further developing (or building on) Marxist studies of social class in Germany as well as the psychological work of Sigmund Freud. In 1933, the institute was closed forcefully by Hitler's Nazi regime. The Frankfurt School as we know it today evolved from the initial forced removal of the institute from Germany to Columbia University, New York.

Today, the "critical" addition to social theory is defined by the problems of privilege, power, and economics and the psychological processes related to those problems.

Some of the core issues of critical social theory involve the critique of discrimination in societies related to ideas such as modernity, capitalism, ableism, ageism, racism, classism, heterosexism, xenophobia, and religion-based prejudice. Critical theory provides a distinct and specific interpretation of social issues, contexts, and individuals as they relate to power relationships. It specifically questions how those institutions, communities, and individuals in power operate. Commonly noted among the most prominent critical theorists of the Frankfurt School's first generation are Max Horkheimer (1895–1973), Theodor Adorno (1903–1969), Herbert Marcuse (1898–1979), Walter Benjamin (1892–1940), Friedrich Pollock (1894–1970), Leo Lowenthal (1900–1993), and Eric Fromm (1900–1980). The second-generation scholars of the Frankfurt School are commonly noted as being led by Jürgen Habermas (1929–). Claudio Corradetti (n.d.), writing in the peer-reviewed *Internet Encyclopedia of Philosophy,* maintains that Axel Honneth symbolically represents a "third generation" of critical theorists in Germany, and early in the 21st century a fourth generation of critical social theorists emerged, led by the work of Rainer Forst. The Frankfurt School has also been strongly linked to the advent of postmodernism, which conveys a critique of modern Western thought, including a questioning of the ability of humans to be "objective" and "neutral." Thus, challenges of taken-for-granted knowledge are associated with the Frankfurt School.

The critical theoretical perspectives in published autoethnography have been informed not only by the Frankfurt School of Germany, but also by French **poststructuralism** (Gannon, 2006). Critical theory from the poststructuralist approach problematizes taken-for-granted knowledge that human subjectivity renders us capable of self-knowledge and self-articulation. The work of poststructuralist theorists such as Michel Foucault (1926–1984) challenges us to rethink our narratives as reflective of our fractured, fragmented human subjectivities and as rhetorical sites of discontinuity, contradiction, displacement, and even estrangement. These notions require us to rethink our ideas about who we are and how we contribute to oppressive formal and informal social structures both consciously and unconsciously. We are called to critique our understandings of who we are and how we relate to others. We are called to question the ways in which decisions are made and who benefits from such decisions. These ideas call for us to deconstruct and examine our understandings of what we think, what we understand, and what we think we know about others and our society. They call for us to not assume we are what we are. Yet poststructuralist theory also justifies the incorporation of the personal into research. Of course, upon further inspection, an intellectual dilemma becomes quite evident at the intersection of autoethnography and poststructuralism—autoethnography starts with the premise that individuals (including marginalized individuals) can speak for themselves, whereas poststructuralism starts with the premise that writing for and against the self is a challenge that in some cases may be insurmountable. French poststructuralists whose works have influenced autoethnography include, but are not limited to, Foucault, Roland Barthes (1915–1980), and Jacques Derrida (1930–2004). Evidence from autoethnographic work based in Australia includes implications and calls for a reconfigured *poststructural autoethnography,* whereby the writing writes the writer as a complex subject in a world where self-knowledge can only ever be tentative, contingent, and situated (Gannon, 2006, p. 474).

The esteemed scholar Paulo Freire, a native Brazilian, is credited with taking the postmodernist movement of critical theory to education and educational research in the 20th century. Freire spent a lifetime advocating for Brazilian peasants, and from this experience he developed theories for conscientious thought and action, or "critical consciousness" (a process known in Portuguese as *conscientização*), in pedagogy. Freirean critical theorizing speaks to pedagogy as a series of dialectical conversations between teachers and students, where the teacher listens to understand what knowledge students already bring to the subject based on their personal learning experiences of the world. This reciprocity is crucial to Freire's influence on theory into practice and practice into theory. Through this approach, in 1962, his critical literacy groups taught 300 impoverished farmworkers to read and write in just 45 days (Gadotti, 1994, p. 15). Unfortunately, Freire was initially exiled from Brazil for this work—not for teaching peasants literacy skills, per se, but for teaching peasants how to read their worlds of oppression so that they might liberate themselves. It was not until the 1980s that Freire was finally welcomed home to national acclaim. Although critical social researchers do not agree on one critical pedagogical form (nor should they, in our opinion), Freire is said to be responsible for much of the way critical pedagogical theory is considered and applied today (Wink, 2005, p. 90).

Freire is well known for his critique of what he perceived as a banking model in education, where teachers learn to put knowledge into students. In opposition to the banking model, he created a notion of teaching as "mining," where first and foremost the teacher's responsibility is to pull knowledge out—to build on the knowledge students bring to the pedagogical situation (Freire, 1974, p. 76). The words *primer* and *priming* are commonly used in education textbooks and are seemingly intended only to reflect the motive of putting something into students' minds, but in a manner distinctly different from the banking model refuted by Freire. *Priming* is a term that reflects Freire's understanding of promising pedagogy as focusing much less on putting knowledge into learners and much more on prompting students as a first step to seeking actively to reveal the knowledge that learners already possess, albeit previously untapped or underdeveloped.

Although most of us do not name it as such, our review of the literature suggests that autoethnographers engage in a similar process of mining and priming that helps (a) to locate social theory in the researchers' daily experiences of privilege and oppression; (b) to read the privilege and oppression of autoethnographers' worlds into the words of social theory; (c) to position social theory in action as "theorizing," which void of practice is rendered "off-base" at best; and (d) to position practice without such theorizing as increasing the potential for shortsighted and preventable errors. These four points essentially involve theory to build a foundation for autoethnography as critical social praxis. Critical theory is enticing to autoethnographers because it speaks to people who are generally excluded from the dominant culture and people who have

A NARRATIVE ON PRIMING

I recall the antique water pump at my grandmother's house. I learned that her family had to literally mine for water in their own yard in order to find a sufficient place for a functional water pump. Once the mining was complete and the water pump was in place, the family used water collected previously to "prime the pump." In the 1970s and early 1980s, I actually helped prime the pump at grandma's house. Priming the pump involved a combination of (a) pouring previously collected water into a hole in the top of the pump, which functions essentially as a lubricant, and (b) moving the handle of the pump vigorously up and down to build just enough air pressure into the pump to suck underground water sources up and out. After enough priming, the pump draws out water well beyond the quantity and quality of that which was used for priming that day.

(Hughes, 2008b, p. 249)

How Can Critical Social Theory Enhance the Work of Autoethnographers?

- Critical social theory can offer a foundation that enables autoethnographers to critique common connotations and definitions of terms, concepts, constructs, and propositions, examining what may have become taken-for-granted knowledge in developed theories.
- Critical social theory can provide autoethnographers with a specific domain to which the phenomenon/problem of interest, theory, or theories in question can be linked and examined for applicability.
- Critical social theory can help autoethnographers identify and critique a set of relationships between constructs in a systematic way that can contribute to established literature in critical social research.
- Critical social theory can afford autoethnographers the language they need to make and critique specific research claims.

learned in the past that their ways of knowing and experiencing the world are unimportant.

In practice, it is ultimately the perspective and epistemological background of the autoethnographer and/or the members of the autoethnographer's academic committee that determine how "theory" is to be framed. A **theoretical framework** can be described as the structure that guides the autoethnographer while he or she refines the central thesis questions, selects the methods, and plans the analysis (Imenda, 2014). In addition, the theoretical framework is constituted by the specific perspective the autoethnographer uses to explore, interpret, or explain lived experiences and the communicative behavior of the participants and events within the larger cultural context under study. At the end of an autoethnography, the researcher can use the framework to check for the existence of discrepancies, and wherever discrepancies emerge, the framework may be used to explain them. Theoretical frameworks can indeed provide maps of the current state of knowledge about problematic phenomena being studied and offer evidence-based explanations for why the particular problems connect to specific phenomena.

Therefore, theoretical frameworks can be essential in preparing autoethnographic research.

Emergent Critical Social Theorizing in Autoethnography

Autoethnographers engaged in critical work consistently create spaces for marginalized voices, identities, and populations through the use of their personal experiences, understandings, and theorizing. We provide the following examples to demonstrate how autoethnographic researchers use and present their work in relation to critical social theories. Please note that this is not an exhaustive list; autoethnographies have examined many additional topics, including studies of indigenous perspectives (using postcolonial theory) and critical White studies (see Table 1.3 in Chapter 1). Employing the notions of pluralist social theory, all of these researchers represent the axiological, ontological, and epistemological stances related to social justice and how autoethnography can resist oppression and create spaces for marginalized voices. The use of various theoretical foundations brings these personal works into larger contexts and illustrates how individual analysis can contribute to, critique, and illuminate existing theories.

What Can Theoretical Frameworks Do for Autoethnographers?

- Theoretical frameworks can help autoethnographers clarify the related constructs and propositions of their studies.
- Theoretical frameworks can give autoethnographers the language for interpreting autoethnographic evidence and thereby serve as tools for guiding data analysis.
- Theoretical frameworks can provide maps of the current state of knowledge about problematic phenomena being studied and offer evidence-based explanations for why the particular problems connect to specific phenomena.

(inspired by Akintoye, 2015)

Feminist Theory

Feminist theory is a movement with ties to postmodernism that came of age in the 1980s, partially as a response to the disparate power, privilege, and penalty between the predominant group of White males conducting social research and those who were the objects of their research (often women, people of color, and people labeled with special needs and/or disabilities; Lichtman, 2013, p. 109). Born and raised in rural Japan, Mayuzumi (2009) highlights the indigenous knowledge of rural Japanese women (p. 508). While these women obviously do possess their own human agency (i.e., the ability to think, feel, and act within and outside prescribed ways of knowing and being), they have been marginalized for much of the history of Japan. Hence, autoethnography provides a means for Mayuzumi to introduce her lived experiences to explore the possibilities that lie in the rural Japanese cultural context and the indigenous-knowledge framework (p. 509). This ontological and epistemological stance permeates her autoethnography as she works through her identity and critiques previous definitions of women's knowledge.

Mayuzumi (2009) relies on a feminist framework that rejects the notion that all women are similar. She shares and clearly unpacks her identity and utilizes her situated self as a key component of her autoethnographic study, citing Spry (2001) as she relies

Three Important Characteristics of Critical Social Theory to Consider in Autoethnographic Work

- Critical social theory can evolve from newly developed or existing concepts, constructs, propositions, and related connotations and definitions that, when considered together as interdependent, represent a systematically constructed point of view about a particular experience.
- Critical social theory comprises two or more related propositions about experiences (i.e., event, encounters, and/or episodes).
- Critical social theory attempts to describe, anticipate, and/ or explain events based on identifiable specific relationships.

(inspired by Akintoye, 2015)

on her "lived experience." Mayuzumi's eloquent integration of her identity, theory, and empirical work, encased in the history of her community cultural practices, represents how autoethnography can maintain a scholarly yet critical interrogation of the construction of women:

> Walking on the land gave me a sense of my community, of the sacredness of the land, and of the spiritual dynamic of the space . . . which I now reclaim as my Indigenous knowledge. Is this not a legitimate knowledge about my land and the community? I did not learn this at school but outside of the classroom. (p. 517)

Mayuzumi ends her argument with a call for more autoethnographic explorations of what she terms "subjugated knowledges." Her use of theory is clear and moves the field forward as she carefully situates her work in feminist theory. Mayuzumi's perspective is aligned with pluralist ideals, and she takes a definitive critical stance. She critiques previous representations of women and in particular the rural Japanese women who are the focus of her study. In many ways, her work can be viewed as an example of mining and priming—Mayuzumi mines and primes the context of her life and work, using it to press the field forward. She states, "Researchers and educators must engage their own sense of agency to resist co-optation by dominant social and political discourses that have become normalized over time" (p. 521).

The complexities of voice, representation, and critique meld into a portrait of how autoethnography can explain, inform, instruct, and create new spaces for new understandings. From another perspective, Coia and Taylor (2013) explore their positioning as feminist educators, asking, "Are we the feminist teachers we think we are?" (p. 5). They rely on six principles of feminist pedagogy related to critical perspectives in their attention to voice, community, diversity, and the relationships between students and teachers. Turning to autoethnography to bring in the sociopolitical context of their understandings, they work through their ideas of teaching, coming to find their conversations and interrogations of their pasts and present through narratives illuminated by their use of what they term "co/ autoethnography." They find their conceptions of being feminist teachers enacting feminist pedagogy to be characterized by "vulnerability, ambiguity, and doubt" (p. 14). While both Mayuzumi (2009) and Coia and Taylor (2013) build their work on feminist theory, they take different stances due to their identities and contexts, reflecting the ethnographic roots of autoethnography's reliance on social context.

Overall, feminist theory can be used to frame autoethnographic work and contribute to existing work.

Black Feminist Theory

Black feminist theory involves a lens for reading critically into the inscriptions of race, class, and gender and how they impose on and intersect in the lived experiences of Black women and the people within their spheres of influence. Clearly connected to pluralist theoretical perspectives, McClellan's (2012) study of her own research work with Black men articulates how her racial and gendered identity is related to her leadership identity. Theoretically rich and firmly ensconced in Patricia Hill Collins's *Black Feminist Thought* (1990, 2000), spirituality, and womanist theology, McClellan's autoethnographic work is, as she describes it, a form of "creative resistance" (p. 92). Weaving her own history into the larger histories of Black women, her narrations of seminal events in her life coupled with connections to leaders such as Septima Clark, McClellan's autoethnography provides a powerful and seamless example of the use of critical theory. Her representation of her experiences through the use of flashbacks and layered theoretical analysis typifies autoethnography's reliance on the researcher as the data source. For example, McClellan presents a detailed description of a meeting with Mr. Aaron that ended with him asking her why she was getting her PhD, noting, "I never answered his question. I responded with a question of my own: 'Why must I choose?'" (p. 96). This is followed by citations of works related to gender relationships in the Black community as well as McClellan's analysis, in which she states, "According to Gordon (1987, 46), sexism in Black men emanates from their lack of power due to racism" (p. 96).

McClellan's autoethnography is writing from a didactic stance—she notes that "a premise in this autoethnography is to challenge readers, particularly men, to interrogate issues of race, gender, and other forms of oppression alongside those of women" (p. 97). Her methodology is transparent and adapted well to her examination of her own research work with Black men. She highlights and theorizes two events and brings meaning to her critical interpretations in ways that instruct and inform. She uses autoethnography to engage in critical reflection and emotional recall of two critical incidents that helped shape her leadership identity (p. 96). Her work as a researcher is the focus, and her attention to the nuances of her own critique demonstrate the ways in which Black feminist autoethnography, when used to mine and prime, is at its best when the researcher is aware not only of herself but of the larger theories, histories, and contexts of her work.

Queer Theory

Closely related to feminist theory and Black feminist theory, with roots in postmodernism, queer theory approaches sexuality and gender identity as social constructs of interest. Some prominent autoethnographers use the metaphor that "autoethnography is queer" (e.g., Adams & Holman Jones, 2008). The autoethnographic example we describe next, the work of Hermann-Wilmarth and Bills (2010), began as an examination of LGBT preservice teachers and moved to a study of how the researchers' own "identities as researchers and teachers were queered" (p. 259). In an autoethnography exemplary of a *confessional tale* (Van Maanen, 1988), Hermann-Wilmarth and Bills detail the chronological journey of their original study and how they as researchers turned to autoethnography to recognize their roles as researchers, participants, and informants. They explain their study's progression and delineate the ways in which their identities were inextricably linked to those of their participants. They detail their original research methodology, which involved interviews and focus groups, and they carefully attend to their role in the research process, from setting up places for interviews that accommodated their students' needs to how they worked to allow the focus groups to drive the discussions. They use autoethnography to queer their data analysis. In common parlance, they use autoethnography to rethink, critique, and reframe their data and analysis.

Hermann-Wilmarth and Bills's (2010) use of autoethnography to offer a critical examination of how LGBT students and teachers navigate their lives within and outside traditional education cultural contexts is uniquely informative. Autoethnography situates the researchers' understandings of themselves and their participants. Their work can be viewed as mining and priming in order to locate critical social theory in daily experiences. Hermann-Wilmarth and Bills conclude with a call for other teacher educators to investigate their own practices and a discussion highlighting the educative nature of many autoethnographies. Their examination of how they had to put themselves into the story illustrates the unique contributions and affordances of autoethnographic research. As do the researchers in the preceding examples, Hermann-Wilmarth and Bills work from a critical pluralistic stance, and they are deliberate in integrating their research and teaching experiences with queer theory and its call for the rejection of stable and binary identity construction.

In another example, we find queer theory and autoethnography as vehicles of expression for LeFrançois (2013), who states, "The autoethnographic 'I' is queered and is reflexively positioned, with the potential to allow me to become someone new through the writing of the story" (p. 109). Her narrations of her thoughts as she works within the child protection and psychiatry instructional systems are powerful and detail the complexities of her work. Stories like these are inherently personal and political; they force a moral inquiry (p. 118). LeFrançois clearly calls for a critical stance through her autoethnographic examination of specific events in her work life that demonstrate the individual enactment of institutional power. Applying the perspective of pluralist social theory, she mines and primes the pump of her work life and encases her lived work experiences in historical and theoretical analysis that illuminates the dominance of the system within which she works. These examples of queer theory clearly detail the ways in which autoethnographers can shape their research based on theoretical tenets.

Critical Race Theory

Critical race theory (CRT) traces its roots to legal examinations of racial discrimination. Brought into social theory research, it provides a framework for critically describing and evaluating the role of race in the marginalization, subjugation, and oppression of people of color. Today, CRT has many permutations and has been adapted to represent more discrete areas, such as critical race pedagogy and Latino critical theory via *testimonios*.

Critical Race Pedagogy

Marvin Lynn developed critical race pedagogy as a way to begin theorizing and acting critically with regard to the environments within which educators engage teaching and learning about race and structural racism. Hughes (2008c) critically addresses the intersections of race, class, and gender in his reflexive autoethnographic study. He blends explanations and calls for autoethnographic work in educational settings while examining his own teaching as a Black professor in relation to his White students. Hughes's work clearly demonstrates the power of mining and priming as he theorizes not only his students' understandings but also his own. In one data excerpt he details an event that took place during a class, when a student questioned his preparation for class asking, "What's the matter, you aren't prepared?" He works to unpack the meaning of his response to her question while considering the student's question in the context of the course, a local race riot, and course readings on "hits" from Swim and Stangor's edited volume *Prejudice: The Target's Perspective* (1998). This use of theory brings the autoethnographer's individual experiences and practices as a teacher educator into the broader realm of critical race pedagogy in order to illuminate how a classroom event can be theorized and examined in relation to response bias work by Swim and Stangor.

Relying on narrative and counternarrative, Hughes (2008c) also applies Collins's (1990) matrix of domination to illustrate the complexities of privilege and oppression inside and beyond his classroom. This intimate work unveils the role of a Black male graduate-level teacher, researcher, and learner as Hughes engages in "good enough" autoethnographic work with his White students. Moving in and out of his positioning as teacher and researcher, he states, "Through 'good enough methods' for autoethnography, my students and I critique personal roles in reproducing ignorance, and the denial of the dynamics of expansion and constraint; privilege and penalty" (p. 141). This work illustrates the power of reading privilege and oppression in relation to theory and daily lived experiences.

Writing as a Black, queer, female teaching assistant for a college undergraduate course, Hill (2014) focuses on the history of race in the United States and details how she "acknowledged positionality and interrogated how my racial positioning, being Black particularly, mediated my decisions, and negotiations around teaching pedagogy and communicating with students" (p. 163). She exposes her teaching and reflections with specific examples and revealing honesty. For instance, she describes her feelings during an interaction between her and her students after they read poetry she had written: "I remain engaged. Still too shaky and nervous to admit, the poems we were discussing were written by the same person, me" (p. 177). In employing critical performative pedagogy, Hill uses her body, experiences, and theory to guide her teaching. As these examples illustrate, CRT can be integrated into autoethnography in powerful demonstrations of racial critique.

Latino Critical Theory via *Testimonios*

Latino critical theory builds on critical pedagogy and critical social theory by centering the distinct and specific experiences of Latinos and seeking detailed descriptions and explanations Latino experiences of common sociocultural phenomena. Chavez (2012) uses autoethnography to critique her experiences in education over time, highlighting its "unconcealed and unapologetic use of emotion utilized by the researcher in the writing style that contains the possibility to position readers in an unconventional spot" (p. 341). Her powerful account of her educational experiences renders a picture of marginalization and racism. Chavez calls for *testimonios* and autobiographical representations as means for resisting and breaking down what she terms the distance of theory as depicted by many academic abstract papers. Her use of autoethnography moves from her childhood neighborhood to her kindergarten teacher and on to her realization of her middle school principal's deficit view of her and her classmates. She begins by stating, "I am an anomaly in higher education: a working-class, Chicana, first-generation college student with a Ph.D." (p. 334). Her intricate use of theory and autoethnographic narration to both articulate and analyze experiences provides examples of how autoethnography can disrupt oppressive voices as well as create space for new interpretations and critiques. Chavez explicitly addresses the use of theory and story as she states, "By weaving theory and narrative together, my *testimonios* aim to problematize the ways in which diverse educational institutions have influenced my ideological perspective regarding race, class, and culture" (p. 344).

Testimonio can be applied with autoethnography to bring the notion of performance into the examination of hybrid/assimilated identities in general. In one specific example, in the work of Correa and Lovegrove (2012), it is used by "a Latina of Puerto Rican descent and a white Chicana" (p. 349). The performance representation of these researchers' interrogation is powerful. Correa and Lovegrove utilize transcripts of conversations and excerpts of letters to provide glimpses into the ways in which their identities are expressed through their lived experiences, demonstrating the nuances and complexities of such work. They state, "These dialogues emerged from our bonds of heritage and our resolve to investigate the ways we could express and theorize our lived experiences" (p. 350). They perform their autoethnography theoretically in the text and in their actual performances of the dialogues at conferences and in courses for students. The performative nature of the piece invites dialogic interactions, a goal of autoethnography as it strives to engage readers in experiencing and theorizing perspectives they may or may not find familiar.

Social Justice Leadership Theory

Social justice leadership theory attempts to frame and explain how leaders perform leadership tasks beyond tradition by honing, practicing, and modeling knowledge, skills, and dispositions necessary to address issues of equity and identity within their spheres of influence. Identity is the focus of the work of Theoharis (2008), who states that he "borrowed from the tradition of autoethnography" (p. 5). Methodologically he included himself as one of the participants in his study of seven school principals. Social justice as it relates to school leadership framed his study; he writes, "Social justice leadership [means] that these principals advocate, lead, and keep at the center of their practice and vision issues of race, class, gender, disability, sexual orientation, and other historically and currently marginalizing conditions in the United States" (p. 5). Each principal is described, and Theoharis does not disclose his own identity as he shares and analyzes the data. The critical theory foundation of the study is clear, and Theoharis delineates its adaptation of autoethnography, noting: "I decided that I could not provide a detailed narrative about each principal and her or his school. . . . The principals in this study were adamant that their social justice work is not context specific" (p. 7). His group of participants, including himself, is broader than the focus of individual autoethnographic studies, and his protection of the principals is crucial. Theoharis's work demonstrates the inherent risk of publishing critical work. Such work is not to be avoided; rather, it is to be respected for what each study touches in relation to the lives of real people in oppressive and at times public contexts.

In contrast to Theoharis (2008), Garza (2008) centers his autoethnographic study of leadership for social justice on his personal experiences, relying on his journaling during his tenure as a superintendent. His dated and chronological entries reveal the day-to-day enactment of his leadership position as it relates to those in his broad district educational context. Less reliant on theory, Garza's focus on social justice leadership is represented in first-person narrations that follow his introductory statement, "Children do not fail, but rather the school system fails them" (p. 164). Both of the studies described above illustrate the precarious position of autoethnographers as they move to critique the systems they inhabit while using critical social theory to frame their critiques.

Transformative Learning Theory

Transformative learning is characterized by altering frames of reference, participating in critical reflection and dialogue, and taking action. Based in adult education, it highlights the notion of breaking through preconceived understandings (Mezirow, 1997). Sykes (2014) examines Native American identity in relation to education. As a Chickasaw adult educator, he proposes "the concept of transformative autoethnography (autoethnography steeped in culture to engage in transformational learning) by extending the existing research on transformational learning by considering the significance of cultural identity" (p. 4). Sykes contextualizes his work by using the history of the oppression of Native Americans in the United States. He integrates transformative learning and phenomenology to explore his experiences in developing and implementing a tribal learning community for Chickasaw students entering a university. He describes several events to demonstrate the ways his critical reflections aided his transformational learning and serve as a call for educators and institutions to "make concerted efforts to provide opportunities for minority learners to engage in culturally relevant learning" (p. 9). The intricacies of Sykes's experiences open up the complexities of his identity and its relationship to his teaching. In its recognition of the intimacy of studying the self, autoethnographic work is powerful in detailing internal strife, doubt, complexity, and vulnerability, all hallmarks of transformative learning, teaching, and research.

Dabrowski Theory

Jane Piirto (2010) displays another way to mine and prime theory and autoethnography—to critique/challenge the assimilationist theoretical tendencies of a major popular theory accepted in the academy. Piirto uses autoethnography to convey how she became disenchanted with a theory that she had studied for more than two decades—the Dabrowski theory of positive disintegration. Kazimierz Dabrowski developed this theory from the mid-1960s to the late 1970s to describe and explain personality attributes, characteristics, and development of so-called gifted and talented youth and adults. It is one of the most popular theories related to the social science of giftedness. A major translator of Dabrowski's work has been Michael Piechowski. A central concept of the theory that has been tested is the concept of *overexcitability* (OE). OE is intended to represent the innate tendency of certain humans with particular gifts and talents "to respond with heightened intensity and sensitivity to intellectual, emotional, and other stimuli, also called psychic overexcitability" (Piechowski, 1999, p. 325).

Piirto (2010) notes her appreciation of autoethnography as particularly conducive to offering a critical reflexive critique of her life's work with Dabrowski theory and her participation in what she calls a cultlike following of the theory. She finds solace in the way autoethnography affords the writer a systemic way to engage her own experiences to garner critical insights into the larger culture or subculture of which she is a part. In sum, culture as described in her autoethnography is explicitly named as *the Dabrowski theory culture within the field of gifted education.* The *auto* is explicitly described as herself and her work within this culture for two decades (1989 to 2010), including her autoethnographic turn to critique the mysterious and mythic adoption of the theory, even when the five OEs are not reflected in her qualitative and quantitative data. She uses the autobiographical component of autoethnography to set the stage for why we should care about her experience with the theory and to build credibility for her critical reflexive gaze upon it. For example, Piirto explains that for the bulk of her career, she administered validated instruments to test Dabrowski theory, including the Overexcitability Questionnaire (OEQ) and the Overexcitability Questionnaire II (OEQ-II). She also informs us of her insider status as the organizer of three of the first Dabrowski conferences in the United States, editor of a newsletter, and adviser of graduate students who used the OEQs in their own studies. So, we learn from Piirto other valuable ways to use autoethnography as a critical reflexive turn on our own life's work in the ways described in the previous sections.

All of the theoretical frames detailed above demonstrate how autoethnographers rely on theory to formulate questions, analyze data, and contribute to their areas of research as they connect their work to previous work and critique and modify the theories as they evolve. In the following section, we propose some guidelines to use when integrating theory into autoethnographic research.

Guidelines for Infusing Theory into Autoethnography

We detail below seven guidelines for infusing theory into autoethnography. During the research process you may find that theory guides your work only initially, or it may be present throughout the data collection. At times theory may become a part of the continuing data analysis and come into focus at the conclusion of the study. The following theory-centered guidelines serve also to separate autoethnography from autobiographical storytelling and to protect the autoethnographer from accusations of narcissistic navel-gazing.

1. Compare, contrast, and analyze salient personal experiences in light of a critical review of the literature *on* theory (primary sources) and the literature *with* theory (secondary sources).

   Theory and theoretical frameworks emerge out of an established research tradition of conducting comprehensive literature reviews to support proposed research (Boote & Beile, 2005; Maxwell, 2006). These reviews are important for autoethnographers because autoethnographic writing is likely to drift in and out of clarity and credibility if it has neither a literature base nor a framework in which the history and big ideas of an area are discussed. For example, a study of one's experiences can be powerful, but if the experiences are not encased in theory, there is no way to apply the information to a larger context. It could be argued that any critical social research must be connected to literature or concepts that support the need for the study and are related to the study's purpose statement in a manner that situates the study in terms of previous work (Rocco & Plakhotnik, 2009, p. 120).

2. State the theory or theories that are the basis of your autoethnographic account.

   One could argue that because qualitative studies are often inductive, there is no place for theory. However, one could also argue that by default all research

Why Is Critical Social Theory Important for the Future of Autoethnography?

- Critical social theory plays the role of identifying the starting point of the autoethnographic research problem and related central research question(s).
- Critical social theory plays the role of informing and directing the autoethnographic research problem and related central research question(s) toward a larger social vision.
- Critical social theory plays the role of clarifying the focus (or foci) and the goal(s) of the autoethnographic research problem and related central research question(s).

(inspired by Akintoye, 2015)

emanates from the researcher's implicit or explicit theory of the problem or phenomenon under investigation. Such inductive research approaches are based on a different epistemology or philosophy of knowledge regarding research that require an a priori announcement of a theory at the outset of a research project.

3. Identify the disciplinary basis of the theory and its proponents.

Even qualitative empirical studies using grounded theory to nurture theory and theoretical frameworks tend to have their foundations in one or more disciplines and the bodies of literature that represent those disciplines. When autoethnography is implemented in the form of critical social research, it may speak to a vast array of disciplines in the social and health sciences. If you are studying literacy instruction you should be well versed in not only the current theories of literacy as a content area in the field but also the current empirical work related to your inquiry. It is crucial that you situate your work within the disciplines to which you intend to make a contribution.

4. Design a figure that represents the theoretical perspective(s).

Some qualitative researchers from the interpretivist and postmodernist paradigms critique the development of visual charts and figures as ways to illuminate such research because of these tools' linearity, simplification, and limitations for adding insight to what can be found in the narrative. In our experience, however, doctoral students have found that such visual figures enable them to gain insight that may not have been evoked through narratives alone. Similar to concept mapping, theory or theoretical perspective mapping can offer both the autoethnographer and the reader greater clarity and transparency by illustrating the components of the theory or theories in question and how they are linked to the problem/phenomenon of interest. Creating such a figure can be a challenging but rewarding exercise irrespective of the autoethnographer's intentions regarding the inclusion of the illustration in the final manuscript.

5. Identify which components of the theory are involved in the investigation.

The theory or multiple theories that constitute the theoretical framework of your autoethnography can serve to situate the problem of the study within a sociocultural context. Autoethnographers can add clarity and transparency to their work by describing which components of theory are involved in their investigations.

6. Use theory to inform and frame your data analysis.

Theory and theoretical frameworks can not only prompt specific research questions but also inform your data analysis techniques and, thereby, how you will interpret your findings (Merriam, 2009, p. 67). In other words, when you introduce theory at the beginning of your autoethnography, your interpretation of the autoethnographic evidence that you gather should also bring the theory back into the research.

7. Cite any rival theories and their authors.

As noted in the cases above, critical social theory in conjunction with autoethnography can serve to refresh, reify, reflect, refute, and/or reconcile theoretical perspectives. The active search for and naming of rival theories and/or rival approaches to the same theory in the literature are particularly useful for autoethnographers to address in order to maximize the credibility of their work. Even a brief mention to inform readers that you know what exists and to explain to what degree, if at all, your work addresses it increases the likelihood that your autoethnographic evidence will be read as trustworthy. Simply dismissing rival theoretical perspectives and explanations of the problem/phenomenon of interest could evoke questions about the integrity and thereby the utility of the research.

Concluding Thoughts

You have a set of theoretical and methodological tools and a research literature to use. That's your advantage. If you can't frame [your autoethnography] around these tools and literature and just frame it as "my story," then why or how should I privilege your story over anyone else's I see 25 times a day on TV? (Mitch Allen, personal interview, cited in Ellis, Adams, & Bochner, 2011, para. 8)

All of the autoethnographers highlighted in this chapter delve deeply into the intersections of their lived experiences within and outside their nuanced cultural contexts. They bring broader meaning into their personal representations by infusing theoretical analysis and historical contextualization by answering the call to share what it means to be, for example, a Black lesbian in a research university or a Chickasaw male creating a curriculum for a tribe. As Mitch Allen so aptly states in the quotation above, we as readers of autoethnography cannot fully know other people's experiences, but we can certainly gain insight about those experiences by learning from their theorizing. The theoretical frameworks guiding these studies press us forward as educators and researchers; they show how autoethnographic work informs and challenges existing theories. The published autoethnographies highlighted in this chapter demonstrate the mining and priming of critical social theory—both for putting in the previously collected substance of thought and for drawing out the yet-unseen thought processes. This dual mining and priming approach can push autoethnographers to take ownership of critical social theory, to adapt and modify it, and to fill their particular space in ways that neither Freire nor we might have imagined or have been able to accomplish in the same way in our cultural contexts.

Individual Activity

Purpose: Involve students in preliminary reading and thinking about theorizing as they consider their own autoethnography projects.

Activity: Journaling; students work to begin theorizing.

Evaluation: Determine whether selected approaches to theorizing for autoethnography projects are defensible for an academic audience.

Individual and Two-Person Group Activity

Purpose: Expose students to individual experiences of theorizing for autoethnography.

Activity: "Think-Pair-Share" in which students first work alone to develop initial drafts that involve theorizing about a supported-salient experience and then work together with other students in a group to identify and critique relevant issues pertaining to their theorizing about the supported-salient experience and to consider alternatives theories to interpret that experience.

Evaluation: Use a rubric regarding theorizing to determine whether students' particular approaches to theory for autoethnographic purposes are relevant, thoughtful, thorough, and defensible to an academic audience.

Note for instructor: Share your own experience with the process of theorizing for autoethnographic purposes.

Sites for Students to Consider

Akintoye, A. (2015, July 3). *Developing theoretical and conceptual frameworks.* PowerPoint presentation delivered at the EDMIC 2015 Research Workshop, Obafemi Awolowo University, Ile-Ife, Nigeria. http://jedm.oauife.edu.ng/wp-content/uploads/2015/03/Akintola-Akintoye_Developing-Theoretical-and-Conceptual-Frameworks.pdf

Internet Encyclopedia of Philosophy, http://www.iep.utm.edu

Rocco, T. S., & Plakhotnik, M. S. (2009). Literature reviews, conceptual frameworks, and theoretical frameworks: Terms, functions, and distinctions. *Human Resource Development Review, 8*(1), 120–130. http://hrd.sagepub.com/content/8/1/120

Doing Autoethnography

From Brainstorming to Guiding Process

The discussion in this part of the book is intended to help you move from brainstorming about phenomena or topics of interest and considering applications of critical social theory to the actual practice, or doing, of autoethnography. These three chapters center on three guiding processes for doing autoethnography: problematizing, legitimizing, and synthesizing. By the end of the part, you should understand how problematizing, legitimizing and synthesizing can serve as integral guiding processes of autoethnography. You should also have gained familiarity with the brainstorming prewriting activities that are essential resources for developing the types of autoethnographies that are published by peer-reviewed journals of social science. The autoethnographies discussed in these chapters are drawn from academic journals with international impact factor rankings that adhere to the blind peer-review process. Additional resources at the ends of the chapters include web links to promising autoethnography preactivities (e.g., Harvard's Implicit Association Test and a cross-cultural simulation called Bafa Bafa).

Chapter 3, "First Guiding Process: Problematizing What You Know for New-Self Insight," discusses the process of moving from brainstorming to (a) finding your relevant phenomenon or topic of interest to pursue and (b) linking your phenomenon of interest to the central autoethnographic research question(s). Chapter 4, "Second Guiding Process: Legitimizing Autoethnography With Three Approaches," discusses the process of moving from brainstorming to legitimizing autoethnography for the larger social scientific audience, including (a) establishing relevant literature to review and critique, (b) considering ethics in relation to autoethnography, (c) confirming/disconfirming criticisms of autoethnography, (d) collecting personal memory data, (e) collecting self-observational and self-reflective data, and (f) collecting external data and member checking. Part II concludes with Chapter 5, "Third Guiding Process: Synthesizing New-Self Insights With MICA," which highlights ways to begin synthesizing understandings across one's own body of autoethnographic work. This chapter also aims to begin constructing a method for synthesizing autoethnography written by other authors known as qualitative meta-synthesis for individualized and coauthored autoethnography, or MICA. Autoethnography is animated by three possible forms of synthesis: (a) refutational synthesis, (b) lines-of-argument synthesis, and (c) the creation of analogies. By the end of Part II, you should be able to articulate these possibilities, name the challenges and describe the promise of constructing a method for meta-synthesizing autoethnography, and detail how this process differs from the meta-autoethnography process developed by Ellis (2004).

3

First Guiding Process

Problematizing What You Know for New-Self Insight

With Esmeralda Rodriguez, Sharon Shofer, Meghan Harter, and Nitasha Clark

●

Focus Your Reading

- One key guiding process of autoethnography involves problematizing what you know for new-self insight.

- Paulo Freire described problematization as a reciprocal teaching and learning project intended to disrupt our taken-for-granted knowledge.

- Michel Foucault applied the term *problematization* in two ways: (a) to describe his preferred method of analysis and (b) to reference a process of producing objects for critical inquiry.

- Initiating research by problematizing what you know is similar to approaches used in related forms of critical cultural studies, in that after one submits to the process, one is expected to consider the self within a cultural context.

W hat is **problematizing** and how can it guide your autoethnography? The first known use of the term *problematize,* meaning "to consider or treat as a problem," was in the early 1900s ("Problematize," n.d.). One way to reveal social power, privilege, and penalty in our cultural contexts is by problematizing how we live our daily lives. It is in the cultural contexts of our teaching and learning communities that our perceptions of common sense are formed, and these in turn affect how we live our lives (Chavez, 2012, p. 339). One of the most important rationales for doing autoethnography is precisely to help reveal power, domination, privilege, and penalty in both the extraordinary and the mundane social issues of our larger cultural contexts. Once those elements are revealed, the thoughts and actions related to them can be translated into critical social research. The process of problematization guides autoethnographers toward a critical and reflexive *new-self* with questions such as the following: Who am I to be making this statement? For whom am I making it? Why am I making this statement here, now? Whom does my statement benefit? Whom does my statement harm? (Crotty, 1998, pp. 156–157). Such a line of inquiry also necessitates an inward, critical reflexive gaze that can be quite useful.

In this chapter we discuss, first, the theoretical foundation of problematization and how that foundation links to autoethnography. We then address the first guiding process of autoethnography—that is, problematizing yourself within the cultural context—through a critique of the utility of traditional triangulation for autoethnography and a discussion of the more promising practice of assemblage data collection. This section also includes information on collecting personal memory data, conducting critical auto-interviewing, collecting auto-observational and auto-reflective data, and collecting external data (Boufoy-Bastick, 2004, para. 1).

The chapter further addresses autoethnography's first guiding process in depth from the perspectives of advanced graduate students from Hughes's doctoral-level autoethnography course, who worked in culturally diverse dyads. In their contributions to the chapter, these students offer glimpses of what is like to feel autoethnography for the first time as social scientists. They discuss anticipating the messiness and pain of finding one's phenomenon of interest, linking the phenomenon of interest to the central question(s), and establishing the relevant literature to review and critique. In addition, the students demonstrate how to begin managing and analyzing the data that autoethnographers gather via assemblage by rendering concept maps into codes, codes into categories, and categories into themes, presenting examples from the most promising practices in member checking and constant comparison analysis. The chapter concludes with a summary, group and individual activities, and some online sources for students to consider.

Theoretical Foundation

Problematizing, as applied in this chapter, has a two-pronged theoretical foundation based on the acclaimed work of both Paulo Freire and Michel Foucault. Similar to Chavez (2012), Freire introduced problematization as a strategy for developing a critical consciousness (Bacchi, 2012). Beyond making politics visible in the general cultural sense, autoethnographers must have a central focus on making their own politics visible. For Freire, problematization is a pedagogic project intended to disrupt taken-for-granted knowledge. This type of problematizing involves posing as problems the myths fed to the people by the oppressors (Freire, 1968/1972, p. 132).

What Is Problematizing?

Problematizing can involve a process of introducing subjects for critical inquiry.

Problematizing can involve a teaching and learning project intended to introduce counterevidence that challenges what we think we know about particular subjects.

Michel Foucault applied the term *problematization* in two ways: (a) to describe his preferred method of analysis and (b) to reference a process of producing objects for critical inquiry. Foucault's (1977, pp. 185–186) notion of thinking problematically does not rest on looking for the one correct response to an issue but moves to examine how the issue is "questioned, analyzed, classified and regulated" (Bacchi, 2012, p. 1). In the second meaning, problematization includes a two-stage process: (a) how and why certain things (behavior, phenomena, processes) become problems (Foucault, 1985, p. 115) and (b) how these things are shaped as particular objects for thought (Deacon, 2000, p. 139). These problematized phenomena become *problematizations*. Autoethnographers can distinguish problematization from other forms of sociocultural criticism in a way that might guide their work:

> What may make problematization different from other forms of criticism is its target, the context and details, rather than the pro or con of an argument. More importantly, this criticism does not take place within the original context or argument, but draws back from it, re-evaluates it, leading to action that changes the situation. (Crotty, 1998, pp. 155–156)

Moreover, what makes problematizing different from other forms of cultural criticism is that after one submits to the process of critiquing old-self-knowledge about a particular phenomenon of interest, one tends to emerge from it, abandoning a focalized viewpoint and moving beyond merely accepting the situation as-is (Crotty, 1998, pp. 155–156). Let us turn now to specifics of designing autoethnography research for the social sciences within the theoretical foundation of problematization.

Designing Autoethnography: Problematizing Data Collection and Analysis Strategies

Problematizing Data Collection Strategies

Collecting Data via Triangulation Versus Assemblage

As one approach to ontological research, autoethnography attempts to come to terms with social complexity through rejection of the hard-bound distinctions between the micro level of analysis (the individual) and the macro level (society as a whole) (Denshire & Lee, 2013, p. 232). Such qualitative research methods come with a heavy burden of proof on the part of the researcher. One way to respond to that burden in the past was to plan for triangulation. Bryman (2004) describes the first allusion to triangulation in 1966 in support of pursuing more than one approach to investigating a phenomenon of interest. The term *triangulation* is derived from a geographic surveying strategy in which a series of three points forming a triangle is used to help map out an area for exploration. In social science, the research strategy of triangulation involves seeking at least three data points and/or three methods for exploring a phenomenon of interest. Why would one use triangulation in autoethnography? For the same reasons that other qualitative social scientists apply triangulation, autoethnographers do so to enhance readers' confidence in the credibility of their interpretations and arguments. The focus is on gathering at least three data points to support the personal narrative of a particular encounter, episode, or event. For example, an autoethnographer's story of racial microaggressions may be supported by the author (point 1), by pertinent documents (point 2), and by a witness who shared the event who has a similar or different interpretation (point 3).

In contrast with triangulation, assemblage involves a collection of multiple items that fit together to provide multiple perspectives and a rich multilayered account of a particular time, place, or moment in the history of the autoethnographer and his or her profession. Assemblage can be considered analogous to the assembling of artifacts from an archaeological site made up of different forms and modes of representation. This approach rivals triangulation as a promising innovation for autoethnography research (Denshire & Lee, 2013). The ultimate goal of assemblage is to foreground an uneasy, unstable relationship between the writer and her- or himself through the juxtaposition of multiple accounts, one against the other, about a particular phenomenon of interest and related central research questions (Denshire & Lee, 2013). A diverse array of qualitative researchers, representing a range of schools of thought from Foucault to Deleuze, have applied the term *assemblage* to their practice (Schatzki, 2002). The eight tasks of assemblage that autoethnographers should consider are listed in Text Box 3.1, and examples of each follow.

BOX 3.1
EIGHT TASKS OF ASSEMBLAGE

There are eight tasks of assemblage that you should consider when doing autoethnography as critical social research:

1. Selecting relevant journal articles

2. Producing twice-told narratives

3. Straddling multiple temporalities

4. Producing personal-professional history

5. Crafting [non]fictions

6. [Auto]ethnographic writing about practice

7. Critical/analytical commenting back to the profession

8. Reinscribing aspects of practice

(adapted from Denshire & Lee, 2013, pp. 225–227)

Task 1. Selecting Relevant Journal Articles

Task 1 involves the selection of relevant peer-reviewed journal articles. For example, scholarly articles on the topic of implicit association bias published in multiple disciplines (e.g., psychology, education, and neuroscience) could inform an autoethnography on that topic from different disciplinary perspectives. Conversely, articles published over multiple decades on the topic could reveal a trajectory across articles that might demonstrate developing understandings of that particular construct.

Task 2. Producing Twice-Told Narratives

Task 2 involves producing a set of retold narratives, each drawing out central ideas from the professional practices described in relevant journal articles. These narratives are then to be told at least twice, once from an initial perspective and then again from a different perspective. When compared to an autoethnographer's original personal-professional accounts of similar experiences in a similar cultural context, these twice-told narratives can render a substantive rewrite of the autoethnographer's original accounts. Moreover, this task can introduce different perspectives on a cultural context described in relevant journal articles located during Task 1.

Task 3. Straddling Multiple Temporalities

Task 3 involves the challenge of writing across multiple time periods when reconstructing what once had been everyday mundane moments of the autoethnographer's lived experiences of a particular setting. An example of Task 3 comes from a coauthored autoethnographic study written in 2010–2011 about the race-related experiences of two professors (one a White female and one a Black male) while they were doing ethnography on school desegregation while matriculating as doctoral students in a rural, post-*Brown* southeastern region of the United States. The original ethnography spanned the period 2000–2004; however, Hughes and Willink (2014) were seeking to document, learn from, and improve experiences of researching, teaching, and learning about school desegregation across the color line in the present for the future.

Task 4. Producing Personal-Professional History

Task 4 focuses on collecting historical materials. An autoethnographer might draw on a range of materials to produce a personal-professional history: texts, course records, memories, and relevant published scholarly articles. This range of materials can then be applied (as in Hughes, 2008c) to construct a personal-professional history that is supported by multiple forms of evidence and, thereby, connected defensibly to each experience as it occurred, was remembered, and was retold.

Task 5. Crafting [Non]Fictions

Task 5 involves the notion of *crafting [non]fictions*—a phrase adapted here from Denshire and Lee (2013) to convey how we can never fully account for every image, smell, taste, sound, and utterance from our lived experiences. What autoethnographers can do, and indeed must do for audiences, is construct the parts of the experiences that they choose to share based on the context and their perception of audience interest, availability, and capability of sharing the stories.

Task 6. [Auto]Ethnographic Writing About Practice

Task 6 involves three options: (a) crafting [non]fictions about practice, (b) crafting [auto]ethnographic writing about practice, and (c) using a combined approach. An autoethnographer doing evocative autoethnography might choose the path toward crafting [non]fictions by dramatizing a narrative and construing it as scenes from a remembered highly emotional personal-professional world. In contrast, an autoethnographer doing analytic autoethnography might choose the path of crafting [auto] ethnographic writing by constructing a narrative solely through recalling and describing relevant moments of professional practice. A researcher who combines evocative and analytic autoethnography might choose to use a combined approach.

Task 7. Critical/Analytical Commenting Back to the Profession

Task 7 involves a path toward revisiting the role that autoethnography can play as stand-alone methodology and the role that it can play when it is drawn from a larger study. This task reminds us that epiphany and transformative self-discovery can come from investigating mundane, everyday professional practices within a given cultural context. Autoethnographers of critical social research may center everyday mundane activities of a profession with the goal to study and comment on the everyday world of practice, thereby commenting back to the profession.

Task 8. Reinscribing Aspects of Practice

Task 8 recognizes autoethnography as problematizing our everyday, mundane professional experiences and then it takes that a step further, toward viewing autoethnography as actually enabling the writing-up (and possible publishing) of those experiences in a manner that can reinscribe the importance of thinking critically about the everyday world of practice. Denshire and Lee (2013) remind autoethnographers that despite their best attempts to explain how the eight tasks might work for individual readers, their representation of such projects actually "sanitize[s] . . . the messy, difficult process of assembling an autoethnography" (p. 226; see Figure 3.1). In addition to the

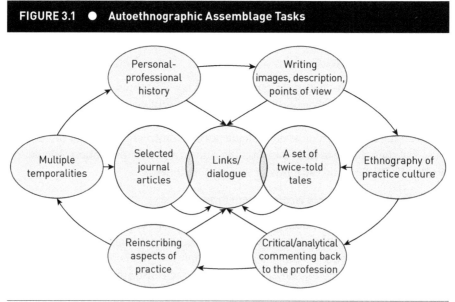

FIGURE 3.1 ● Autoethnographic Assemblage Tasks

Source: Denshire and Lee (2013, p. 227).

eight tasks of assemblage discussed above, autoethnographers may reframe their data collection approaches in terms of *collecting external data* (e.g., Anderson, 2006) and *collecting internal data* (e.g., Boufoy-Bastick, 2004). Moreover, we find these two tasks (detailed below) to be consistent and compatible with the tasks of assemblage.

Collecting External Data

Autoethnographers can contribute further to problematization by collecting defensible data from external sources, which may include observations, interviews, documents and other artifacts, audio and video recordings, standardized instruments like surveys and tests, structured interview protocols, and categorical demographic information that permits future aggregation and disaggregation of data across cases or units of analysis. Additional examples of autoethnography also detail rich sources of empirical evidence (Anderson, 2006)—which may include interviews, field notes, observations, journals, surveys, legal documents, recordings, audiovisual media, and Web 2.0 correspondence—toward advancing sound, logical, and credible designs for autoethnography (e.g., Hughes, 2008c; Laubscher & Powell, 2003). Hughes (2008c), for example, delineates data focusing on a White female student and himself as her Black professor using course events, journal notes, correspondence, and reflections to weave a narrative of how educator biases can not only inform experiences of race, class, and gender but also inadvertently influence data coding, interpretation, and analysis.

Collecting Internal Data

Critical Auto-Interviewing Data

Although collecting external data can enhance the credibility of autoethnography, collecting internal data is the sine qua non of autoethnography research. Boufoy-Bastick (2004) introduces critical auto-interviewing as a way for autoethnographers to purposefully seek gaps in their self-awareness by collecting internal data. This data collection method originated in oral history for the construction of individual history. With auto-interviewing, autoethnographers must be cognizant of what catches their attention, what stirs their emotions, and how what they choose to report is an expression of their own cultural codes. The questions that autoethnographers ask themselves should exemplify critical reflexivity, demonstrating the researchers' understanding of themselves, their society, and the value systems within which they have been acculturated to some degree. For example, an autoethnographer might ask her- or himself: "In what ways are my values of living, learning, and teaching for equity and justice challenged by my participation in the capitalist (win–lose) rules and norms of our democracy? How might this challenge influence my approach to equity and justice in the college classroom?" In critical auto-interviewing, autoethnographers can use their reconstructed life histories to explore and facilitate insight into their evolving worldviews. This data collection tool can help autoethnographers discover and problematize assumptions that give meaning to their thoughts about what cultural conditions are, the way cultural conditions are, and why cultural conditions are interpreted in certain ways.

Two-Step Emic Process for Critical Auto-Interviewing in Autoethnography

Autoethnographers can pursue critical auto-interviewing through a two-step emic process (i.e., a process of working from an insider's perspective) that consists of (a) memory recollection and (b) transcription of those memories into words to induce vicarious experiences (Boufoy-Bastick, 2004). Memory recollection is used to gather baseline data for transcription. Autoethnographers can engage a visual mode of response to past lived experiences to prompt immediate sensory responses in the form of colorful, vivid images from the different cultural contexts within which they interact with others. They may experience visual flashes in their minds—faces, objects, places, and rituals, as well as photographed images. These self-generated emic raw data can be used for transcription. The second step in this process involves transcribing those fleeting visual memories into words linked to thick, rich descriptions of memorable events that ultimately create vicarious experiences and culturally contextualized narratives for analysis.

Collecting Personal Memory Data: Emic Reporting/Etic Exploratory Analysis

Subjectivity is integral to the emic process and emic reporting. Autoethnographers can use narratives from the emic data collection process as descriptive and interpretive methodological tools to construct their personal histories and thereby (re)create reality. The narratives can evoke "real" transformative experiences, yet in revising emic reports autoethnographers must remain aware of how they are portraying themselves and why. A clear detailing of how and why the narratives are constructed is helpful. Readers must understand that the autoethnographic researcher has reasons for her or his narrations and is cognizant of the self-image being projected to the reader and back to the researcher.

Once the emic narratives are collected, the autoethnographer can subject them to etic exploratory analysis. Such analysis requires the autoethnographer to begin separating narration from analysis. To achieve this challenging task, the autoethnographer must deliberately separate the emotionally loaded reporting from the interpretive analytical reporting. In other words, the autoethnographer can give an analytical etic rationalization of her or his emotional emic experiences. This technique involves two methodological considerations of which autoethnographers of critical social research should be aware: (a) recollected emic reporting is subjective, and this subjectivity can be rendered in the open coding process; and (b) when the researcher is the only source of data and is the only one interpreting the data, there is limited opportunity for assemblage or triangulation, and therefore limited reliability and trustworthiness (Boufoy-Bastick, 2004, para. 12).

In a sense, autoethnographers must take care to be as clear about their data analysis as any other researchers. Each of the considerations noted above can be addressed if researchers remain aware of the need to detail and justify their data analysis methods. The importance of considering these issues stems from the autoethnographer's position of being both the researcher and the researched. Therefore, autoethnographers should at least consider naming and explaining how the emic/etic duality plays out in their studies, rather than attempting to hide it. Further, autoethnographers should consider developing research designs that engage the multiplicity of assemblage data collection techniques to improve the possibility that readers will view their work as a useful contribution to their given field.

Designing Autoethnographic Coding of Dual Emic/Etic Data

Autoethnographic design can include narrative deconstruction, a process of seeking and selecting key components in auto-interview narratives, such as metaphors and key events (Boufoy-Bastick, 2004). Data from those metaphors, key events, episodes, and encounters are the focus of the coding process. These data can be coded using broad key concepts, such as equity and gender role differentiation, achieved status versus ascribed status, individual versus group, social interaction, kinship relationships, language and culture, and related linguistic capital (Boufoy-Bastick, 2004, para. 14). Autoethnographers must also anticipate that their emic narrative data may be replete with overtly expressed emotions and that these emotions may taint their ability to be subjective in data coding. The strength of autoethnographers' work relies on the researchers' ability and willingness to anticipate how their value judgments may be reflected during the open coding process (Boufoy-Bastick, 2004, para. 11). Researchers must be aware that their interpretation of narratives will tend to reflect values related to the cultural contexts in which they were acculturated.

Problematizing Coding and Data Analysis Strategies

Qualitative research studies traditionally use coding and particular data analysis strategies. For our purposes, we will draw from exemplars of coding from grounded theory, a systematic approach to collecting and analyzing data for emergent or divergent theoretical analyses (Bryant & Charmaz, 2007). Interviews, audio and video recordings, observational research, open-ended questionnaires, and other data collection methods are common in grounded theory studies. A researcher identifies codes by scanning the data and completing an open coding, in which each data artifact is assigned to a category. The researcher then organizes the codes into conceptual categories. The next step is to develop hypotheses to explain the relationships between the categories. As the grounded theory is developed and refined, and data are revealed that contradict the hypotheses, data collection methods evolve and change. Thus, data collection and analysis are intertwined until all examples are explained.

Autoethnography problematizes grounded theory's data collection and analysis techniques in some important ways. First, autoethnography enables researchers to remove their academic armor for scholarship (Lerum, 2001) while placing themselves into academic analyses of certain phenomena (Hughes, 2008c; Hughes, Pennington, & Makris,

2012). Next, autoethnographic methodology allows researchers to systematically and scientifically assemble their data in a way that is not linear yet is semistructured and acceptable within the academy (Denzin, 1978; Hughes et al., 2012; Maxwell, 1992; Mitra, 2010). Third, despite the assertions of critics that researchers' voices within the research itself are not relevant, autoethnography permits researchers to be at the center of their research (Delamont, 2007; Ellis, 2004).

The analytic techniques of autoethnography also problematize those of ethnography (Goodall, 2000; Noblit, Flores, & Murillo, 2004). The shape and pattern of lived experience are related closely to the ethnographer's personal, political, and poetic experiences, choices of narrative forms, and uses of language (Goodall, 2000, p. 77). Thus, when engaging traditional ethnography, the author (a) forms overarching questions, (b) chooses ways to answer those questions, (c) analyzes his or her research, and (d) places the analysis within a historical context and/or theoretical framework (Atkinson, Coffey, Delamont, Lofland, & Lofland, 2001; Bacchi, 2012, p. 1; Coffey & Atkinson, 1996; Foucault, 1977, pp. 155–156). Autoethnography, in contrast, does not necessarily follow the same order where analysis is concerned. It can start and end with the order listed above, and it often does. However, it may instead start with a framework and end with data analysis. The process may be very circular, and it is possible that the author will continue to analyze the data until the very end of manuscript writing and beyond (Ellis, 2004; Hughes, 2008c; Mitra, 2010). Once a phenomenon of interest is identified and/or the researcher is placed within the phenomenon of interest or the phenomenon of interest surrounds the researcher, an autoethnography can live continuously in the fieldwork, past and present, and this adds a unique layer to traditional discussions of analysis. What does this type of problematizing look like in practice? Figure 3.2, in which Hughes details his data coding in one study, provides an example.

From the example in Figure 3.2, we learn that it is imperative for autoethnographers of critical social research to problematize their data coding and interpretations by recognizing, acknowledging, and naming how subjectivity influences their coding, for both their readers and themselves. It is perhaps counterintuitive, but this imperative problematization-style thinking, feeling, and writing for the audience is a crucial aspect of conveying the type of thoughtful, careful, and thorough work that is the hallmark of credible autoethnography in critical social research.

The following sections of this chapter present the analytic thinking and writing processes of four doctoral students of education—Esmeralda Rodriguez, Sharon Shofer, Meghan Harter, and Nitasha Clark—for one autoethnography project. These students, coauthors of the material that follows, highlight several potential techniques toward rethinking, analyzing, and initial writing for autoethnography. The Esmeralda/Sharon and Meghan/Nitasha dialogic format is intended to show the multiplicity and cyclical analyzing process in an autoethnography.

While the processes demonstrated by all of these doctoral students were grounded in the same general goals, objectives, and values, they differ based on the nuanced approach that each student brings to her autoethnographic project. Esmeralda and Sharon describe the promise and challenges of doing autoethnography, and they urge

---

FIGURE 3.2 ● An Example of Problematizing Codes, Interpretations, and Analyses

Despite our attempts to be our most critically reflexive selves, our value judgments and those of our students will inevitably be reflected in our open coding of the data. For example, while engaged in the open coding of data used for the *Educational Foundations* article titled "Maggie and Me" (2008a), Hughes, a Black male professor, initially coded his journal notes about an episode in a graduate course with White high school educator, Maggie, through an a priori critique of the educator as *White, privileged, dysconscious, charismatic, racist, savior narrative.* His interpretations of the narratives then reflected his current experiences, taken-for-granted knowledge, and values rooted in equity, excellence, and social justice. He undoubtedly translated his value-laden open codes into constructs such as *charismatic racist, dysconscious racist, White privilege,* and *White savior narrative.*

Upon critical reflexive inspection following member checking with Maggie, it became clear to Hughes that the constructs he used were essentially a subconscious way for him to express his disapproval of any unique challenges that he faced as a Black male professor teaching race-related graduate courses with White high school educators at a predominantly White institution of higher education. This interpretive stance was also reflective of "the clusters of common concepts, emotions and practices" associated with his experiences at that time (Boufoy-Bastick, 2004, para. 11). Therefore, his [non]fictional recollected narrative was replete with implicit and explicit emotion-evoking language that was corrected by member-checking dialogues with Maggie that revealed her as charismatic but not dysconscious and as privileged but not self-aggrandizing as a White savior. In fact, those dialogues led Hughes to recode his dialogues with Maggie to include constructs to describe some of her narratives instead as *critically reflective* and *anti-racist.* This new coding ultimately led to Hughes's interpretations and analyses of Maggie as being cognizant about and critical of her own privileges, as well as more of an authentic White ally than Hughes had initially anticipated.

---

fellow researchers to anticipate that it will be messy (i.e., nonlinear). They also describe bearing the burden of confronting the oft-hidden self and then struggling to decide what to share other others. In one of their most poignant and instructive statements, these two students challenge us to consider that "writing an autoethnography means jumping into a problem knowing that you will get wet." Esmeralda and Sharon also challenge us not to de-emphasize the fact that "engaging in this form of critical and reflexive work can be messy and painful." They note that "this turn [to studying ourselves] can be an unnatural process for researchers because we have been trained to see others, not ourselves, as our data." While Meghan also acknowledges the messiness, her project began with the most structure, which included concept mapping followed by comprehensive outlining followed by coding. Meghan also revisited oral history narratives from her native cultural artifacts to make sense of herself. In contrast, Nitasha's analytic thinking and writing processes consisted of (a) researcher-based narrative writing, (b) triangulation with multiple perspectives, (c) coding with emic and etic approaches, and (d) collaboration for member checking.

Although at the time of this writing none of the doctoral students has moved to publish her autoethnography, comments and questions about ethics, informed consent, and institutional review board approval were raised each day during the course in which the students produced their work. Therefore, following the four students' contributions, we end this chapter with a discussion of ethical issues for autoethnographers of critical social research to problematize alongside issues related to IRB approval.

Deciding to Do Autoethnography: Problematizing a Linear Approach to Self-Exploration

Anticipating the Messiness

Esmeralda and Sharon

Going back to Chavez's (2012) discussion of problematizing how we live our daily lives, the act of writing a critical autoethnography is a step toward uncovering how oppressive systems inform what we think of as "common sense." However, autoethnography is not just about discovering these oppressive systems. Hughes (2008c) notes that autoethnography "may teach one about self in that it challenges assumptions of normalcy [and] forces us to be more self-reflexive and [can instruct] us about our professional and personal socialization" (p. 127). As scholars, we must not only analyze the cultural context but also understand ourselves as part of it. Writing an autoethnography should be about challenging what is "common sense" and should make us analyze the lenses through which we interpret our own reality and, by extension, our research. Autoethnography is not meant to be a benign process, and it is not just a process of discovering the self—it is about confronting the self. For example, Pennington acknowledges her White privilege and racism throughout a previously conducted study, stating, "Throughout the study, Julie inhibited any racial dialogue that did not reflect her own views. . . . Julie's role illustrates the cost of relying on assumptions" (Pennington & Prater, 2014, p. 19). Not only are we dissecting ourselves, but we are also, as the subjects of our own ethnographies, turning the academic gaze inward. This turn can be an unnatural process for researchers because we have been trained to see others, not ourselves, as our data. Engaging in this form of critical and reflexive work can be messy and painful. For many, this can present a sort of problem. For example, there are more opportunities to second-guess our analysis, and we can become overwhelmed by issues of fairness and ethics in our depictions. Consequently, it is possible for us to be overcome with "paralysis by analysis" (Juan Carrillo, personal communication, April 2014).

However, writing an autoethnography means jumping into a problem knowing that you will get wet. In order to critically engage any research process, researchers must drop the veil that serves to separate participants from researchers. Warren and Hytten (2004) argue that it is important for researchers to be reflexive and interrogate what they bring to the research process. Fine (1994) posits that as researchers "we need to position ourselves as no longer transparent, but as classed, gendered, raced, and sexual subjects who construct our own locations, narrate these locations, and negotiate stances with relations of domination" (p. 76).

What we communicate as autoethnographers is not free of our own underlying assumptions and interpretations of the world. We must be in constant dialogue with ourselves in order for any of our research projects to serve as pedagogical encounters (Warren & Hytten, 2004). However, these encounters can be part of a messy, painful, and uncomfortable process. By wading through critical introspection, we can shed light on the major ideological principles underlying our worldviews (Boufoy-Bastick, 2004). The autoethnographer's gaze has been described as focusing outward, on social and cultural aspects of the researcher's personal experience, and then turning inward, exposing a vulnerable self that is moved by and may move through, refract, and resist cultural interpretations (Ellis, 2004). As we zoom backward and forward, inward and outward, distinctions between the personal and the cultural become blurred, sometimes beyond distinct recognition (Ellis, 2004, p. 38). The experiences described in this section of the chapter came out of our participation in an autoethnography graduate seminar. While some of us initially thought that this methodology would involve a fairly straightforward exercise, the autoethnographic process proved to be rigorous work—a rigor defined by the act of reframing the personal as political (Hanisch, 1969), just as our predecessors were encouraged to do during the second-wave women's liberation movement.

The seminar transformed into a community where the professor and students critically engaged each other. Thus, our phenomena of interest—the personal lived experiences we had each decided to unpack, confront, and challenge—began to take form. Our phenomena of interest underwent moments of transformation during which they would unravel and be sewn together only to unravel again in the next session. While others were able to identify their phenomena of interest and research questions early on, one member of our dyad jumped back and forth between subjects whenever a phenomenon proved to be too uncomfortable. Once we began to analyze our own experiences, naming and recognizing things we once held as common knowledge, we were ready to begin the search for our central questions. It is through the autoethnographer's gaze that the phenomenon of interest either comes into focus or is recognized for the first time by the writer. Once the phenomenon of interest is located, diving deeper into the literature might be required for the researcher to recognize what the guiding central questions are. We wish to remind readers that the autoethnographic process is not a linear one, nor does it look the same for everyone, as the following accounts reflect.

Giving Meaning to the Messiness

Sharon

I started our autoethnography seminar knowing what my general phenomenon of interest was. I had been grappling with my identity as a White, half-Latin@, middle-class woman ever since I was a teenager. I had never really felt that I fit in within the world of Latinidad where I grew up, and yet I also did not feel entirely comfortable identifying completely with the dominant White culture in which I was unquestioningly accepted, largely due to my phenotype. This issue of my identity had become more pertinent as I began doing ethnographic research in a school where one of the important subtexts was the fact that the needs of the Latin@ students and those of the White students were often at odds. It became a necessity for me to explore my conflicted identity between the White and Latin@ worlds I felt a part of not only for the eventual positionality statement that I would be writing but also for my own psyche as I naively struggled to maintain some sense of researcher neutrality between the two populations in my study.

I began my autoethnographic study with narratives based on memories of incidents pertaining to my identity formation. As is often the case, it was the painful memories that were the clearest in my mind. In our seminar, our professor encouraged us to share what we were working on, even if it was just short, unfinished narratives like the ones I had. My classmates listened intently as I recalled incidents from my past. The seminar conversation and analysis of these incidents ended up being transformative for my autoethnography. Whereas previously I could see the incidents only through my own lens, my classmates were able to help me identify larger contextual aspects that I was not seeing. Using these insights I was able to go into the literature and find a theoretical framework that I could use to examine my identity. But the process was not complete. I did not yet have my central question identified. I felt like I was dancing around it but couldn't pin it down.

Delving into the literature, I realized that there were voices missing from my autoethnography. I decided to interview family members formally to use their memories of my history as data. From this bit of data gathering, I went back to the seminar and again shared with my classmates and professor. It was they who helped me "turn the gaze inward" and again identify issues that I was having difficulty seeing. My central question was finally coming into focus. This recursive process of writing, analyzing, and returning to the literature occurred a few more times before I was able to finally locate my elusive central question. Instead of the "navel-gazing" exercise that I might have written had I been forced to put pencil to paper on the first day of the seminar, I was now able to see my own ethnography in terms of how it played out against the larger issues of hegemony, linguistic oppression, and hybridity. Importantly for me, I was able to relate these issues to the context of the research that I was conducting. I was now able to return to my my narratives and interview data and analyze them with a focus that I did not have earlier. For me, the laser focus that I felt after finally identifying a central question enabled me to use my autoethnography as more than an end unto itself. Instead of being an indulgent piece of self-analysis, it helped me to study the larger cultural issues that were pertinent to my study. As a step toward understanding my own positionality, it was critical in assisting me in locating myself within the cultural context that I was studying.

Esmeralda

Chavez (2012) argues that autoethnography can be an emancipatory process for those researchers on the margins of academia. Like Chavez, I too am a Chicana—one of the few to enter the ivory tower. White privileged males have had the utmost authority in the telling of my story, and my voice has, for the most part, remained largely absent in this world. I borrow from Chavez, who asserts that "producing autoethnographic research acknowledges and validates my Chicana presence as well as draws attention to my marginal position inside dominant structures of education" (p. 334). Throughout my graduate career, I have questioned to what ends I have used the master's tools (Lorde, 1983) and whether academia has been conducive to dismantling oppressive systems. These questions, along with grappling with my colonizer/colonized ethnographer positionality, became the phenomenon of interest I wished to explore.

While I ultimately decided on this topic, I confess that I was the aforementioned student who changed her subject multiple times. These changes can be linked to my increasing discomfort and anxiety about sharing my experiences working with a social justice–oriented summer reading program. I not only wanted to address questions of how I can continue to engage in my scholarship while problematizing the nature and racist history of academic research, but I also wanted to look specifically at how I have participated in the same oppressive system I wished to dismantle. This autoethnography was meant to be exploratory, reflexive, and confessional. I was uncomfortable discussing some of the issues surrounding my participation in what I recognized as the "oppression olympics" (Martinez, 1993). Writing it down seemed to make it real in ways for which I was not ready. I was afraid that by possibly saying things the wrong way, without a full critique, I was going to harm the way my colleagues (past, present, and future) viewed me. While I knew my critique of myself was valid, and the topic was pertinent and timely in a space like the new Latino diaspora (Hamann & Harklau, 2010), the fear of misrepresenting memory, along with revealing what I was problematizing, paralyzed me. Thus, I spent most of my time formulating verbal arguments and (re)writing the positionality component of my paper. Although reading pertinent literature was of utmost importance (as in any other research project), I was using this process to actively avoid the very phenomenon I had chosen to explore.

While the looming due date provided the push I needed to finally start writing the autoethnographic part of my autoethnography, what helped me compose my thoughts and ease my anxiety was not necessarily using the literature to support my arguments; rather, it was using the literature to have a critical conversation with myself. I looked toward using critical race theory to provide the framework to problematize, analyze, and critique my experiences. CRT allowed me to shed light on my own contradictions in the struggle for social justice in a way that was needed to unpack my phenomenon of interest. Mainly, I focused on CRT's fundamental tenet that racism is endemic and its acknowledgment that the omnipresence of Whiteness creates a hegemonic system where Whiteness is not only the norm but also the governing power. In my case, theory provided the language through which I could articulate my critiques and discomforts.

The vague manner in which I have described my phenomenon of interest and subject is intentional. I am still not comfortable publicizing the products of my autoethnography. In some ways, I chose a phenomenon of interest that I was not ready to address. However, that does not mean that the autoethnographic and problematizing process was not a beneficial process for me. Chavez (2012) argues that autoethnography can be an emancipatory process for those researchers on the margins of academia, and that certainly has been the case for me. This work serves to place me in dialogue with myself and positions my work within a larger cultural context.

Let us now turn to the specifics of directing autoethnography work from process to product. As you have seen in the section above and will find in the next section of the chapter, written with graduate students Nitasha Clark and Meghan Harter, the Kenyatta/Leakey question of representation that emerged at the very birth of autoethnography permeates every facet of autoethnographic work by social scientists. While reading about the detailed processes that guide Clark's and Harter's autoethnography work, you might ask yourself an additional practical question: How do I apply this technique to my own research?

Directing Autoethnography: Problematizing Uniformed Applications

Different Strokes for Different Folks

Working as two emergent autoethnographers, we, Meghan and Nitasha, produced critical dialogues that revealed the complex cyclical nature of analysis in autoethnography. What follows are examples of our work, which are intended to speak to emergent autoethnographers like ourselves who are learning to identify with and engage in this genre with a particular focus on its unique analytic processes. Each autoethnography we present (the first by Meghan and the second by Nitasha) in this section bears some resemblance to traditional grounded theory and ethnographic analysis techniques, yet each also exposes unique analytic techniques and processes that build on those traditions as we problematize ourselves within our respective cultural contexts.

Meghan

First Attempt. I am discovering that each autoethnography project I undertake is uniquely analytically processed and written according to (a) what I want to communicate and (b) how I want to communicate the topic. With hopes of exposing an additional possibility for approaching autoethnographic analysis, I describe below how I begin with the analytic thinking/writing techniques I learned in grade school, which essentially are the techniques with which I am most comfortable. Typically, for each of my thinking/writing projects, I start with a topical outline, because that process is most familiar and comforting for me. However, for my first autoethnography project (as detailed below), I initially had difficulty imagining how concepts interacted, and thus I had limited familiarity and comfort with which to propel a cogent autoethnographic analysis. Dr. Hughes, the course instructor, suggested that I develop a concept map.

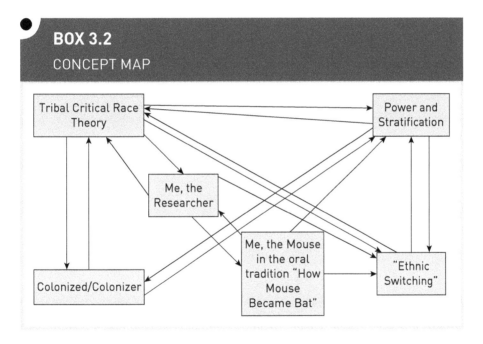

BOX 3.2
CONCEPT MAP

I took his advice and constructed a concept map (see Text Box 3.2) in order to show myself the intersection of concepts. Afterward, I created a topical outline, a technique that I learned in middle school, to illustrate chronologically for myself how the paper would be written. Creating such an outline benefits me because it forces me to list the main ideas (denoted by uppercase Roman numerals) and supporting details (each with sublevels as needed), using brief phrases indented below the main ideas. I can then split the computer screen so that the document I'm writing and the outline are side by side. All I have to do is fill in the outline with complete sentences in the written document, and I have cut the time needed for my writing process into half of what it would normally take me if I had been writing without an outline. Text Box 3.3 shows a small portion of the topical outline that I used. My complete outline was a total of 5 pages in length; however, those 5 pages turned into 30 pages of writing as I filled in the outline with details and sentences.

BOX 3.3
TOPICAL OUTLINE

I. "How Mouse Became Bat"

   a. Retell story

II. Brief family introduction

   a. Unconventional

      i. Jewish

      ii. Native American

         1. These ethnic/cultural/racial groups do not normally mix

   b. Contradictory

      i. Jewish people normally do not intermarry (Chabad/Talmud sources)

   c. Controversial

      i. Shawnee Nation, United Remnant Band

      ii. Explanation later in paper

   d. Do not fit into both cultures/worlds completely

III. Thesis

   a. Using my Native American "glasses," I analyzed and explored the following question: Why did my chance interaction with a reference librarian propel me into an academic identity dilemma?

      i. What I assume/what I know

         1. List these

      ii. What I will do in the paper

1. Brief history of autoethnography in educational research

2. My positionality

3. A dilemma

4. Emerging epiphanies from crisis

5. Concluding thoughts

IV. Why autoethnography?

   a. Helps me investigate the dilemma

   b. Helps me create an ethnographic study on myself

   c. Helps me understand my role in what is happening

      i. Cite articles here from class

After outlining the text of the manuscript with the content I wanted to explore, I started to code the texts I wanted to analyze. The texts I coded included the Ohio Constitution, a joint resolution of the Ohio State Legislature, and conversations that I remembered that surrounded the Ohio Constitution and the joint resolution. One of the memories was not member checked by the other person. In cases like this, where an autoethnographer has to analyze a memory without the ability to member check (or member checking may be a problem because the memory would have negative consequences for the researcher or the other person), the researcher should be sure to note in the manuscript that the memory was not member checked. I did so in this case, and afterward I was able to triangulate the information.

Finally, I constructed a framework to help the reader understand my main points. The frameworks for autoethnographies vary. All of the autoethnographies that I have written have been based on different frameworks. For this particular one, I used the oral tradition "How Mouse Became Bat." The lens of how I analyzed my information reflected back on that oral tradition to explain my thought processes, which can be seen in an example in Text Box 3.4. In the next section, I discuss how my autoethnographies' frameworks differ.

Second Attempt. I believe that writing autoethnographies becomes easier after you have made your first analytic thinking and writing attempt to draft one. However, I am finding that while autoethnographies have guidelines, there are limited texts available that address how to write them in set ways. My second autoethnography's writing process did not start or end in the same way as my first. First, I did not construct a

BOX 3.4
FRAMEWORK: "HOW MOUSE BECAME BAT"

Oral Tradition Within My Autoethnography

This is my retelling:

> One day, the animals in the animal kingdom decided to play stickball. They were divided between the land animals and those who had wings. Mouse wanted to play with the land animals. However, Bear, who was the leader of the land animals, denied Mouse's request. Mouse, confused and emotionally distraught, went to the winged animals and pleaded with them to let him join their team. Eagle, the leader of the winged animals, looked at Mouse and said, "We would love for you to join, but all of our team members have wings. We must create wings for you so you can fly and join our team." So, Eagle created wings for Mouse. When the game started, Mouse used his new wings and flew to score the winning goal for the winged animals. And that's how Mouse became Bat.
>
> Mouse then proceeded to say, "If you do not include an individual in your life, that person might reject you and turn against you."

Oral Tradition Reflection in My Autoethnography

Referring back to the oral tradition "How Mouse Became Bat," I felt like Mouse in this situation. I was rejected by the land animals (Bear, the librarian), and I wanted to score points for the winged animals (Eagle, Shawnee Nation) while I "acted" with the cultural capital I understood. Ironically, like Mouse, I took revenge by choosing to discuss what happened in this manuscript. In the meantime, I confided in Eagle (my adviser).

concept map for the second autoethnography. I felt that I knew how the themes overlapped from the beginning, so I believed it was unnecessary to make a map. I also did not start with a topical outline. I knew that my topic would require an in-depth qualitative analysis. As a result, I started with coding my data, which typically occurs in the middle of my writing process. Coding my second autoethnography required an unusual approach. I had two interviews that I had conducted during an independent research project. I wanted to capture my reflections between my interactions with the interviewee and her responses to my interview questions. As a result, I decided to code the interviews two ways: (a) according to how I asked the questions and (b) according to how the interviewee responded. I printed out the interviews twice and tried to code the transcriptions according to the themes I sensed throughout the interview process. I created a legend for the coding processes, and I used highlighters to code the various themes I found. Several lines were highlighted multiple times with different colors, which represented the different codes that overlapped with each other. It is difficult to illustrate the overlaps of highlighting in a Word document, but I believe I represented the the codes in the best way I could. Text Boxes 3.5 and 3.6 offer examples of my initial coding for the two-way coding method I employed.

BOX 3.5
EXAMPLE OF CODING: RESPONSES OF THE INTERVIEWEE

Legend:

Italics = Wrong Path

Caps = Free Spirit/Rebellion

Dark Shading = Native

Light Shading = Expectations

Underline = Family/Exclusion

Responses of the Interviewee

Interviewer: Do you know how long he was mayor?

Interviewee: No. I don't. 'Cause I think he was still mayor some when he left home. I just didn't pay attention to anything back then. I didn't care about nothing.

Interviewer: So, how did you get interested?

Interviewee: I didn't. I just didn't. I didn't get interested in it until I got into it. *'Cause, like I said, I didn't care about anything back then.*

Interviewer: Is there anything else that you would like to say?

Interviewee: Not that I know of.

Interviewer: Thank you for telling me what you remember of everything.

Interviewee: . . . which ain't much . . . *I just didn't care about anything in my life.*

Interviewer: So, when did you start to care?

After I stepped back from my coding methods, I realized that I had overlooked several themes. So, using the same technique, I printed out the interviews twice again, created a legend of the new themes, and began coding. I then compared the two coding processes and analyzed what I found. What resulted turned out to be the body of my manuscript. This process occurred several more times. From the previous steps, I was able to add all the codes together to view the different categories I had created. For example, in the first coding process, I used black underlining to demonstrate the code "family." In the second coding process, I used blue underlining to display the code "exclusion." By adding them together within one interview transcript, I was able

---

BOX 3.6

EXAMPLE OF CODING: INTERACTION OF
THE INTERVIEWER WITH THE INTERVIEWEE

Legend:

Italics = Wrong Path

Caps = Free Spirit/Rebellion

Dark Shading = Native

Light Shading = Expectations

Underline = Family/Exclusion

Interviewer:	Do you know how long he was mayor?
Interviewee:	No. I don't. 'Cause I think he was still mayor some when he left home. I just didn't pay attention to anything back then. I didn't care about nothing.
Interviewer:	So, how did you get interested?
Interviewee:	I didn't. I just didn't. I didn't get interested in it until I got into it. 'Cause, like I said, I didn't care about anything back then.
Interviewer:	Is there anything else that you would like to say?
Interviewee:	Not that I know of.
Interviewer:	Thank you for telling me what you remember of everything.
Interviewee:	. . . which ain't much . . . I just didn't care about anything in my life.
Interviewer:	So, when did you start to care?

---

to see the interactions between the two categories. Only then was I able to go forward with finding my theoretical framework.

The analysis pointed to a framework that was theory based instead of one based in an oral tradition. However, the theory that I wanted to use was outside my field of study. Therefore, I had to research that theory in depth to analyze my coding. I could then use the theory that I researched to explain the historical and cultural intersections that occurred. As a result, I had to create an extensive literature review within the autoethnography in order to understand the theoretical phenomena within the interview transcripts. The coding processes also allowed me to create my topical outline. Normally when I write a paper, I create a topical outline first, but in this autoethnography I used the outline to help me organize the coding and analysis of the two interviews. I found that outlining last made it easier for me to write the manuscript. As in the first autoethnography, all I needed to do was fill in the topical outline with sentences. However, in the second autoethnography I needed to change the outline to meet my needs for the manuscript during the writing process. I adapted my outline a few more times before the format of the manuscript was finally written, demonstrating the shifts in my thought processes and the complexity of the multilayered topic.

Nitasha

Clarifying the Focus of the Autoethnographic Reflection. My autoethnography is a reflection on my tenure as a multitiered system of support facilitator and a response to intervention (RTI) facilitator at two Title I elementary (K–5) schools in a large urban/suburban school district in the mideastern region of the United States. The positions were supported by the district with Coordinated Early Intervening Services (CEIS) funds distributed under the Individuals with Disabilities Education Act (IDEA; see Text Box 3.7 for an explanation of such funding). Funding was available due to the district's significant disproportionality in race or ethnicity with respect to the identification of children with disabilities; the identification of children in the district in specific disability categories; and the district's incidence, duration, and type of disciplinary actions, including suspensions and expulsions. I chose my two-year tenure experience as the phenomenon of interest because I needed to gain a critical perspective to explain my implementation challenges as an RTI facilitator. My analytic thinking and writing process consisted of researcher-based narrative writing, triangulation with multiple perspectives, coding with emic and etic approaches, and collaboration for member checking.

Researcher-Based Narrative Thinking and Writing. In my initial drafting of my autoethnography, I emphasized my personal narrative with emotional writing. I intended to start with the "red" (i.e., resentment, irritation, rage, anger, agitation, and so on), "orange" (i.e., anxiety, fear, and the like), "purple" (i.e., disgust and loathing), and "blue" (i.e., depression, dejection, and so on) memories. During the writing process, I realized I was experiencing something like post-traumatic stress disorder. I wanted to avoid recalling those thoughts, feelings, and conversations as traumatic events. It was easier to write about the "green" emotions of respect, appreciation, and trust. Writing helped me explore and investigate the alternative or counternarratives of RTI implementation.

Red Writing

From 8:30 a.m. to 2:30 p.m. at Bay Elementary School, Tuesday is Intervention Day. Throughout the day, teams of educators (each consisting of general education teachers, a school administrator, a language translator, a school psychologist, and a social worker) gather with parents of students in a small conference room for student intervention meetings. Each meeting of a student intervention team with a parent lasts approximately an hour, with the stated purpose of determining appropriate interventions for the child experiencing difficulty in school. The meeting begins with introductions. Then, the educational team reports on the child's academic or behavioral deficits. With minimal

(Continued)

(Continued)

input from the parent, the team develops a professionally driven intervention. The over-all tone of the meeting blames the child and the parent for the child's school failure. With the printed notes of the meeting, the parent then retreats to a daily life that lacks a good, family-supporting job that would enable the parent to maintain a roof over the family's heads and provide healthy food for both children and adults. The teachers on the intervention team depart to their classrooms, maintaining their institutionalized power, privilege, and classism. This ritual is repeated four or five times every Tuesday.

Each time the ritual occurs, I can't believe I'm a participant in this disenfranchise-ment. I see and feel crimson red. I wish I had a dollar for every time I heard "below grade level." The persistent and overwhelmingly condescending tone of the intervention team members disables my voice. Inside I scream, "The customer is always right! Stop blam-ing the child. Stop blaming the family." Instead, little acts of agency turn my mood from crimson red to orange. I attempt to speak for the child. I share the results of interest surveys and preference assessments. I ask empowering questions to assert the parent as expert: child/family background, critical events, medical issues, major developments, important relationships, community participation, and so on. Those simple acts provide me with some optimism to rejuvenate my spirit throughout the Tuesday ritual.

Triangulation Toward Assemblage. My concern with writing an autoethnog-raphy was that I would be giving my perspective only. However, the purpose and nature of the autoethnography methodology is to give voice to marginalized popula-tions. My memories alone were powerful counternarratives, but I wanted to establish validity or understanding through triangulation (Maxwell, 1992). Many qualitative researchers develop understanding with multiple perspectives or data sources. Since it was not possible to triangulate my data with the voices of my colleagues, I triangu-lated with documents that outlined the expectations of employment. I triangulated data not to arrive at consistency across data sources but to find inconsistencies that would uncover deeper meaning in the data. The inconsistencies strengthen rather than weaken the analysis (Denzin, 1978).

BOX 3.7
WHAT ARE COORDINATED EARLY INTERVENING SERVICES?

CEIS are services provided to students in kindergarten through grade 12 (with a particular emphasis on students in kindergarten through grade three) who are not currently identified as needing special education or related services, but who need additional academic and behavioral supports to succeed in a general education envi-ronment. The IDEA (20 U.S.C. §1413(f)(2)) and its regulations (34 CFR §300.226(b)) identify the activities that may be included as CEIS: (1) professional development for teachers and other school staff to enable such personnel to deliver scientifically based academic and behavioral interventions, including scientifically based literacy instruction, and, where appropriate, instruction on the use of adaptive and instructional software; and (2) providing educational and behavioral evaluations, services, and supports, including scientifically based literacy instruction.

For example, an LEA might use CEIS to provide behavioral interventions to nondisabled students who receive a certain number of disciplinary office referrals, perhaps as a part of a Positive Behavioral Interventions and Support (PBIS) initiative. CEIS also might be used to help fund reading or math specialists to work with nondisabled students who have not reached grade-level proficiency in those subjects, or to fund after-school tutoring for nondisabled students who score below "basic" on Statewide assessments.

Section 613(f)(5) of the IDEA also states that CEIS funds may be used to carry out services aligned with activities funded by and carried out under the Elementary and Secondary Education Act of 1965, as amended (ESEA), if IDEA funds are used to supplement, and not supplant, funds made available under the ESEA for those activities. Thus, if the IDEA funds do not supplant ESEA funds, they may be used to supplement school improvement activities conducted under other programs, such as Titles I or III, that are being implemented in an LEA.

(U.S. Department of Education, 2008)

Coding Emic and Etic. I placed my color-coded memories in a matrix with the district job description for the intervention specialist position and the federal guidance on use of CEIS funds. I recognized my alignment with the posted job expectations but also noticed a misalignment with the actual needs of schools. The frequent themes of need were related to issues of race, culture, language, class, gender, and sexuality, and their intersections. The themes emerged from my interpretation and then from the literature. Using the literature in determining themes helped to balance emic and etic dilemma coding. The emic approach codes were what I saw as the participant. The etic, researcher-oriented, codes were from the research literature on best practice strategies for implementing RTI with diverse student populations. Next, I used theory and perspective triangulation. Using multiple theoretical perspectives, I examined and interpreted the data to explain the misalignments and inconsistencies of the matrix. Learning sociocultural theories, identifying a few appropriate theories, and applying them to my own autoethnographic process was challenging. Moving from a positivist epistemology to writing with a theoretical perspective and self-reflexivity requires transcendence. The researcher moves from past to present, inward and outward, with the theory and without the theory, to frame an analysis. The matrix helped me to see that my emotional frustration was rooted in my silent witnessing to fulfill a job description that had potentially harmful effects on low-income and culturally and linguistically diverse learners and their families.

FIGURE 3.3 • Feedback From Instructor

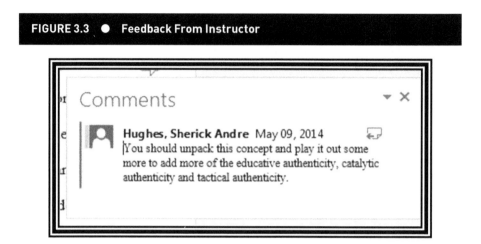

Collaboration for Member Checking. In qualitative research, member checking is a technique used to help improve the accuracy and credibility of a study. Member checking allows participants to affirm and/or challenge the data collected and the summaries of the researchers. The member-checking process decreases incorrect data and increases accurate interpretations and study credibility. In my autoethnography, I did not conduct any member checking with my colleagues who were employed at the same time as me. However, my course instructor and fellow classmates helped me to turn the lens inward and even to recognize and contextualize the absence of member checking for this circumstance (see Figure 3.3). The member-checking component of autoethnography continues to challenge me, as intended. Many autoethnographers have written about how reviewers and colleagues have compelled them to engage in further critical self-analysis (e.g., Holt, 2003).

Problematizing Ethics and Institutional Review Board Approval

Qualitative researchers have an obligation to address ethical decisions that shape research design, methodology, and analysis and to report on consent and confidentiality agreements (Duran et al., 2006). In addition to these obligations, it is incumbent on all qualitative researchers in the academy, including autoethnographers, to determine the necessity and parameters of approval from an institutional review board (Duran et al., 2006). Although autoethnography translates across the other standard obligations quite seamlessly, obtaining IRB approval is complex when this method is applied. Conventional qualitative research methods require an informed consent form for each adult and child observed (during focused observation) and interviewed during the course of the research.

However, if autoethnography is to continue offering a venue for unveiling and critiquing underrepresentation, marginalization, and oppression, how might autoethnographers go about obtaining informed consent from the individuals, groups, and institutions that subject the subaltern to underrepresentation, marginalization, and oppression? Would we be remiss to ignore the unique ethical dilemmas, risks, and social costs to be considered by subaltern autoethnographers, who may act to protect themselves and their families in ways that challenge ethical reporting as interpreted by some of the more powerful and privileged members of the academy? In other words, how do autoethnographers request permission to use information about themselves that rests on their interactions with those around them? Do autoethnographers ask for consent from anyone they encounter and may mention as they reflect on their work? How are human subjects protected throughout the process when the study is focused on the researcher? Is using pseudonyms enough? At the center of the discussion of relational ethics and IRB approval remains the problematic question driving autoethnography since its inception: How might one defend the academic right to study cultural phenomena, experiences, and artifacts (including episodes, events, and encounters) that are integral to one's own native cultural affiliation, and through what methodological means might this defense be credible?

There are no simple responses to this line of inquiry; however, it may be sufficient to say here that autoethnographers have traditionally considered *relational ethics concerns*—that is, concerns that involve "doing what is necessary to be 'true to one's character and responsible for one's actions and their consequences on others'" (Ellis, 2007, p. 4). Relational ethics also recognizes and values "mutual respect, dignity, and connectedness between researcher and researched, and between researchers and the communities in which they live and work" (Ellis, 2007, p. 4). Since the study of the self is rarely done in a social vacuum, relational ethics emerges "as a crucial dimension of inquiry . . . that must be kept uppermost in [autoethnographers'] minds throughout the research and writing process" (Ellis, Adams, & Bochner, 2011, para. 31).

In pursuit of ethical reporting, autoethnographers have presented research and findings in ways that honor site access agreements and consent from participants. They have also been aware of potential conflicts of interest and researcher perspectives that may influence how the empirical research is reported. However, even with identifying information seemingly omitted by the researcher, direct and indirect disclosure of participant identities can occur. In response to this type of ethical threat, autoethnography has evolved into a method that can allow participants "to talk back to how they have been represented in the text" (Ellis et al., 2011, para. 31). In fact, in their review, Hughes, Morant, Lawrence, Jacobs, and Smith (2010) found that autoethnographers have implemented one or more of the following strategies to protect confidentiality and anonymity: pseudonyms applied to all proper nouns and pronouns (e.g., Berry, 2005), member checking (e.g., Pennington, 2007), and coauthorship with a key informant (e.g., Laubscher & Powell, 2003). These three practices are consistent with relational ethics concerns, as well as with the typical concerns for qualitative research posed by IRBs. However, these practices are less useful for autoethnographies in which member checking may be impossible (e.g., a deceased relative), implausible (e.g., a movie star met in passing at an airport), and/or ill-advised (e.g., an abusive ex-partner). Given the information provided throughout this chapter, autoethnographers of critical social research would be wise to at least consider relational ethics and

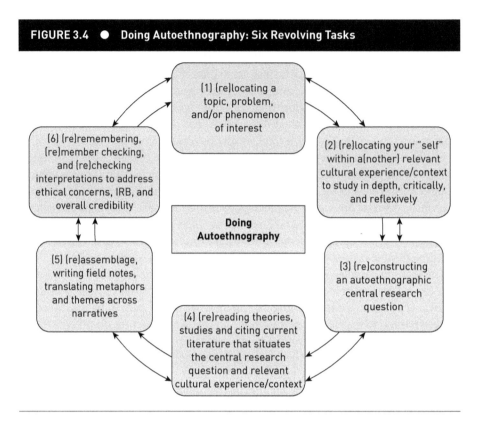

FIGURE 3.4 ● Doing Autoethnography: Six Revolving Tasks

(1) (re)locating a topic, problem, and/or phenomenon of interest

(2) (re)locating your "self" within a(nother) relevant cultural experience/context to study in depth, critically, and reflexively

(3) (re)constructing an autoethnographic central research question

(4) (re)reading theories, studies and citing current literature that situates the central research question and relevant cultural experience/context

(5) (re)assemblage, writing field notes, translating metaphors and themes across narratives

(6) (re)remembering, (re)member checking, and (re)checking interpretations to address ethical concerns, IRB, and overall credibility

Doing Autoethnography

IRB approval as part of the guiding process of problematizing. Moreover, evidence from the autoethnography projects of the doctoral students who contributed to this chapter supports an argument for the emergence of six key revolving tasks at the center of doing autoethnography, as illustrated in Figure 3.4.

Concluding Thoughts

This chapter has provided evidence to support the notion that the problematizing process is a complex but necessary guide in the application of autoethnography as critical social research. We do recognize that the chapter presents this complexity in a stepwise manner at times, and we ask you to interpret these times as our attempts to convey the complexity of this guiding process, and of doing autoethnography, in the most teachable manner we could devise. Clearly, the evidence of this chapter (and others) indicates that, given its foundation in lived experiences, autoethnography is not only complex but also "messy." Our evidence suggests consistently, however, that it is messy in a good way, in a way that can illuminate, as we attempt to make meaning and sense of our lived experiences. Ultimately, in this chapter we are speaking to emerging and advanced researchers and speaking back to critiques of the possibilities of autoethnography by problematizing what we know for new-self insights.

Individual Activity

Purpose: Involve students in preliminary thinking about problematizing as they consider their own autoethnography projects.

Activity: Auto-interviewing; students write and respond to questions that purposefully challenge their taken-for-granted knowledge about a topic of interest.

Evaluation: Determine whether selected auto-interviewing questions and responses reflect problematizing in the manner described in this chapter.

Individual and Group Activity

Purpose: Expose students to individual or small-group experiences of problematizing for autoethnography.

Activity: Think-pair-share in which students first work alone to develop an initial design for an autoethnography with *triangulation* described as its central data collection approach (two to three paragraphs). Each student then drafts a second design with *assemblage* described as its central data collection approach (two to three paragraphs). Finally, students work in groups to compare and contrast the two data collection approaches. Students practice *problematizing* in this activity by engaging the process of producing a subject for critical inquiry (Foucault, 1977) and by disrupting taken-for-granted knowledge (Freire, 1968/1972).

Evaluation: Use a rubric regarding problematizing to determine whether students' approaches to problematizing are relevant, credible, thoughtful, thorough, and defensible to an academic audience.

Note for instructor: Share your own experience with the process of problematizing as a prompt for students to begin sharing.

Sites for Students to Consider

Introsocsite: Lesson Plan for Bafa Bafa: A Cross-Cultural Simulation: http://www.asanet.org/introtosociology/LessonPlans/BAFABAFALesson%20Plan.htm

Project Implicit: Harvard Implicit Association Tests: https://implicit.harvard.edu/implicit/takeatest.html

4

Second Guiding Process

Legitimizing Autoethnography
With Three Approaches

Focus Your Reading

- Legitimizing (or legitimation) is important to autoethnography because of the high level of scrutiny applied to autoethnographic studies.

- Legitimizing is the process of making something "legitimate" or accepted, whereby many of the preferred practices of individuals with legitimate authority are adopted as cultural standards, benchmarks, and criteria for establishing credibility.

- Integral to the process of legitimizing is the understanding and implementation of rules and norms, and distinct approaches that comply with those rules and norms.

Legitimizing (also known as **legitimation**) is the process of making something "legitimate." In the context of scholarly research, it involves the existence and prevalence of habitual social acts, positions, structures, and practices that become taken-for-granted (legitimated) objects with established rules and norms for participation (Johnson, 2010). When autoethnography is applied as critical social research, a particularly high level of scrutiny is applied to it by public audience members. This level of scrutiny was perhaps first amplified when Louis Leakey critiqued the work of Jomo Kenyatta (1938/1965) in a London public forum, in what has come to be known as the first autoethnography debate (as discussed in Chapter 1). From that day forward, autoethnography in the social sciences has been subjected to the process of legitimizing by the author(s) and ultimately by the reading public.

As we have noted previously, autoethnography assumes multiple forms, including spoken-word poetry, digital storytelling, monologues, memes, diary entries, notes, and blogs, as well a vast array of other private formats. Critical work in autoethnography involves these modes related to self-questioning. Self-questioning about the perils and promise of legitimizing in critical social research is indeed important to consider if the work toward equity and justice is to continue. Such questions include but are not limited to the following: Is my autoethnography a legitimate representation from my life? Is anyone privileged by how I go about legitimizing my autoethnography, and, if so, how? Is anyone penalized by how I go about legitimizing my autoethnography, and, if so, how? These questions reflect the essence of how autoethnography relates to the crisis of legitimation via representation (Denzin & Lincoln, 2008b; Holt, 2003). *Representation* refers to how the self and others are interpreted and described. Indeed, like other social science methods, autoethnography in critical social research is often seeking to align with the expectations of the research community. There are ways to legitimize autoethnography with signature characteristics that lean toward either evocative or analytic autoethnography (as described in Chapter 1). Moreover, there are at least three distinct approaches to legitimizing critical social research autoethnography from peer-reviewed literature. All three identifiable approaches to legitimizing autoethnography share the embedded credibility-seeking criteria of rigor and reflexivity by linking autoethnography to the following:

- Existing qualitative constructs (Starr, 2010)
- Traditional qualitative methodology (Anderson, 2006)
- Established professional association standards (Hughes, Pennington, & Makris, 2012).

The following section digs a little deeper into the theoretical foundation of legitimizing and a key metaphor of legitimizing autoethnography: reflexivity as rigor. We then discuss three common approaches to legitimizing autoethnography in the academy as they manifest as evocative and analytic autoethnographic products. Interwoven within the text that follows is a discussion of the promise and perils that researchers may anticipate when attempting to legitimize autoethnography. The chapter concludes with some strategies for any autoethnographer to consider while deciding which one of the three approaches to legitimizing to use when pursuing autoethnography as critical social research.

Theoretical Foundations of Legitimizing

Traditionally, researchers have ensured the value of their work by adhering to existing research traditions and methods. They have been able to make their work legitimate and, therefore, accepted by using familiar tools and theories of research common to their fields of study. Autoethnography is not a part of the traditional research canon—it is still finding its way. Therefore, legitimizing is a key factor in autoethnographic work. We begin here with a conceptual view of legitimizing, followed by a discussion of the ways rigor and reflexivity contribute to legitimizing. Finally we apply these notions of legitimizing to three ways of specifically linking autoethnography research components. The three approaches to legitimizing autoethnography named above, and subsequent examples of those approaches, tend to be informed by the pioneering work of Max Weber (1958) and the team of Peter L. Berger and Thomas Luckmann (1967). The way in which we apply the term *legitimizing* in this chapter is based on a two-pronged theoretical foundation that employs the influential work of

Weber (1958)

Legal authority is based on a system of rules and norms that are applied administratively and judicially in accordance with known principles. The persons who administer those rules and norms are appointed or elected through legal procedures. Superiors are also subject to rules and norms that limit their powers, separate their private lives from their official duties, and require written documentation.

Traditional authority is based on a system in which authority is legitimate because it "has always existed." People in power usually enjoy that position because they have inherited it. Their prerogatives are usually similar to those of the ruler above them, just reduced in scale, and they too are often selected based on inheritance.

Charismatic authority is based on the charisma of the leader, who shows that she or he possesses the right to lead by virtue of magical powers, prophecies, heroism, or the like. The leader's followers respect her or his right to lead because of the leader's unique qualities (charisma), not because of any tradition or legal rules or norms.

these researchers. This work is seminal because it was among the first widely disseminated scholarship in Western thought to explain how groups develop and sustain what is to be considered "legitimate." The concept of legitimizing is particularly important in the current academic climate, where the acceptance of autoethnography as a legitimate form of critical social research has grown tremendously, and yet debates continue about its legitimate place in dissertations and in first-tier publications that adhere to the peer-review process.

Max Weber, a 20th-century sociologist, argues that humans feel obligated to obey the rules and norms associated with a legitimated object (e.g., the rules and norms of a professional research organization/association), even when they may disagree with those rules and norms. He posits three pure types of human legitimation strategies used to justify the rights of authorities: (a) legal, (b) traditional, and (c) charismatic. Both legal authority and traditional authority are central to legitimizing autoethnography. Legal authority is perhaps most visible in the example of the appointment and election of editors and associate editors of journals and book publishers. Journals and books that are considered legitimate in the academy are the products of legality, which thereby renders the text therein as supported by legitimate authorities. The research community considers research published in particular journals and books to be legitimate because of the peer-review process, a traditional authority of prestige that has been inherited in the academy. The peer-review process for journal articles represents the utmost level of scrutiny for studies, and the publication of studies in peer-reviewed journals demonstrates their legitimacy. The related traditional authority at play in legitimizing autoethnography also involves the notion of rejection rates (whereby the "best," or most legitimate, academic journals reject 75% or more of submitted articles) and the advent of the use of impact factor ratings (calculated using widely accepted formulas) to determine journals' merit and worth in the academy. As you may have guessed, the foundation for legitimizing autoethnography as critical social research is publishing in venues recognized by the aforementioned legal and traditional authorities.

Berger and Luckmann (1967), also 20th-century sociologists, discuss legitimation via socialization, which occurs because people identify with significant others and those identifications can lead to them to develop new social identities and acquire new institutional memberships. In their book *The Social Construction of Reality* (1967), Berger and Luckmann interrogate the social constructions of human conduct to unveil how individuals, groups, associations, teams, and societies socially construct, reproduce, and reinforce the rules and norms for legitimate participation across generations. Their text is credited with introducing the term *social construction* into the social sciences. Human conduct, from the social construction

Berger and Luckmann (1967)

First order of objectivation of meaning: Prearranged patterns of thought and action that seem objective to us when we enter a given everyday life context (p. 35). The problem is that "the reality of [the individual's] everyday life is taken for granted *as [the]* reality" (p. 37).

Second order of objectivation of meaning: Seen in the process of legitimation. Legitimation provides meaning that can be sustained by later generations, those who did not share firsthand in the events and experiences that led to the currently accepted understanding.

perspective, involves a cyclical process of (a) objectivation of experiences, habitual thoughts, symbols, and actions related to that objectivation; (b) typification of thoughts and actions via language, symbols, objects, roles, and other representations; (c) institutionalization of those thoughts and actions, and (d) the legitimation of the institution, followed by further objectivation—and the cycle continues (Berger & Luckmann, 1967, p. 79). Berger and Luckmann describe two orders of objectivation. Objectivation is sustained through the ongoing process of legitimation (pp. 92–93). Berger and Luckmann's main point that is most relevant as an additional element of the theoretical foundation of this chapter is that one tendency of human conduct is that we find ways to objectify, typify, and ultimately institutionalize the meanings of our experiences, our tendencies, our preferences, and our habits of thought and action, and we support and sustain these tendencies by legitimizing them. Therefore, critical social researchers engaged in legitimizing autoethnography logically follow the human tendency to sustain the method's development, while those who seek to de-legitimize autoethnography follow the human tendency to sustain previously established qualitative methods of the institution (e.g., Delamont, 2007). Legitimizing autoethnography is a crucial aspect of understanding autoethnography and its place in the research community. Given these two ideas about the ways in which autoethnography can be legitimized, it should be clear that it is crucial for autoethnographers to review their own work.

Applying These Concepts to Your Own Autoethnography

The following are some questions regarding legitimation (inspired by Denzin & Lincoln, 2008b; Holt, 2003) that you may consider:

- Is my autoethnography a legitimate representation of critical incidents from my life?
- Is anyone privileged by how I go about legitimizing my autoethnography, and, if so, how?
- Is anyone penalized by how I go about legitimizing my autoethnography, and, if so, how?
- Is my autoethnography linked to specific research traditions, methods, and associations?

Understanding how to frame and interrogate your work in relation to venues of authority and community requires questioning your work in ways that examine your representation and its relationship to the representations of others. We now turn to a deeper discussion of reflexivity as an integral part of legitimizing autoethnographic work, with a particular focus on its link to rigor, prior to offering our interpretation of how reflexivity is embedded within the three major approaches to legitimizing autoethnography.

Reflexivity

Reflexivity has been variously defined, and its implications have been widely discussed in interpretive sociology, education, cultural studies, and cultural anthropology over the past 15 years (Anderson, 2006, p. 378). Reflexivity as a central criterion of autoethnography provides researchers with a forum for expressing their awareness of their integral connection to the research context and thereby their influence on that context. Reflexivity involves an in-depth level of awareness of the reciprocal influence between ethnographers and their settings and informants (Anderson, 2006). It entails self-conscious introspection guided by a desire to better understand both self and others through examining one's actions and perceptions in reference to and in dialogue with those of others (Anderson, 2006, p. 378). While this description is formidable, *The SAGE Encyclopedia of Qualitative Research Methods* addresses reflexivity in terms that may seem more palatable to readers who may be new to the concept, explaining that reflexivity can be broadly described as qualitative researchers' engagement of continuous examination and explanation of how they have influenced a research project. This source goes on to note that qualitative researchers have adopted essentially four types of reflexivity, and that the form used is dependent on the methodology adopted (Dowling, 2008, p. 1).

Reflexivity can be viewed on a continuum with an objectivist end and a constructivist end (Dowling, 2008). For years, the term *reflexivity* as applied to critical social research was considered poorly described and elusive; however, the authors cited here took up the task of conveying a more comprehensive understanding of the concept. Today, reflexivity is applied toward closing the door on a belief that researchers and participants must fear and hide the distances that separate them, by providing momentum for a move toward a position where boundaries between the two are surrendered (Dowling, 2006).

Reflexivity as Rigor

If reflexivity can be understood as a concept to name an underlying goal of the researcher's understanding and critiquing his or her own role in the study, then **rigor** might be understood as a related concept to name an underlying goal for the research to be conducted with systematic, trustworthy, and credible methods. Considering the two concepts together, we propose that reflexivity is a factor in relation to the rigor of autoethnography. One important characteristic that seems to separate autoethnography from its predecessors in educational research is its foundation in reflexivity as rigor (including authors naming their complicity), whereby the rules and norms of engagement require an adherence to the pursuit of equity and justice as the standard for adequate participation. *Reflexivity as rigor* is such an integral metaphor of autoethnography in critical social research that it can be found embedded within the three approaches to legitimizing this alternative qualitative method. Boufoy-Bastick (2004) is among the few scholars during the past decade to discuss the notion of rigor for the purposes of legitimizing autoethnography.

Rigor alone can be defined as adhering to strict standards of implementation, yet qualitative work embraces the need to adjust methodology to the needs of the inquiry. The work of Boufoy-Bastick (2004) actually "brings together some more modern tools of qualitative enquiry to suggest a more rigorous process for uncovering the royal road to self-knowledge—to shed light on ethical and ideological principles which have forged from lived experiences" (para. 3). Moreover, autoethnographers can apply auto-interviewing, auto-ethnography, and critical incident methodology in the manner Boufoy-Bastick proposes "for eliciting [a] self-conceptualised worldview" (para. 1) in a manner that implies rigor and thereby is an important step toward legitimation. In critical qualitative work, rigor is considered in relation to design and methods. Kincheloe, McLaren, and Steinberg (2011, p. 170) highlight the idea of a bricoleur (one who recognizes the blurred lines of disciplines and methods) to describe how researchers must attend to how research design and methods are used in concert with a deep understanding of the complexities of the context and area of inquiry. Autoethnographers strive to clearly delineate their purpose, research designs, and methods as one way of addressing what some traditions term rigor (Holman Jones, Adams, & Ellis, 2013b, p. 31).

Moreover, the advent of radical reflexivity, as addressed in the work of Wanda Pillow, has augmented our understanding of reflexivity as rigor by conceptualizing it as the process of monitoring and reflecting on all aspects of a research project, from the formulation of research ideas through to the publication of findings and, where this occurs, their utilization. Sometimes the product of such monitoring and reflection is a reflexive account. Reflexivity, then, can also be described as prevalent and growing, not only in autoethnography but also in qualitative research in general. Reflexivity is commonly used in qualitative research and has been posited and accepted as a method qualitative researchers can and should use to legitimize, validate, and question research practices and representations. For example, Pillow (2003) "examines the role of reflexivity as a methodological tool as it intersects with debates and questions surrounding representation and legitimization in qualitative research, within modernist and postmodernist ideologies, and pays close attention to how reflexivity is being defined and used in present-day research" (p. 175). There are four common trends in present-day uses of reflexivity that researchers may consider problematizing in their autoethnographic work: (a) reflexivity as recognition of self, (b) reflexivity as recognition of other, (c) reflexivity as truth, and (d) reflexivity as transcendence (Pillow, 2003). In fact, within some qualitative research, less conventional uses of reflexivity are being replaced by a more reflexive writing practice that challenges topics of equity and social justice and can expose uncomfortable feelings, like guilt and complicity (Pillow, 2003).

With the theoretical foundation and key metaphor of reflexivity as rigor in mind, let us lean forward to a more in-depth discussion of the three distinct approaches to legitimizing autoethnography. The foundations of the *reflexivity as rigor* metaphor are unmistakable upon deeper inspection of each approach.

Three Approaches to Legitimizing Autoethnography

As noted above, at least three distinct approaches to legitimizing autoethnography can be identified from the literature. These approaches reflect autoethnography applied as critical social research by linking it to one or more of the following:

- Existing qualitative constructs (e.g., Guba & Lincoln, 1989; Starr, 2010)
- Traditional qualitative methodology (e.g., Anderson, 2006)
- Established professional association standards (e.g., Hughes et al., 2012)

It is important to note that these links are not exclusive. Many autoethnographers utilize all three or other combinations in order to situate and validate their work.

Claiming Links to Existing Qualitative Constructs

One approach to legitimizing autoethnography in critical social research can be identified by its characteristic style of claiming links to existing qualitative constructs. This means simply that writers attempting to legitimize autoethnography with this approach do so by connecting it with key qualitative research requirements (or criteria) that are already in use and thereby already familiar to members of the qualitative research community. For example, Starr (2010) works at legitimizing autoethnography by addressing the qualitative requirements for authenticity introduced by Guba and Lincoln (1989, pp. 245–249). This approach challenges previously described criteria for legitimacy in autoethnography (e.g., Ellis & Bochner, 2000) by providing evidence that those criteria do not fully address the requirement for authenticity in research (Starr, 2010, p. 5). In working toward more fully addressing this authenticity requirement, Starr (2010) adapts Guba and Lincoln's (1989) fairness criterion alongside six additional authenticity, methodological, and rigor criteria and reframes them as essential to addressing and evaluating the legitimacy of autoethnographic studies in a manner that keeps intact the "tenets of constructivist inquiry" (pp. 5–7). Starr presents samples from autoethnography that have addressed each criterion in order to enable readers to locate instances that may ring true to their own experiences (p. 5). This evidence suggests that a sound academic argument can be made that the legitimacy of autoethnographic research in the social sciences is contingent on the application of the following requirements (Table 4.1 provides some key details about the proposed requirements):

- Fairness
- Ontological authenticity
- Catalytic authenticity
- Educative authenticity
- Tactical authenticity
- Methodological rigor
- Aesthetic rigor

Overall, the notion of autoethnography in relation to existing qualitative constructs connects the traditions and methods in ways that recognize and emphasize similarities. This form of legitimizing is key to presenting autoethnographic work to those unfamiliar with the methodology.

TABLE 4.1 ● Toward Criteria for Legitimizing Autoethnography		
What Are the Defining Criteria?	**What Do the Criteria Involve?**	**Examples and Advice**
Fairness: The extent to which the presence of different values and different social constructions of reality are named during the evaluative writing process. This self-evaluation process is integral to credible writing that represents conflicts over claims, concerns, and issues. *Related question:* Is this part of my story and construction fair or unfair, and to whom?	Identifying key stakeholders and different social constructions of reality from within/between groups. Investigating and naming (communicating) any emergent value system(s). Writing a detailed account of conflicting values and social constructions of reality and the social context and conditions that may inform or influence those conflicting differences.	Fairness is illustrated by autoethnographic study of teacher development conducted by Austin and Hickey (2007). In the initial stages of the study, students were asked to engage in memory work to recollect evocative events. Some students expressed frustration that their conception of race was limited by their self-professed Whiteness. One student, through a series of guided discussions, was able to identify her home space as being one affected by race and class differences. The previously unrecognized conflict not only highlighted her family and home constructions as raced spaces but also further emphasized the presence and plight of indigenous Australians, but only when referenced through violations of White cultural mores.
Ontological authenticity: The extent to which a researcher's own values and social constructions of reality are improved, matured, expanded, and elaborated, in that they now possess more evidence-based information and have become more comprehensive, complex, and/or sophisticated. *Related question:* Is there evidence of any changes in who I think I am versus who I think I want to become?	Improving pedagogical practices and policies by facilitating change that begins with critical self-study of how one teaches and who one is as a teacher. Examining the space between critical self-reflection and action.	By actively engaging her memories of race as a child, locating herself within a racial-social dynamic, and then reflexively engaging more recent memories, Maryanne has moved from the recall and telling of a tale, a story from her life, to actively and critically engaging issues of race in her professional practice. At this point in her life, Maryanne has not only summoned up the courage to transgress the racialized borders that had operated with decreasing strength to contain her within safe White space, but she is also now actively dwelling within the space of the Other (Austin & Hickey, 2007, p. 7; Starr, 2010, p. 6).

What Are the Defining Criteria?	What Do the Criteria Involve?	Examples and Advice
Catalytic authenticity: The extent to which action is stimulated and facilitated by the evaluative writing process, whereby the purpose of the self-evaluation is some form of action or decision making. *Related question:* Is there evidence of change in who "they" want to become?	Energizing participants (i.e., autoethnographers and their readers) to engage in critical conscientious action, which mirrors Patti Lather's (1991) call for *catalytic validity*, a reality-altering, channeling state of mind, through which participants ultimately gain more critical self-understanding and more self-determination than typically experienced.	Boyd's (2008) autoethnographic research demonstrates a catalytic learning experience that is illustrated in the following text: "The difference now is that I am aware of those tendencies coming out of my place of White privilege, and I am seeking to forge a new way for myself. I am trying to live in that tension between cautious action and critical reflection, between the need to engage in dialogue for mutual understanding and the need to actively listen to the experiences of colleagues and friends of color" (p. 223).
Educative authenticity: The extent to which participants' (i.e., autoethnographers' and their readers') sense(s) of understanding and appreciating the social constructions/assumptions of *others* outside their stakeholding affinity groups are challenged and enhanced. *Related questions:* Is there evidence of empathy and validation of the constructed/assumed *other* in relation to the constructed/assumed *self*? To what extent can any revealed constructions/assumptions be linked to greater insight about and/or strengthened relationships with *others*?	An evolution of critical self-reflexive awareness and dialogue, and a greater sense of understanding the self as mediated by a closer critical examination of the experience of the *other*. For example, autoethnographers such as Pennington (2007) ask questions like the following: What assumptions about children from marginalized groups are revealed during interactions with my preservice teachers? How might my preservice teachers and I begin to develop more honest and genuine understandings of how our White privilege is viewed in the observed school community?	Through self-reflexive analysis, Pennington's (2007) participants were able to develop an honest and genuine understanding of how their White privilege was viewed by parents and families in the community. In addition, assumptions held by preservice teachers about children belonging to essentialized groups were revealed, leading to greater insight and strengthened relationships (Starr, 2010, p. 6).

(Continued)

TABLE 4.1 ● (Continued)

What Are the Defining Criteria?	What Do the Criteria Involve?	Examples and Advice
Tactical authenticity: The extent to which stimulation and facilitation of action are evoked by the critical self-evaluation process to the next step of empowerment to act on the needed change(s) that emerged. *Related question:* How did I (and/or my students) want to or need to act and how did I (and/or my students) stimulate, facilitate, and proceed to action (if at all)?	Moving participants beyond desires and feelings about the need to act on a problem and toward critical self-evaluation strategies that can actually empower participants to act.	Using journal writing as a data collection method allowed Pepper to reflect on the ineffectiveness of her leadership style. In her analysis, Pepper identified that she was subscribing to and had been enacting an authoritarian leadership style with negative effect. As a result of Pepper's self-analysis, she repositioned her practice toward a more transformational, and arguably more effective, style of leadership. The process had a positive impact on her ability to lead but also helped the author create a more positive and caring school environment. A climate of collaboration, including a cycle of support and feedback, was instrumental in establishing realistic, attainable school goals in which the stakeholders were willing to invest (Starr, 2010, p. 6).
Methodological rigor: The extent to which methodological self-evaluation standards provide a bridge between more traditional conceptions of validity, reliability, and generalizability and standards for methodological rigor that are more reflective of interpretive and constructivist inquiry. *Related questions:* To what extent does my voice as an external interpretive researcher (i.e., me as autoethnographer) replace my voice as an internal participant (i.e., me as subject of my autoethnography)? To what extent does my voice diminish or even negate the value of constructivist inquiry for revealing critiques of personal experience and critical perspectives on knowledge?	Moving beyond traditionally understood evaluation methods as externally imposed, generalized rules or procedures that overshadow specific research, whereby the voice of the external researcher (i.e., me as autoethnographer) replaces the voice of the internal participant (i.e., me as subject of my autoethnography), at times diminishing and even negating the value of personal experience and knowledge.	Methodological rigor is linked closest to constructive inquiry, which is a type of research inquiry that (a) relies on a more cyclical exchange that is not present in interpretive, responsive methods and (b) does not rely on isolating cause or effect (Starr, 2010, p. 7). *Rationale:* Discerning what people think exists and why they think so is at least as important as verification of some a priori postulate about cause-effect relationships that the evaluator thinks exists (Guba & Lincoln, 1989, p. 232).

What Are the Defining Criteria?	What Do the Criteria Involve?	Examples and Advice
Aesthetic rigor: The extent to which an accepted standard for literary quality is adhered to, including the standard juxtaposition between critical social research and evocative literature. *Related question:* What can my writing represent about a communal sense of what is real and how might it resemble a provocative weaving of story and theory?	Writing that does the following: • Remains accessible and evocative. • Represents a satisfying, complex, and intriguing literary accomplishment. • Renders an impact, where it speaks to the overall effect of the text on an emotional and intellectual level and the ability of the text to inspire or motivate the reader to some form of action. • Represents an *expression of a reality*, which requires the researcher to ensure that the text is a credible representation of a cultural, social, individual, or communal sense of what is real. • Reflects how methodological and literary criteria bridge the distance between the scholarly and the creative.	Aesthetic rigor is rooted in the particularities of "standards of literary quality that further legitimize autoethnography in its juxtaposition between scholarly research and evocative literature"(Starr, 2010, p. 7; citing Richardson, 2000). Thus, "good autoethnography" engages a "provocative weave of story and theory" (Starr, 2010, p. 7; citing Spry, 2001). This criterion is an "aesthetic requirement of autoethnography" that cannot be dismissed (Starr, 2010, p. 7). *Rationale:* Both the scholarly and the creative have a place in research and are essential to the success of autoethnography (Starr, 2010, p. 7).

Source: Adapted from Starr (2010).

Reclaiming Links to Traditional Qualitative Methodology

A second approach to legitimizing autoethnography in critical social research can be identified by its characteristic style of reclaiming links to traditional qualitative methodology. Perhaps the most widely read work by a researcher engaging this approach is Leon Anderson's article "Analytic Autoethnography" (2006), which as of August 2014 had been cited by more than 640 other authors (according to a Google Scholar search). According to Anderson, this approach to legitimizing autoethnography positions the researcher as follows:

• A full member in the research group or setting
• Visible as such a member in published texts
• Committed to developing theoretical understandings of broader social phenomena (p. 373)

The type of autoethnography most closely associated with this approach is *analytic autoethnography,* which was developed and articulated, Anderson (2006) notes, in the hope that other scholars would join in reclaiming and refining autoethnography as part of the analytic ethnographic tradition (p. 392). In the discussion that follows, we consider the specific goal of reclaiming autoethnography as part of the ethnographic tradition (Anderson, 2006, p. 392), alongside an exploration of how this argument for reclamation may serve essentially as another approach to legitimizing autoethnography. It is an approach that relies on (a) linking to classic ethnographic texts, (b) making an explicit critique of evocative autoethnography, (c) presenting five key features of analytic autoethnography as links to the classics and as resolving most of the pitfalls of evocative autoethnography, and (d) addressing key limitations of all autoethnography work.

Linking to Classic Ethnographic Texts

Situating autoethnography in the context of classic historical ethnographies is the signature characteristic of a second form of legitimizing autoethnography that we call *linking to classic ethnographic texts.* It is a step that even goes so far as to label some elements of early works as signs of proto-autoethnography (i.e., previous iterations of autoethnography in practice prior to the term's introduction to many educational researchers by Hayano, 1979). Sociologists who became pioneers in the field also collected and shared autobiographical experiences. However, their work was done without the impetus for the in-depth self-reflexive critique of today's analytic autoethnography. As Anderson (2006) explains:

> Student sociologists [at the University of Chicago] often lived in the settings studied, walked the streets, collected quantitative and qualitative data, worked for local agencies, and had autobiographical experience emerging from these locales or ones similar to them. . . . While analytically more sophisticated and focused than the first wave of Chicago School studies, these later . . . studies continued the earlier tendency to downplay or obscure the researcher as a social actor in the settings or groups under study. So, for instance, none of the researchers just cited incorporated any self-narrative or explicitly personal anecdotes in their substantive writings. The only examples of self-narrative from these scholars came in the form of occasional methodological notes . . . "confessional tales" of fieldwork experiences. (p. 375)

Proponents of this logic also suggest that the history of autobiographically related ethnography in the historic Chicago School, as well as the autoethnographic examples provided by Hayano (1979) and Zurcher (1983), offered a potential direction for the development of autoethnography in the realist or analytic tradition (Anderson, 2006, p. 375). Even the acclaimed sociologist Louis Zurcher actively practiced and advocated for autobiographically situated and self-observant research, while collected essays on role enactment included an extended discussion of methodological issues related to the autobiographical role (Anderson, 2006, p. 376). Some supporters of this role of autoethnography seem annoyed that in the intervening years, from the 1980s to the present, the term *autoethnography* has become linked almost exclusively with the descriptive literary approach known as evocative autoethnography (e.g., Denzin, 1989, 1997; Ellis & Bochner, 2000). What are the explicit critiques of evocative autoethnography, and why does this form of autoethnography induce such disdain?

Explicit Critiques of Evocative Autoethnography

The explicit critiques of evocative autoethnography are "critiques" in the sense of the word as it tends to be applied in academia—that is, discussions of promise and limitations. Anderson's (2006) critique begins by describing evocative autoethnography's promise, and more specifically by praising some of its pioneers; for example, "Evocative autoethnography requires considerable narrative and expressive skills— exemplified in the well-crafted prose, poetry, and performances of Carolyn Ellis, Laurel Richardson, Carol Rambo Ronai, and others" (p. 377). One of the strengths of these scholars' contributions is that they have not just produced discourse about evocative autoethnography. They have also modeled autoethnographic scholarship and mentored students and colleagues (p. 377).

There is an important paradox at work in the world of autoethnography. On the one hand, disparities exist, whereby evocative autoethnographers have published extensively and yet remain largely marginalized in mainstream social science venues due to their rejection of traditional social science values and styles of writing (Anderson, 2006, p. 377). On the other hand, evocative autoethnography has gained traction in many traditionally realist qualitative research journals (e.g., *Journal of Contemporary Ethnography, Symbolic Interaction,* and *Qualitative Sociology*) (Anderson, 2006, p. 377). In addition, evocative autoethnographies have been influential in the creation of newer postmodern-friendly journals (e.g., *Qualitative Inquiry*), handbooks (e.g., Denzin & Lincoln's several editions of *The SAGE Handbook of Qualitative Research;* see Denzin & Lincoln, 1994, 2000, 2005, 2011), and even book series such as AltaMira Press's series Ethnographic Alternatives (Anderson, 2006, p. 377).

As Anderson (2006) observes, "The evocative autoethnographers' critiques of traditional social science—and realist ethnography in particular—are well-catalogued, as are realist or analytic ethnographers' critiques of evocative ethnography" (p. 377). A major goal of analytic autoethnography "is not to revisit these debates but rather to clarify an approach to autoethnography that is consistent with traditional symbolic interactionist epistemological assumptions and goals rather than rejecting them" (p. 377). Sometimes, scholars align themselves with other analytically oriented qualitative researchers en route to further legitimizing autoethnography. For example, Anderson writes, "I share with Paul Atkinson, Amanda Coffey, and Sara Delamont" a move to allude subtly to the point that only the analytic autoethnography scholars have sustained "an interest in critically examining new forms of inquiry and practice to assess their potential value for improving and expanding the analytic ethnographic craft" (p. 378). However, the evidence we have presented in Chapter 3 does not support this allusion. Following his critique of evocative autoethnography and the arbitrary separation of analytic scholars from evocative ones, Anderson (2006) presents what he terms five key features of analytic autoethnography, ultimately as a better way to go about legitimizing autoethnography.

Five Features of Analytic Autoethnography: Linking Classics to Resolve Evocative Shortfalls

Anderson (2006) proposes and describes in depth the following five key features of analytic autoethnography in an effort to legitimize autoethnography as a "viable and valuable subgenre in the realist ethnographic tradition" (p. 378):

- Complete member researcher (CMR) status
- Analytic reflexivity
- Narrative visibility of the researcher's self
- Dialogue with informants beyond the self
- Commitment to an analytic agenda

He justifies each feature by drawing upon several realist ethnographic texts that exemplify the autoethnographic impulse—albeit often only partially—to further legitimize analytic autoethnography (pp. 378–387). It is not within the scope of this chapter to discuss each of the five features of analytic autoethnography in depth, but Table 4.2 situates the features for quick reference. (For more details, see Anderson, 2006.)

Addressing Key Limitations of Analytic Autoethnography Work

A final strategy toward legitimizing autoethnography involves addressing key limitations of analytic autoethnography work. This means not only being explicit about the limitations of such work but also being adamant about its possibilities and strengths, so that researchers are not deterred from pursuing autoethnography and, more important, the limitations are not perceived as strong enough to de-legitimize autoethnography. For example, some autoethnographers justify (and thereby legitimize) the use of analytic autoethnography by noting its connection to all methodological approaches, "but it is not particularly damning to acknowledge that analytic autoethnography has limitations. All methodological approaches have their limitations" (Anderson, 2006, p. 390). Conversely, another strategy to legitimize the advantages of analytic autoethnography is by presenting them as superior to any anticipated disadvantages. These advantages include the following:

- Autoethnography has methodological advantages that relate to the ways in which being a CMR facilitates the availability of data.
- The autoethnographer has multiple reasons to participate in the social world under study, and thus multiple incentives to spend time in the field.
- The access that autoethnography provides researchers is invaluable for identifying and describing insider meanings, as long as the researchers assiduously pursue other insiders' interpretations, attitudes, and feelings as well as their own.
- The advantage of being personally identified and involved in the social world under study is a characteristic of autoethnography that gives the researcher an added vantage point for accessing certain kinds of data. (Anderson, 2006, p. 389)

TABLE 4.2 ● Five Features of Analytic Autoethnography

Feature	Characteristics and Links to Traditional Ethnography
Complete member researcher (CMR) status	The first and most obvious feature of analytic autoethnography is that the researcher is a complete member in the social world under study. There are two types, *opportunistic* and *convert*: • *Opportunistic CMRs* (by far the more common) may be born into a group, be thrown into a group by chance circumstance (e.g., illness), or have acquired intimate familiarity through occupational, recreational, or lifestyle participation. • *Convert CMRs* begin with a purely data-oriented research interest in the setting but become converted to complete immersion and membership during the research.
Analytic reflexivity	While ethnographers have long recognized the importance of understanding relationships between researchers and their data, most traditional ethnography has not focused on this issue in a particularly sustained reflexive manner. Chicago School ethnographies, including such classics as William Foote Whyte's *Street Corner Society* (1943), significantly include the researcher in the ethnographic story.
Narrative visibility of the researcher's self	By virtue of the autoethnographer' s dual role as a member in the social world under study and as a researcher of that world, autoethnography demands enhanced textual visibility of the researcher's self. Such visibility demonstrates the researcher's personal engagement in the social world under study. Autoethnographers should expect to be involved in the construction of meaning and values in the social worlds they investigate.
Dialogue with informants beyond the self	The ethnographic imperative calls for dialogue with "data" or "others." Even ethnographic reflexivity, which has been treated at times as a purely subjective phenomenon, is more appropriately understood as a relational activity. It should be seen not in terms of self-absorption, but rather in terms of interrelationships between researcher and other to inform and change social knowledge.
Commitment to an analytic agenda	The defining characteristic of analytic social science is to use empirical data to gain insight into some broader set of social phenomena than those provided by the data themselves. This data-transcending goal has been a central warrant for traditional social science research.

Source: Adapted from Anderson (2006).

While this section has explored the notion of reclaiming autoethnography in the realist tradition of qualitative research as a route to legitimizing it, a third legitimation strategy involves linking autoethnography to established professional association standards. That strategy is the focus of the final section of the chapter.

Naming Links to Established Professional Association Standards

A third approach to legitimizing autoethnography as critical social research can be identified by its characteristic style of naming links to established professional association standards. In 2012, we published an article in *Educational Researcher* (the fourth-ranked journal in the field at that time) with coauthor Sara Makris that exemplifies this approach to legitimizing autoethnography (Hughes et al., 2012). This article represents an approach that is less common than the two approaches discussed above, but it continues to make a unique contribution, since it was the first article to feature autoethnography in that high-impact journal in approximately 13 years. Moreover, it calls for the legitimizing of autoethnography with evidence from the 2006 standards for reporting on empirical social science research that were approved by a majority of the more than 25,000 members of the American Educational Research Association (AERA). In the remainder of this chapter, we explain the argument that we made and discuss important ways that this approach works for legitimizing autoethnography in educational research.

Brief History of the Standards for Reporting on Empirical Social Science Research in AERA Publications

In an effort to add transparency, clarity, and uniformity to the guidelines for articles published by AERA-sponsored journals, members of the association developed reporting standards that were adopted by the Council of the American Educational Research Association in June 2006. The AERA Task Force on Reporting of Research Methods in AERA Publications was instrumental in the preparation of draft standards for council consideration. Task force members included acclaimed scholars in the field such as Richard P. Duran, Margaret A. Eisenhart, Frederick D. Erickson, Carl A. Grant, Judith L. Green, Larry V. Hedges, Felice J. Levine (ex officio), Pamela A. Moss (chair), James W. Pellegrino, and Barbara L. Schneider. The preamble to the AERA standards document developed by this task force speaks to the overarching principles that underlie its inception:

> Two overarching principles underlie the development of these reporting standards: the sufficiency of the warrants and the transparency of the report. First, reports of empirical research should be *warranted*; that is, adequate evidence should be provided to justify the results and conclusions. Second, reports of empirical research should be *transparent*; that is, reporting should make explicit the logic of inquiry and activities that led from the development of the initial interest, topic, problem, or research question; through the definition, collection, and analysis of data or empirical evidence; to the articulated outcomes of the study. (Duran et al., 2006, p. 33)

The guidelines are inclusive of, but not limited to, qualitative and quantitative methods (Duran et al., 2006). This statement is important because additional forms of scholarship, at least in theory, are appreciated as equally important to education research, including "reviews of research; theoretical, conceptual, or methodological essays; critiques of research traditions and practices; and scholarship more grounded in the humanities (e.g., history, philosophy, literary analysis, arts-based inquiry)" (Duran et al., 2006, p. 33). The task force states clearly that authors' work representing different methodological or intellectual traditions may vary in the modes, order, or form of presentation. They add the following thoughts for additional clarity regarding the audiences for which the standards are intended:

> While these standards are directed to authors, editors, reviewers, and readers of AERA journals, the substance of the standards and the breadth of methodological coverage are not particular to education research. Thus, in publishing these standards, the Association seeks to offer an educational document that can be useful to other research societies and journal publishers that disseminate empirical work using these same social science methods. Also, as part of AERA's broader educational mission to advance high-quality research in education and to foster excellence in reporting on empirical research, the Association commends use of these standards in the training and preparation of researchers in publishing research. (Duran et al., 2006, p. 33)

The primary audience for these standards is intended to be researchers who wish to publish reports of empirical research and researchers who also serve as manuscript reviewers (Duran et al., 2006). AERA's 2006 reporting standards are divided into eight general areas:

1. Problem formulation

2. Design and logic of the study

3. Sources of evidence

4. Measurement and classification

5. Analysis and interpretation

6. Generalization

7. Ethics in reporting

8. Title, abstract, and headings

Given that AERA is the flagship association for critical social researchers in the discipline of education, a logical way to engage the legitimizing process for autoethnography is to link autoethnography to AERA's professional standards. Hughes et al. (2012) set out to make that link by asking: How does autoethnography stand up to scrutiny when relevant areas of the 2006 AERA publication standards for empirical research are applied to assess the utility of the method as critical social research? We thought that such a translation of autoethnography across AERA's own standards could make an argument that ultimately works for legitimizing autoethnography in a unique fashion. And it did!

An Alternative Rubric for AERA Researchers, Editors, and Reviewers of Autoethnography

Table 4.3 illustrates how Hughes et al. (2012) collapse the AERA standards into four compatible central focus areas of autoethnography, noting the related AERA

TABLE 4.3 ● **Autoethnography Evaluative Checklist**

Researcher, Reviewer, Editor: _____

Objectives Evaluated

To analyze the relationship between a particular autoethnography and the potential contributions to the field produced from it.

To compare and contrast autoethnography with the 2006 AERA Standards for Publication.

Focus	Indicators	Publishable (clear, engaging, and convincing presentation)	Publishable w/ Minor Revisions (clear presentation)	Major Revisions (limited presentation)	Rewrite or Reconceptualize (little or no presentation)
Formulating social scientific problems	• The manuscript summarizes the author's key claims. • The manuscript describes the author's study design and methodological choices. [2006 AERA Standards 1, 2]				
Facilitating critical, careful, and thoughtful discussion of methodological choices and claims	• The manuscript asks critical questions about the autoethnographic text's design and logic, including epistemological, ontological, and/or axiological moorings. • The manuscript guides discussion and/or other activities on the relationship between the author's methodological choices and the truth claims made in the text. [2006 AERA Standards 2, 3, 6]				

Focus	Indicators	Publishable (clear, engaging, and convincing presentation)	Publishable w/ Minor Revisions (clear presentation)	Major Revisions (limited presentation)	Rewrite or Reconceptualize (little or no presentation)
Offering multiple levels of critique, naming privilege, penalty, units of study, and classifications; and criteria for selected units and classifications	• The manuscript guides discussion about the units of study (sites, groups, participants, events, or other units), and the means through which they were selected is adequately described; the manuscript offers adequate information regarding the collection of data or empirical materials. • The manuscript names and offers multiple levels of critiques (i.e., personal, dyadic, group, and institutional); it discusses the relevant methodological dilemmas and complications of the position of the researcher as the center of the project. (2006 AERA Standards: 3, 4, 5)				
Conducting credible analysis and interpretation of evidence from narratives and connecting them to researcher-self via triangulation, member checks, and related ethical issues	• The manuscript guides discussion on the relationships between the researcher-based narratives and other texts/narratives explored in the manuscript. • The manuscript addresses the practical aspects of the autoethnography (e.g., ethical considerations, logistical issues, political realities, and related confidentiality issues). (2006 AERA Standards: 5, 6, 7)				

Source: Hughes, Pennington, and Makris (2012).

standards. This checklist was developed as a rubric for reviewers and editors and to show how the method can be translated across the AERA standards toward legitimizing autoethnography as empirical research. This alternative rubric is intended for assessments of the empirical social science format of autoethnography used in critical social research.

Concluding Thoughts

Autoethnography can be painstaking and yet refreshing. Perhaps as the growth of this method continues to increase as critical social research, it will have a more permanent influence on school and society. In this chapter we have called for engagement in a critical reflexive thought exercise that centers a key tension in autoethnography—legitimizing standards for the method in education and the social sciences. Readers may ask themselves:

- How do I engage in the legitimizing of standards for autoethnography?
- Is it my intent to demonstrate that autoethnography falls well within the rigorous standards expected of scholarly research but is also reflective of the continuous negotiation throughout evaluation, analysis, and interpretation? (Starr, 2010, p. 7)
- If this demonstration of legitimacy is my intent, then why, and what trade-offs might I anticipate?

A final important point on the legitimacy of autoethnography is that maintaining the rights of the researched should be at the heart of autoethnographic inquiry (Ellis & Bochner, 2000). With the tenets discussed in this chapter in mind, legitimizing autoethnography in educational research in the social sciences has the potential to share and extend privilege or penalty. It is our sincere hope that the approach to legitimizing that you take closely aligns with your research goals and values and that those goals and values lean consistently toward equity, justice, and peace.

Group Activity

Purpose: Involve student dyads in preliminary thinking about legitimizing their own co-constructed autoethnography projects.

Activity: Journaling; brainstorming about the possibilities and pitfalls of at least two approaches to legitimizing autoethnography.

Evaluation: Determine whether students' selected approaches to legitimizing autoethnography projects are defensible for an academic audience.

Individual Activity

Purpose: Expose students to individual experiences of legitimizing autoethnography.

Activity: Think-pair-share in which students first work alone to develop the initial drafts of their own autoethnographies and then work with other students in groups to unpack and identify relevant issues pertaining to their selected approaches for legitimizing their own autoethnographic work.

Evaluation: Use a rubric regarding legitimizing autoethnography to determine whether students' drafted plans to select particular approaches to autoethnography are plausible and defensible to an academic audience.

Note for instructor: Students are sometimes shy, or even reticent, about participating, so prepare to participate and share your own trials and triumphs regarding the approach you take to legitimizing autoethnography.

Sites for Students to Consider

Encyclopedia of Group Processes and Intergroup Relations (SAGE Publications), http://sk.sagepub .com/reference/processes

The SAGE Dictionary of Social Research Methods (SAGE Publications), http://srmo.sagepub.com/ view/the-sage-dictionary-of-social-research-methods/SAGE.xml

The SAGE Encyclopedia of Social Science Research Methods (SAGE Publications), http://sk.sage pub.com/reference/socialscience

5

Third Guiding Process

Synthesizing New-Self Insights With MICA

With George Noblit

●

Focus Your Reading

- Qualitative meta-synthesis is akin to quantitative meta-analysis, but there are key differences, including a focus on interpretation versus a focus on generalization and a focus on understanding relationships toward a better understanding of the topic of interest (i.e., how does interpreting X help with interpreting Y?) versus a focus on naming causal relationships (i.e., to what extent is X related to or causing Y?).

- Meta-ethnography was developed and introduced by Noblit and Hare (1988) as a systematic way to explore what can be learned from multiple pieces of qualitative research by translating across them. Meta-ethnography offers at least three possibilities that pieces may work in relation to each other: (a) *reciprocal translations* (essentially similar and subject to direct translation), (b) *refutations* (involving translation of refutations as well as accounts), and (c) an analogic *line of argument* (an analogy about a set of parts to some whole). Each account involves a different assumption and thus a different approach and process.

- Meta-autoethnography was developed and introduced by Ellis (2009) as a way for autoethnographers to reassess their own bodies of autoethnographic work in order to gain more ideas, more insights, updates, and a renewed sense of self.

- Meta-synthesis of individualized and coauthored autoethnography, or MICA, is a method through which qualitative researchers can synthesize two or more autoethnographies of interest by other authors and thereby gain emerging insights from considering how the pieces work in relation to each other.

> The major problem yet to be resolved is developing usable and communicable systematic approaches to conducting metasynthesis projects that maintain the integrity of individual studies. (Sandelowski, Docherty, & Emden, 1997, p. 365).

How can we make sense of autoethnographies as bodies of intellectual work, and thereby respond to the problem of meta-synthesis asserted in the quotation above?

Thus far, we have looked at autoethnographies as unique studies using specific methods. Now, we turn to one way to examine autoethnographic studies that share specific phenomena of interest or topic areas. We begin this chapter with a brief comparison of meta-synthesis (commonly applied in qualitative work) and meta-analysis (commonly applied in quantitative studies). We then introduce meta-synthesis of individualized and coauthored autoethnography, or MICA, as a systematic approach to conducting

---

Authors' Note: This chapter is derived in part from an article titled "Meta-ethnography of autoethnographies: A worked example of the method using educational studies" and published in *Ethnography and Education,* 2017, by Sherick Hughes and George Noblit, copyright Taylor & Francis, http://www.tandfonline.com; it is available at the following permanent link: http://dx.doi.org/10.1080/17457823.2016.1216322.

meta-synthesis that maintains the integrity of individual studies (Sandelowski et al., 1997, p. 365). We consider the MICA method in relation to meta-autoethnography (Ellis, 2008) before demonstrating an example of it that engages this method of synthesis with four autoethnographies.

Autoethnography has much to teach us about how social and cultural contexts shape and are shaped by the lives of humans. In centering the self, autoethnography serves as both a critique of the colonial origins of ethnography (and its objectification of the other while hiding the subjectivity of the colonial author) and an assertion of relational knowing. *New-self* insights often emerge from autoethnography when it is applied as critical social research. The concept of the new-self, introduced by Hughes (2005), is meant to convey the notion that while insights into a cultural context may be new to an individual, with the potential of evolving over time, those insights are not necessarily new to others. In light of this point, autoethnography can illuminate the way life works both individually and socially. It is this conjunction that can make autoethnography powerful and revealing. Nevertheless, critics might reasonably ask: How can we make sense of autoethnographies as bodies of intellectual work? Within this question is both a challenge and a possibility for autoethnography. The challenge is a veiled critique of autoethnography as too isolated, too subjective, and too self-absorbed. In this the challenge ignores that all qualitative research is about individual accounts and experiences, which are then contextualized. The challenge ironically accepts the positivist critique of all qualitative research. Given this logic, the challenge must be rejected as it stands. Yet the question does point to the possibility of a worthy direction for future research. It asks for a way to consider sets of studies and what meaning they have as a "body of work," as a *qualitative meta-synthesis*.

What Is Qualitative Meta-Synthesis?

Qualitative meta-synthesis is akin to quantitative meta-analysis, but there are key differences, including a focus on interpretation versus a focus on generalization and a focus on making insight claims versus a focus on making causal claims (see Table 5.1). One prominent example of qualitative meta-synthesis is meta-ethnography. Noblit and Hare (1988) developed meta-ethnography as a systematic way to explore what can be learned from multiple pieces of qualitative research by translating across them. Meta-ethnography offers three possibilities to consider when working to determine how two or more qualitative studies can be translated and, thereby, synthesized: (a) *reciprocal translations* (studies are linked by obvious similarity and subject to direct translation), (b) *refutations* (studies can be linked by a translation of refutations as well as accounts), and (c) an analogic *line of argument* (studies can be linked by an analogy about a set of parts to some whole). Each account will involve a different assumption and thus a different approach and process, as we will explore later in this chapter. The advent of meta-ethnography provided the blueprint for the development of meta-autoethnography (the focus of the next section) and the MICA method, which is the centerpiece of this chapter.

TABLE 5.1 ● Quantitative Meta-Analysis Versus Qualitative Meta-Synthesis

Quantitative Meta-Analysis	Qualitative Meta-Synthesis
Focus on generalization	Focus on interpretation
Focus on making causal claims	Focus on making insight claims
Asks: What can synthesizing X studies tell us about what is causing phenomenon Y?	Asks: How does synthesizing X studies help with understanding phenomenon Y?
Expectation: To "predict" the meanings of lives lived in certain cultural contexts and under certain conditions	Expectation: To anticipate possibilities of lives lived in certain cultural contexts and under certain conditions

What Is Meta-Autoethnography?

Ellis (2009) developed **meta-autoethnography** as a way to explore a set of autoethnographies by an individual researcher. She describes the impetus for meta-autoethnography as linked to first-person accounts, "occasions in which I revisit my original representation, consider responses, and write an autoethnographic account about autoethnography" (p. 13). Meta-autoethnography is situated, again, in the first-person voice and through the lens of "text in motion" (Sutton-Brown, 2010, p. 1308). As Ellis (2009) puts it, meta-autoethnography offers "opportunities to alter the frame in which I wrote the original story, ask questions I didn't ask then, consider others' responses to the original story, and include vignettes of related experiences that have happened since I experienced and wrote the story and now affect the way I look back at the story" (p. 13).

Clearly, Ellis's meta-autoethnography is an invaluable contribution to the field, but it is limited as well—recall the quotation from Sandelowski et al. (1997) that opens this chapter. Meta-autoethnography assumes that autoethnography is the characteristic methodological choice of a researcher. In this book, we have argued that autoethnography may be used strategically as one methodology among others in a program of methodologically varied qualitative studies. For example, one may do an autoethnography as an early step in a research program so that one's positionality in subsequent studies is more carefully deliberated and understood. In addition, autoethnography may be used by people who would not necessarily think of themselves as professional researchers. Teachers, for example, might use autoethnography to better understand the meanings they enact in their practice; while they may find it useful to do this repeatedly, their work is not about repeated research studies per se. Thus, we have a host of autoethnographies from different teachers, and it seems reasonable to ask what these, as a set of studies, offer to our understanding of being a teacher or doing teaching as a lived experience.

The remaining text of this chapter reflects Noblit and Hare's (1988) meta-ethnography as the basis for an approach to synthesizing autoethnographies from authors beyond the self. Because Ellis uses the term *meta-autoethnography* in her work, we differentiate the approach offered here as a qualitative **meta-synthesis of individualized and coauthored autoethnography**, or **MICA**. There are, indeed, other approaches to qualitative research synthesis (e.g., Thorne, Jensen, Kearney, Noblit, & Sandelowski, 2004), but the MICA method emerges as the most appropriate and preferable logic for the synthesis of autoethnographies that are not of the researcher's own making.

Introducing MICA

Doing the MICA method requires a particular mind-set. First, it begins with an acknowledgment that simply adding studies up is insufficient and undercuts the unique contributions of each autoethnography. Instead, the focus is on how the studies translate into one another. Thus, the synthesis takes the form of an analogy rather than an aggregation (we will explain this in more detail later in the chapter, when we present our example of a MICA synthesis). Second, autoethnographic studies are, at their very base, interpretive. In other words, a data set does not stand separate from its meaning. In accounts of one's experiences, fact and value are bound together. Thus, MICA is primarily a synthesis of interpretations. The meanings of life experiences of different authors in relation to other people, in various conditions and contexts, are what we are trying to understand. When we look at a number of autoethnographies, all of these relational issues are to be taken into account. Thus, such synthesis is not for the faint of heart. It is an ambitious and decidedly difficult undertaking. Third, the goal of synthesis should not be taken to be an end in and of itself. So many attempts at synthesis wish to put some contention to rest. "Research says . . ." becomes a way of stopping the development and refinement of understanding. For MICA, our goal is to learn what authors' lives taught them and evoke in us while relating these lives and learnings to each other. Through this method, we come to say something about the meanings of people's lives, including our own. MICA produces analogies that allow readers to anticipate possibilities rather than "predict" the meanings of lives lived in certain contexts and under certain conditions. It is intended to serve agency over structure.

Finally, synthesis, like all research, is organized around a purpose followed by a rationale. There must be a reason for someone to take on the onerous task of synthesis and for someone else to begin reading it with an anticipation of finding use in it (an anticipation that has the potential of being fulfilled). We will argue that it is helpful to think about purpose in terms of a phenomenon of interest. Each autoethnography obviously encompasses many possible phenomena of interest. Thus, the interest of the

Phases of MICA

- Phase 1: Getting started
- Phase 2: Deciding relevance
- Phase 3: Reading the studies
- Phase 4: Determining relationships
- Phase 5: Synthesizing translations
- Phase 6: Expressing the synthesis

synthesizer is understood in the context of the other phenomena in an autoethnography and across a set of autoethnographies. In this intellectual move, the purpose/rationale focuses but does not exclude. In the discussion that follows, we adapt the general approach in Noblit and Hare's *Meta-Ethnography* (1988) to fit the special purposes of MICA. Since synthesis is best learned through example, we end this chapter with a description of how we applied the MICA method to engage a sample meta-synthesis on teaching race to largely White groups of students in higher education. The comprehensive sample is followed by concluding thoughts on the past, present, and future of MICA methods in critical social research.

Phase 1: Getting Started

When we wrote that a synthesis is organized around a purpose, and that purpose should specify a phenomenon of interest, we perhaps underemphasized what this process involves. Our experience is that getting a MICA started is actually a quest of sorts. It is easy to say that we are interested in something, but as a synthesis proceeds, we learn much more about what is interesting to us in the lives of others. Thus, getting started is actually a provisional endeavor. We may start a bit inchoate, but our effort to articulate a purpose and a phenomenon of interest begins to set some boundaries that can be interrogated as we proceed.

Our purpose for the synthesis presented here was in the first instance driven by the need to demonstrate an application of the MICA method for the readers of this textbook. This purpose led us to a rather open-ended search for autoethnographies with the hope that one would be of interest to us. We considered, for example, autoethnographies in nursing and nursing education. This search was interesting because the field of nursing is strongly qualitative in methodology and thus represents a potential market for this book. However valuable this synthesis could have been, it fell short, for us, of a central connected phenomenon of interest. We both work on issues of race in education, and this work is compelling to us. Furthermore, we have both taught social justice–related courses—including courses in race, equity, and education—at predominantly White institutions of privilege throughout our entire careers. We know both from the literature (Bell, 2002; Laubscher & Powell, 2003; Pennington, 2007; Rodriguez, 2009) and from personal experience that teaching race makes students uncomfortable and often leads them to reject the message and the messenger.

Finally, a number of our graduate students were just about to start teaching their own social justice–related courses in education, and we felt an obligation to help them prepare for the unique challenges and possibilities of this experience. We did this preparation in many ways, including sharing teaching materials, discussing course planning, advising them on how to manage their students' emotions and their own, and so on. All of these elements helped us to determine the phenomenon of interest: to understand what autoethnographies have to say about teaching social justice–related courses. We offer this example to achieve two initial purposes:

- To reflect critically on our own teaching of social justice–related courses
- To provide an account for our graduate students that may help them manage their critical reflections as they are teaching social justice–related courses

In this way, the phenomenon of interest was provisionally specified and then was refined as we learned more. During this part of the MICA process, Phases 1 and 2 overlap and work together to specify the content of the synthesis and what it will actually entail.

Phase 2: Deciding What Is Relevant to the Initial Interest

The initial phenomenon of interest drives the search for autoethnographies to be studied. In much research synthesis there is pressure to be exhaustive in the search for possible studies to be included. Here the interest is in searching as broadly as possible. However, qualitative research has demonstrated repeatedly that context matters, so the initial drive to be exhaustive leads usually to increased specification of that which is of interest. Contextual differences are clearly one form of specification. Ellis (2008), for example, specifies some of her autoethnographic work as related to rural communities. Institutional locales, such as educational settings and hospitals, are key contexts. Some autoethnographies are about specific types of people (e.g., marginalized and indigenous group members; occupational groups such as first-year health care providers, first-year teachers and administrators). There are other possible specifications as well, including the character of the author, the situations being faced, social and emotional relations that are implicated in the story, and the story lines themselves. Of course, autoethnographers also have explicit and/or implicit purposes, rationales, and theses for their accounts. The search for what is relevant to the initial phenomenon of interest inevitably then scaffolds the support of a refinement of purpose and, ultimately, a refinement of the phenomenon of interest. This scaffolding also necessitates that Phases 2 and 3 (reading the studies) overlap as do Phases 1 and 2. However, the reading in Phase 2 is different from that in Phase 3. Phase 2 is about deciding what is relevant and specifying the central purpose of the observed studies.

To decide what is relevant, one needs to be fully engaged in the search process. In many cases, online searches will be the primary vehicle. Since autoethnography is a form of academic discourse, searching libraries and journals, exploring Google Scholar, and the like are likely to be productive. It is important to keep in mind, however, that *autoethnography* itself is a relatively recent term in qualitative research, and, as we noted earlier, different texts use different terms for rather similar forms of work (e.g., *reflexive ethnographies, indigenous/native ethnographies, co-constructed narratives*) and different forms of the same term (e.g., *auto-ethnography, auto/ethnography, auto ethnography*). Thus, it is necessary to use multiple search terms to find relevant examples of this kind of work and to investigate substantive interests. When we were considering nursing education for our synthesis, we found that *nursing, nursing education,* and *nursing care* were all terms that needed exploration. The most promising search method is to start broadly, using sets of terms in various combinations. We should note, however, that not all possible resources are available on the web, at least not yet. For example, the published proceedings of the meetings of various professional associations may well be vital sources for personal, critical accounts, particularly given that in years past journals were less likely to publish autoethnographic texts. Hence, these accounts would be more likely to be accepted for presentation at association meetings and then collected and published in book form.

Scholars of critical social research tend to view publication in a peer-reviewed journal as a good standard for inclusion of a work in their studies. Having some assurance that scholars with a high level of expertise have recommended the piece for publication suggests a certain level of study quality. Peer-reviewed journals are also well covered in computer databases, so critical readers can search out the texts either to attempt replication or to issue critiques. However, the history of autoethnography also attests to the proposition that refereed journals can be reluctant to embrace new forms of scholarship. Again, volumes of proceedings and/or other edited and authored books may be better sources for those seeking autoethnography and other emerging forms of scholarship.

Dissertations are often excluded from research syntheses because they are initial works by novice scholars and done under the rather close direction of advisers and committees. Expectations for dissertations also vary across universities. However, dissertations can be seen as fuller works than articles, able to present larger interpretations. In some fields, books may result from reworked dissertations, but in other fields with weaker book-writing traditions, dissertations may be the best sources for the full studies. Interestingly, while some universities may not yet embrace autoethnography as an acceptable dissertation form, it is often the case that reflective personal accounts can be found embedded in qualitative dissertations, either in methodology chapters or in appendixes. Depending on the phenomenon of interest, the purpose, and the relative acceptability of autoethnography-type accounts in a field or university, dissertations may be important sources of relevant studies. Regardless of the types of sources used to identify relevant studies, the references in each work should also be searched for other possible studies and possible search terms.

The MICA method does not require any particular number of studies. It literally depends on the number that can be found and the subsequent specification of what the studies address. At the end of our initial nursing exploration, we had but a few autoethnographies to consider, and we found them to be about rather different phenomena. Counterintuitively, that paucity of literature helped us decide to follow our specific interest in the teaching of social justice–related courses, particularly those that center race and education. Many meta-ethnographies start with a rather large number of **candidate studies** (i.e., studies with the potential to be selected for meta-synthesis), but subsequent specification reduces those actually included in the synthesis to a much smaller number. Noblit recently blind reviewed a meta-ethnography paper for a journal. The authors of the paper began with 490 studies and in the end synthesized 7 of them. In doing the specification, they were able to discuss what they learned about the field, independent of what the synthesis revealed. As qualitative research has become more popular, more studies with the potential to be included have become available, thus there is little reason to talk about the number of studies as some sort of standard or even expectation. Rather, the expectation is that the search will identify all the studies potentially relevant to the purpose and phenomenon of interest, and subsequent review of these studies will lead to specification and consequently reduce these numbers.

One additional consideration is important to consider relative to the number of studies. Given that the MICA method is based in translating studies into one another, each study requires a section of text to be discussed adequately, and then the studies have to be translated into each other. Tables are often used to summarize studies. Thus, as the number of studies increases, so will length of the text required to accomplish the synthesis. This may mean that some syntheses will exceed the maximum article page lengths set by some journals. Noblit and others are currently preparing an edited book in order to take on a set of syntheses related to identity theory.

The point, then, is that syntheses do not require large numbers of studies and that reviews of the studies will lead to specification of the phenomenon of interest and purpose of the synthesis, thereby reducing the number of studies. As we note within the example provided below, we found multiple possible syntheses in the studies that we reviewed and simply picked the one that was of greatest interest to us and our graduate students at the time. A final point concerning the MICA method: Since autoethnography is a relatively new field of inquiry, it is possible that there will be few studies available for synthesis no matter what is of interest. This condition may lead to MICA sometimes serving more as a way to help develop what the field should be addressing and less as a way to offer an overall statement of what we now understand. This condition, of course, is changing rather quickly as autoethnography is becoming increasingly popular as critical social research.

As we were deciding what was relevant to our synthesis concerning teaching social justice–related courses, particularly race- and equity-based courses, we used sets of search terms and conditions to generate an initial list of studies via the Articles+ software available through our university library. We searched the terms *autoethnography, teach, teachers,* with the following conditions: items with full text online, and limited to articles from scholarly publications, including peer review. The first searches yielded some 545 candidate studies. These helped us refine and specify our interest. First, we realized that we were really interested in autoethnographic studies of teaching race in higher education. Second, we found that the studies involved teaching race both to students of color and to White students. This information left us in a quandary. We think that both phenomena are important to understand, and we are interested in both of them. However, we concluded after considering the studies that the differences between teaching race to White students and teaching race to students of color are such that each phenomenon deserved its own synthesis—and then we would need to do a comparative synthesis of the two sets of studies. This task, we concluded, would be more like a research program than an example for this book. We decided to limit ourselves to the former—teaching about race to Whites in higher education.

We conducted a new search with this decision in mind, using only the following set of search terms: *article, autoethnography, sociology, education, ethnography, teachers, teaching, pedagogy, race, education & educational research, racism, teacher education*. The conditions we set were as before: items with full text online, and limited to articles from scholarly publications, including peer review. This search yielded 195 candidate studies. We then read through the abstracts of those studies to search for autoethnographies that were written by faculty teaching predominantly White students about difference, particularly related to race and equity, while also seeking to improve their craft. Moreover, our interest in informing ourselves and our graduate students' craft for teaching largely White students in higher education courses on race was the most pressing. Thus, we decided to specify our MICA example to involve only autoethnographies of teaching race- and equity-based courses to mostly White groups of students in higher education. The resulting set of four studies does have variability in it, as we will discuss in what follows. The authors vary by racial identity and by discipline taught, among other things. Our two purposes remained largely the same, but they were now more specified: (a) to critically reflect on our own teaching of race- and equity-based courses to White students in higher education contexts, and (b) to provide an account for our students that may help them manage their critical reflections as they engage in teaching race- and equity-based courses to White students in higher education contexts.

Phase 3: Reading the Studies

Phase 3 builds on the reading of the candidate studies discussed above. MICA requires repeated reading of the studies identified as relevant. This repetition is intended to ensure that the synthesizer gains a rather intimate familiarity with the texts. We find it useful to download texts when possible and color code potential **tropes** (commonly repeated words, phrases, and images that may be used as rhetorical devices to provide clarity and for informative and persuasive purposes) for authors and readers to interpret research findings with familiar language. The specific tropes of interest are metaphors and the myriad ways they appear in texts.

Moreover, it is important here to note that in interpretive accounts, authors often contend that the characteristics they have experienced are metaphors—not literal descriptions. In essence, we come to know something new through the terms we have for what we have already experienced (Lakoff & Johnson, 1980). We use a term "as if" it works to characterize that which is new to us. Such terms are rendered tropes, and many of those tropes are then metaphors. In qualitative research, scholars usually offer sets of terms that organize their interpretations and are meant to convey the meaning of their experiences. Thus, in reading the autoethnographies to be part of the synthesis, it helps to search for, identify, and determine the definitions and meanings of these metaphors.

Focusing on the interpretive tropes underlying contemporary autoethnography as metaphors is also helpful for the later synthesis effort, when accounts are compared. Here the "as if" nature of metaphor allows us to think more broadly about any author's characterization and its relation to other authors' characterizations, and/or to generate new metaphors that enable the translation of the studies into one another. Since metaphors are inexact, there is room to "play" with them interpretively. But in Phase 3, the important thing is to look for the words meant to convey the meaning of what occurred and not limit oneself to only those words highlighted by the author as themes or concepts. Sometimes words that authors use in a matter-of-fact manner are later quite helpful in the translation of studies into one another.

Phase 4: Determining How the Studies Are Related

After the possible metaphors in each study have been highlighted, it is helpful to generate a list of them and the relations the author offers between them. Important questions to ask at this phase include, but are not limited to, the following: Are some metaphors subsumed under others? Are some metaphors conceptually prior to others? Are some metaphors consequences of others? Are some metaphors parallel and work together? Are some metaphors contradictions of others? What about dilemmas, paradoxes, and slippages among the metaphors? Once this task of locating and separating metaphors is complete for each study, the goal then is to juxtapose the sets of metaphors and to see how the studies are related.

As noted above, Noblit and Hare (1988) argue that there are at least three ways in which studies can be related. First, studies may be "reciprocal" in that the metaphors and their relations are **commensurate**. This need not be exact—rather, the metaphors of one study may seem to parallel those in the other studies. Reciprocal studies clarify how different experiences may be similar in key ways. Second, studies may be "refutational" in that the accounts are not commensurate and one or more seem to undercut the accounts offered in others. Refutations are important because they open up possibilities and suggest new lines of inquiry. Third, studies may be related in terms of a "line of argument." In this case, different interpretations do not refute but rather speak to different aspects of experience and, when taken together, suggest a larger interpretation than any one of the studies allows individually. Lines of argument suggest layers or linkages not seen in the individual accounts and address experience more broadly.

In each phase discussed so far, there is a possibility that the studies found may no longer be useful for the purposes of conducting MICA. This caveat is also true in Phase 4. You may complete Phase 4 and find that the selected studies are no longer conducive to the MICA method. So, you may decide to seek additional studies if your purpose and rationale are strong but there are relatively weak connections among the studies you initially selected. At this point, you may have (and likely will have) selected a particular autoethnographic study that exemplifies your purpose, rationale, and phenomenon of interest. You may use that study as the central study to which any other selections should relate. Phase 4 concludes, however, with the study set that you designate for a MICA methodological application.

Phase 5: Synthesizing Translations

In Phase 5, the synthesis is actually accomplished. This phase involves the following four steps:

1. Inductively examining autoethnographies

2. Comparing and contrasting identified metaphors from those autoethnographies

3. Creating defensible analogies based on those metaphors

4. Synthesizing studies by way of the created, defensible analogies

Translation, in a MICA, is of a particular form, because it begins with an inductive (specific to general) examination of each selected autoethnography (Step 1). This examination is driven by the goal of locating sets of metaphors to compare and contrast in each study (Step 2). The identified metaphors will be more or less explicit in the autoethnographies selected for meta-synthesis. Step 3 commences with the creation of defensible analogies based on those metaphors. A defensible analogy is one that the author can back up with, at the very least, evidence from the current autoethnography, evidence from related literature on the problem/phenomenon of interest, and evidence from previously published qualitative meta-synthesis work. Steps 2 and 3, involving metaphors and defensible analogies, are based on the work of Turner (1980) and Noblit and Hare (1988). Turner (1980) proposes that all social explanation is comparative in the sense that what we expect in that which is studied is based on what we as social scientists and humans would expect of our own behaviors and/or experiences. He calls this proposition the "same practices hypotheses" (p. 97). Noblit and Hare (1988) expand on this proposition to allow for a comparison based on expected differences, a "different practices hypothesis" (p. 30). As they clarify, "We solve the interpretive puzzle (that raised by the observation of similar or differing social practices in interpretive accounts) by explaining how the observed practice is alike and different from our own" (p. 31).

In Step 4, the final step of Phase 5, the metaphors of one autoethnographer's observed practice and the metaphors of another autoethnographer's observed practice are treated as analogies and thereby translated into each other (Noblit & Hare, 1988, p. 31). MICA requires that the sets of metaphors used to characterize each study be kept whole. In fact, the goal is not to say one concept in one study is like or different from one concept in another study. Rather, the focus is on the full interpretation offered in each study and how the full interpretations *translate* into one another. In MICA, the metaphors and related analogies we seek are between individualized and coauthored autoethnographic studies. Ultimately, these metaphors and analogies are identified and framed so that differences (and similarities) among autoethnographies with similar problems and phenomena of interest can be "explained in a way that a different rule of a game is explained" (Turner, 1980, p. 97). So, how do we go about expressing our new synthesis in a way that adheres to the MICA method?

Phase 6: Expressing the Synthesis

Most MICA applications in the foreseeable future will be expressed through the adaptation of the standard form presented in pioneering texts on qualitative meta-synthesis (e.g., Sandelowski & Barroso, 2003). Speaking generally, qualitative research syntheses tend to mimic standard research papers, with a general form as follows:

1. Introduction to the phenomenon of interest

2. Purpose and rationale

3. Potential significance of a synthesis based on the proposed phenomenon of interest

4. Description of the MICA method

5. Review of the autoethnography literature and description of what was learned in the review process

6. Summary of autoethnographies to be synthesized (may be presented in a chart)

7. Identification of each autoethnography's metaphors (use of direct quotations with citations within the text is recommended; also, another chart may be used for clarity and transparency)

8. The synthesis: translation of the autoethnographies across each other through the creation of defensible analogies from identified metaphors and interpretation of the analogies for readers

9. Statement of what the MICA findings mean in terms of knowledge and the phenomenon of interest

10. Suggestions for future research on the phenomenon of interest, MICA, and qualitative meta-synthesis

We recognize that this process of translation is very different from traditional rules and norms of practice. Perhaps some examples of how MICA looks in practice may help to clarify the process of translation. We have selected the autoethnographies noted in Table 5.2 to illustrate one promising way of expressing a synthesis of research on teaching about race and equity through the MICA method.

Sample Application of the MICA Method

It is fortunate for MICA that autoethnographies often take narrative forms, and thus they often explicitly offer metaphors. For the purpose of synthesis, however, it is important to search beyond the metaphors that authors explicitly offer. In autoethnographies, authors depict their own experiences, but all depict their situations and other actors as well. Each of these depictions offers potential metaphors. Thus, our process was to

TABLE 5.2 ● Selections for MICA: Autoethnographies from Peer-Reviewed Academic Journals and Books			
Author(s)	**Year**	**Title**	**Journal/Book**
Rodriguez	2009	"The Usual Suspect: Negotiating White Student Resistance and Teacher Authority in a Predominantly White Classroom"	*Cultural Studies ↔ Critical Methodologies, 9*(4), 483–508.
Hughes	2008	"Teaching Theory as 'Other' to White Urban Practitioners: Mining and Priming Freirean Critical Pedagogy in Resistant Bodies"	J. Diem & R. J. Helfenbein (Eds.), *Unsettling Beliefs: Teaching Theory to Teachers* (pp. 245–272). Greenwich, CT: Information Age.
Pennington	2007	"Silence in the Classroom/ Whispers in the Halls: Autoethnography as Pedagogy in White Pre-Service Teacher Education"	*Race Ethnicity and Education, 10*, 93–113.
Laubscher & Powell	2003	"Skinning the Drum: Teaching About Diversity as 'Other'"	*Harvard Educational Review, 73*(2), 203–224.

identify a large number of potential metaphors in each piece and then determine what set of metaphors seemed to adequately represent the account offered by the author(s). The metaphors that we identified are primarily emic in nature, which means that they are drawn directly from the autoethnographers' writings. The metaphors in the studies selected for our example of MICA are displayed in Tables 5.3, 5.4, 5.5, and 5.6.

When we had completed our search for metaphors in each piece separately, we then began to consider how the metaphors lined up with each other across studies. We found that the studies are largely reciprocal. There are salient similarities and differences in the accounts, but this salience only made the reciprocal translation a bit more complex. It did not suggest a different form of synthesis (i.e., refutational or line of argument). We then translated the studies into one another by developing an analogy that reveals what these studies say as a set. We followed this translation by using the MICA method of summarizing the metaphors in each study, which, in turn, can be compared and synthesized.

Laubscher and Powell

Laubscher and Powell (2003) title their article with the metaphor of "skinning the drum" and return to it at the end, noting the importance of the body in the

TABLE 5.3 ● Autoethnography of Interest: Laubscher and Powell (2003)

Laubscher, L., & Powell, S. (2003). Skinning the drum: Teaching about diversity as "other." *Harvard Educational Review, 72*(2), 203–224.

Metaphors Identified	Pages	Metaphors Identified	Pages
Skinning the drum	210	Students being othered	216
Colored, marked	204–205	Marginalized students	216
Competence and authority	209, 213	Students reflect on behaviors: oppressive, patriarchal	216
Silenced, marginalized voices	205	Student denial of bias	217
Teaching as "Other"	204	Oppositional reaction	217
White student stance	207	White student benefits	218
Fruitful strategy	204	Emotionally draining	218
Laying ourselves bare to teach race-equity-based courses	210	Rich discussion	218
Objectified as having baggage	213	Professor resists impulse to: lash out in hurt manner; lash out in a defensive manner	218
"Marked" faculty may see themselves as imposters	214	"Marked," yet with privilege	219
Persistent battle	214	Students select sites of active struggle	219
Engaging the body	215	Social activism as working	219
Self-experience as learning text	215	Social activism as freeing oneself of constraints of bias	219

account and that there are many ways to skin a drum. This metaphor works as title but hides much of the richness of these authors' account of their experience. They use their "critical, reflexive auto-ethnography" (p. 205) as a way to represent their stories, providing an in-depth view of their teaching of multicultural content in psychology courses. These two authors identify differently from each other and say explicitly, "We shout the presence of our difference to challenge attempts to silence, marginalize, or represent us by standards not of our making" (p. 205), but they also share in their current status as professors and in their pedagogical approach. Their differences offer a rich account. In the experiences they recount, their respective differences, "colored" and "deformed," make them "marked" by both society and their students. In their account, the wider society and the students both work against the "competence" and "authority" that normally should be accorded professors in their teaching role (pp. 204–205, 209). Furthermore, this identification of difference leads to "particularly unique dynamics that accrue if the teacher who addresses such issues as sexual orientation, ethnicity, class, religion, or gender is marked by the very aspect(s) of difference about which he or she teaches" (p. 204). Given this experience, Laubscher and Powell suggest that "a fruitful strategy is to take a position in the discussion" in their classrooms (and the wider institution) by using experience with marginalization in the face of the "stance" of White students (pp. 204, 207). The professors confess, "The moment we step into the classroom, we are immediately marked as 'different' by some of our students" (p. 213). In this condition, they must respond to this stance individually and privately, interpersonally and publicly. They "seek to integrate private experiences into pedagogical approaches" and note that such an integrative approach can lead to experiences of vulnerability and exposure associated with "laying ourselves bare" in the classroom when teaching about difference (p. 210).

Pedagogically, then, for Laubscher and Powell (2003), "the praxis translation of critical multiculturalism involves a pedagogical stance that constantly rethinks what and how we are teaching" (p. 211). Yet they experience being "objectified" as having "baggage" that students believe the professors should move beyond (p. 213). In this questioning, the pressure to become and identify with the projections of otherness is immense for Laubscher and Powell, leading them to feel like "imposters," which "demands a persistent battle" (p. 214). In the face of this struggle to educate and be educated, they "see the possibility of pedagogic transformation" and respond "by engaging [students] at all levels of the body, the affect, and the cognitive" (p. 215). The professors name the othering dynamic as well as use the "presentation of [themselves] and [their] experiences as learning texts" (p. 215). This naming and presentation in turn allow students who have been marginalized "to speak up about their experiences of being othered," while other students have then said that "they had not realized that some of their behaviors were perceived as oppressive and patriarchal" (p. 216).

Laubscher and Powell (2003) explain that teaching in this way involves a measure of skill and comfort and demands a willingness to be vulnerable and to face uncertainties. It is also "anxiety provoking," they lament. Nonetheless, they persevere, using

> a variety of strategies, including responding to all questions and comments so that students feel attended to; challenging misinformation without shaming the source; and validating students' discomfort by sharing our own struggles and growth related to difference. In doing so, we are careful to proceed delicately so that the class does not become a therapy session. We allow students to share at their own pace, rather than forcing self-disclosure. Further, we speak individually with students who seem to be struggling with course content rather than publicly confronting them. (p. 217)

The professors also "challenge students to select their sites of active struggle" (p. 219). In these moments of self-selection, "students are challenged to consider that social activism is not simply about working for the other, but perhaps more importantly about freeing themselves from the constraints of bias, prejudice, and unthinking collusive relations to oppressive practices" (p. 219).

In the face of this pedagogy, though, "white students too often deny the possibility of prejudice and stereotyping in their lives" and challenge the professors by minimizing and disputing assertions of societal discrimination and oppression (p. 217). The professors have also "witnessed some students contesting the experiences of their classmates marked as different" (p. 217). This "oppositional reaction" is directed at the professors and the content of the course (p. 217). White students do find some benefits, including an increased appreciation for difference, an understanding of their own privilege, and a fuller sense of the implications of that privilege for their personal and professional development. Still, Laubscher and Powell admit, "it can also be saddening and emotionally draining to witness the power of denial and bias," and "it can be a challenge to stay in the present moment and facilitate rich discussion when our impulse might be to withdraw or to lash out in a hurt or defensive manner" (p. 218). The message for those people not marked as different is promising, in that they can

> teach the various components of their own identities, both those that result in marginalization and those that result in privilege. From such understanding, the instructors can recognize and challenge their biases, areas of discomfort, and manifestations of power dynamics related to difference in the classroom. (p. 219)

Furthermore, instructors marked as different may be able to use their experience with marginalization to connect with othered students, but they must also work to understand all components of their identities, including those that afford them privilege.

Pennington

Julie Pennington's (2007) related autoethnography is rife with metaphors (see Table 5.4). With her metaphorical title, "Silence in the Classroom/Whispers in the Halls," Pennington signals how Whiteness was at work in her teaching and in her work with three preservice teachers in the same school. "Whiteness" left the classroom silent about the dynamics of race, but outside the classroom race was being spoken of furtively (p. 95). Pennington's account has a query she offers from her own teaching that guides the study: "I wanted to help him, to save him. But was he praying for me not to be there?" (p. 94). She chooses a strong metaphor, "conquered," drawn from the work of Merwin (1988), which signals students who "came to adopt my culture" (Pennington, 2007, p. 94). Pennington frames her autoethnography as "a possible method of engaging White pre-service teachers in dialogues about race in schools" (p. 94). She begins with her own teaching experience, which she characterizes as "torn between a love for the children and an uncertainty as to my place in their culture" (p. 94). She admits that she "took two contradictory positions, all children were the same, while I acknowledged that at-risk children, like those of Marquez, needed more support" (p. 94).

Pennington's (2007) class of preservice teachers mirrored these views in many ways, and in the teacher education program Pennington and her students "spoke of the

TABLE 5.4 ● Autoethnography of Interest: Pennington (2007)

Pennington, J. L. (2007). Silence in the classroom/whispers in the halls: Autoethnography as pedagogy in White pre-service teacher education. *Race Ethnicity and Education, 10,* 93–113.

Metaphors Identified	Pages	Metaphors Identified	Pages
Silence in the classrooms	94	Race education work is two steps forward one step back	100
Whispers in the halls	94	White teachers of children of color as outsiders	101
Whiteness	95	White teachers are construction of families of children of color	101
White savior	94	The transforming White teacher martyrs herself	101
Conquering "Others"	98	White teachers with lack of awareness of privilege harbor racism	102
Torn between love of children and uncertainty about their culture	94	White teachers as guests with societal power and yet, in a school community of color, with a lack of cultural power	102
Children are at risk	94	Counternarrative resistance as "White talk"	103
Race is a construction	95	White teacher view of neighborhood of color as unsafe	104–105
Race education is an exploration	96	White teacher in community of color is defensive, fearful, and helpless	104–106
Custodial positioning of teachers	97	White teacher in critical reflection on this context from sympathetic to martyr to victim	106
White teacher rescuer	97	Whites teachers can be activist alongside communities of color	107
White teacher acting: conquering via saving	97	Autoethnography is conquering	108
White teacher of children of color is a pre-scripted, ritualistic acting role: savior	97	White teacher in a school of color is to live in a place of immunity by birthright	108
Children of color acting role: heartbreaking lives	97, 99	White teacher hyperpoliteness increases silence	108

(Continued)

TABLE 5.4 ● (Continued)

Metaphors Identified	Pages	Metaphors Identified	Pages
Race education is breaking the fourth wall	99	Race-educated teacher is open to vulnerability	108
Professor of race is pedagogue and yet feeling	99	White culture is an unnamed factor in teacher education content matter	110
Saving narrations as boundaries to go beyond	99	Teacher educators need narratives opened up to scrutiny	110
Professor is bewildered, manipulative, and coercive, exposing her biases	100	Inherent lack of White confessions in nonmulticultural courses	110
Professor becomes the student as "one of them"	100	White preservice teachers' self-study can become indulgent self-aggrandizing and isolated, with old view validated	111

children without openly recognizing the role race played in our constructions" (p. 95). What changed for Pennington? "I had entered a doctoral program, began to study race and was more aware of how my racial positioning played into my constructions of my students" (p. 95). As a result, her work with preservice teachers changed. Using autoethnography, Pennington began "bringing the personal life into the professional life . . . an effective way to broach topics such as personal explorations of race" (p. 96).

Pennington (2007) uses a set of metaphors as subheads that explain the trajectory of her interpretation. Under the subhead "Saviors," she begins with how she and the preservice teachers saw their role as teachers, thereby characterizing their understanding as "the custodial positioning of teachers" (p. 97), using Gloria Ladson-Billings's (1995) term. As a result, "we saved them before we even got there by our own histories" (p. 97). Yet saving has a dark side: "We were trying to save the children from their own culture by bringing them into ours, or 'conquering them' . . . with our own role being cast as the rescuer" (p. 98). In "conquering via saving," the White teachers were playing out "pre-scripted roles in dealing with cultures of color . . . 'acting as individuals but . . . in fact acting as part of a White pattern'" (p. 98). Pennington (2007) elaborates on this point:

> Our identities as privileged teachers did not force us to explore the role we played in the institution of the school that mimicked the roles we played in the larger society. Roles designed to maintain our position of power that lacked any mechanism for empowerment of the families and children. Our ritualistic attention to narrating their lives in reference to our own was not disrupted at all in the school or during the university coursework experiences. Their role was to have heartbreaking lives and our role was to save them from those lives. Our ritual was to maintain distance but be helpful. (p. 99)

Pennington "had to bring up race, Whiteness specifically, as a means of exploring our own identities and understandings" (p. 99). She writes of "breaking the fourth wall," which "denotes when the plot of a story calls for an event to shatter the barrier between the fictional world of the story, and the 'real world' of the audience watching the story" (p. 99). Pennington describes this wall breaking: "I shattered the fourth wall and shifted from my position as the pedagogue and moved into an admission of my personal thoughts about teaching" (p. 99).

Here autoethnography was "crucial and necessary to expose the positions and attitudes" that Pennington (2007) held before she "disrupted [the] saving narrations" present in her classroom (p. 100). She had "an overwhelming feeling that I was going beyond certain boundaries" (p. 100). Her feelings were "negative," as she explains further: "I felt bewildered, manipulative and coercive exposing my biases to them," but to "encourage the openness necessary for reciprocity, I had to reveal my thoughts about race" (p. 100). Pennington describes the growing pains and promise of transformation in the following passages: "I used my own stories to reposition myself racially as 'one of them,'" and in the end, "it opened up a space for a counternarrative about our experiences," a "two steps forward, one step back progress" (p. 100). Pennington reveals the salient moments during her race education pedagogy, in which the "feeling of being an outsider manifested itself as reverse bias," and yet "it was also the beginning of turning our gaze onto how we are constructed by the children and families" of the school (p. 101).

As race pedagogy infused Pennington's work with students inside and outside class, she reflects critically, the positions of Pennington and her students "as saviors were disrupted. We became martyred, in our own eyes, by our good intentions. We were caught between the stages of conflict and disequilibrium" (p. 101). Pennington explains further: "Even as we saw race, we were unaware of the pervasiveness of White privilege and our lack of awareness harbored White racism" (p. 102). The White teachers also began to realize that the "power of our decision-making status as teachers . . . contrasted with our lack of cultural power" in the setting where they were White teachers in a school of color (p. 102). The teachers' "tentative conversations alluded to our realizations that we were guests and we must be respectful of the neighborhood and the families" (p. 102). Then Pennington and her students "began to disrupt our positions as saviors by talking about how people of color might view our perspectives" (p. 103). This form of "'counternarrative' resistance" was a form of "White talk" that insulated the teachers from considering their own roles in racism (Pennington, 2007, p. 103). These "counternarratives revolved around two common experiences, the physical and relational" (p. 103). Pennington observes that the White teachers had "biased views of this neighborhood as being unsafe" (p. 104) and also states, "Negotiating relations with parents was stressful and the added realization of not being accepted brought out defensive, fearful, and helpless reactions" (p. 105). The counternarratives moved from "sympathetic stories" to "constructing ourselves as martyrs" to being "victims" (p. 106).

This process became "more 'enlightened' over the course of the semester" (Pennington, 2007, p. 106). The realization that "Whites must move to activism alongside people of color" led to "opening up our minds as to how to engage as Whites in schools of color" (p. 107). Pennington ends by considering whether her autoethnographic approach is itself a form of "conquering" (p. 108). Noting what was learned along the way, Pennington professes, "To be a White teacher in a school of color is to live in a place of immunity by birthright" (p. 108). She also asserts that "White women's tendency toward politeness as hyperpoliteness increases the silence in classrooms" (p. 108). In the end, the group has a shared achievement: "We were all willing to be vulnerable" (p. 108). Pennington also reconsiders autoethnography involving teacher educators as "opening up a first person dialogue to examine diversity in the classroom with their students" (p. 109). She laments the fact that too many "education programs have yet to mainstream the idea of examining White culture as a factor in teacher education in courses related to content" (p. 110). However, "for active involvement in breaking the silence of Whiteness in education . . . teacher educators should open up their own narratives to scrutiny" (p. 110). Pennington finds that the challenge of implementing this suggestion comes in the form of "an inherent lack of White confessions in courses not declared multicultural" (p. 110). In this effort, autoethnography can help, but Pennington cautions readers that "narrating personal stories can err on the side of indulgent self-aggrandizing" (p. 110), and "White PST [preservice teacher] educators and researchers . . . can become isolated and validated by the very views we are attempting to disengage" (p. 111). Pennington ends on a somber note: "I still wonder about White teachers teaching children of color. . . . I end asking not *if* we should be there, but *how* we should be there" (p. 112).

Rodriguez

Rodriguez (2009) finds autoethnography to be an appropriate methodology to convey her experiences of teaching race- and equity-based coursework. With a similar phenomenon of interest as Laubscher and Powell's (2003) and Pennington's (2007) studies, Rodriguez's work is also replete with metaphors that help her and readers to make sense of her experiences of the phenomenon of teaching White students about race as "Other" (see Table 5.5). Rodriguez's autoethnography is also metaphorically titled: "The Usual Suspect." This metaphor signals that from her perspective, supported by related research, "female faculty of color are held suspect" (p. 484). Rodriguez uses autoethnography to address "what happens when the teacher is the 'Other.'" She notes that female teachers of color often work "under the climate of suspicion," and their "power and authority . . . are often questioned . . . challenged, held suspect, and disrespected" (pp. 483–484). In autoethnography, Rodriguez argues, "the author becomes both subject and object" (p. 485). She uses the method "to understand Whiteness as a social location of power" (p. 486).

Rodriguez (2009) argues that "White innocence maintains White racism" and "perpetuates a sense of *White arrogance*" (pp. 487–488). She also maintains that "it is this White superiority that is the foundation for *White arrogance*" (p. 488). Rodriguez

TABLE 5.5 ● Autoethnography of Interest: Rodriguez (2009)			

Rodriguez, D. (2009). The usual suspect: Negotiating White student resistance and teacher authority in a predominantly White classroom. *Cultural Studies ↔ Critical Methodologies, 9*(4), 483–508. doi:10.1177/1532708608321504

Metaphors Identified	Pages	Metaphors Identified	Pages
Female faculty of color are the usual suspects	483–484	Female faculty of color as suspect for not knowing or at least not knowing what majority students want to hear	495
Faculty of color teaching as "Other"	483–484	White students as verbal challengers of lecture material, assignments	495
Working in climate of suspicion	483	White students as users of White talk	495
Faculty of color as "Other" with suspect power and authority to be challenged	483–484, 492	White talk as freeing responsibility for racism, resisting in the classroom, dismissing White privilege, and recentering Whiteness	495
Author is subject and object in autoethnography	485	Female faculty of color benefit from faculty distance, and yet also from faculty closeness, where instructors center themselves in courageous conversations	496
Whiteness as a social location of power	486	Female faculty of color as movers of students into critical consciousness	496
White innocence maintains White racism	487	White students as White entitlement	496
White innocence perpetuates White arrogance	488	Social cost to being White	496
White superiority is a foundation for White arrogance	488	Perception of people of color as taking away the unearned rewards from Whites	496
White arrogance permeates the classroom every semester	489	White entitlement as myth of meritocracy, yet with a priori White rewards	497–498
White arrogance plays out in student re(actions)	489	Professorial authority makes White students uncomfortable and resistant to accepting professors of color	498
White arrogance as threat to female faculty of color	489	White colleagues as brokers to decrease White student resistance	498

(Continued)

TABLE 5.5 ● (Continued)

Metaphors Identified	Pages	Metaphors Identified	Pages
White student friendliness sometimes is a mask for racism	491	Female faculty of color as negotiator, controller, and disrupter (negotiating power in the classroom, controlling a classroom, and disrupting White dominant narratives)	498–499
Female faculty of color experience confusion and rage	490	Female faculty of color act a role, dress the part every week in a play sometimes titled *A Poor Attempt to Gain Respect From Students*	499
Racial inequity as needed food to be shoved down the throats of White student arrogance	490	Female faculty of color as exerting big authority (not afforded to them by White students) and, thereby, as partly responsible for the negative reactions of White students	499
White student racist	491	Female faculty of color as exerting small authority: small ways making credentials known, reminding students of position, and questioning comments to make it a pedagogical moment for all	500
Female faculty of color as difference makers	491	Academy as seeking to separate cultural and linguistic identity from professional identity	500
Location of teaching social justice as uncomfortable space	492	Changing the system by learning how to live within it	500
Historical-structural issues as barriers for White students to not see their positions of privilege	492	Autoethnography as disrupting "business as usual" in the White academy	501
Critical pedagogy as giving up authority, yet female faculty of color are afforded no authority and misinterpret any use of experimental pedagogy	493	Female faculty of color as speaking out against the normalized discourse that perpetuates inequality	501
Female faculty of color as misread by White students	493	Female faculty of color as alienated	501
Female faculty of color as filtered through White eyes	493	Teaching race as creating spaces: for students to challenge existing paradigms	501

Metaphors Identified	Pages	Metaphors Identified	Pages
Approachable style misread as weakness and as an inability to control class	493–494	Female faculty of color as necessarily negative challengers of racist assumptions	501
Female faculty of color opening opportunity for White ridicule on evaluations	494	Female faculty of color as explorers in search of reasons for why they see the world as they do	502
Female faculty of color as "oppressed" yet teaching about White supremacy and patriarchal forms of domination	494	Female faculty of color as frustrated workers	502
White students fear confronting their own White privilege and domination	494	White students as living in subjective social locations	502
Whites have "sincere fictions"	494	Female faculty of color as conveyors of hope essential to learning	502
White students minimize reality of racism and invest in racial denial	495		

confesses from her experiences in the professor role: "*White arrogance* also permeates my classrooms every semester, and most often this plays out in re(actions) of White students" who do not ask or request but demand justifications and offer "a threat" (p. 489). White arrogance is asserted regularly, and sometimes Rodriguez is caught unawares "to discover a student's friendliness was simply a mask for racism" (p. 491). In such instances, Rodriguez confesses, she is not always her most critically reflexive thinking self (and who is?); she describes how "confusion quickly became replaced by rage," and in her rage she once contemplated, "if I could do anything in this world, I would cram every last bit of information down my students' throats about racial inequality" (p. 490). Rodriguez explains how she remains steadfast and resists the urge to quit: "Every time I think about giving up, I think that I refuse to be intimidated. . . . Nor will I hate the racist student, therapist, administrator, the racist professor, nor the racist person next door" (p. 491). Still, occasional self-doubts ensue: "Am I *really* making a difference?" (p. 491). In the face of self-doubts, Rodriguez reminds herself "that teaching social justice issues will always take place in an uncomfortable space" (p. 492).

Rodriguez (2009) offers an analysis: "White students' experiences, based on the structural hierarchy as well as historical forces that place them at an advantage, hinder students from recognizing their own subjective positions" (p. 492). For Rodriguez, this historical evidence means that "when considering female teachers of color, the assumption of authority becomes problematic at many levels" (p. 493). Rodriguez notes the paradox that "critical pedagogy is the argument that an effective teacher must give up authority in the classroom" and yet White "students are usually unwilling to grant me any authority in any way and most often misinterpret my use of experimental pedagogy" (p. 493). In her experience, Rodriguez is "read a particular way by White students" because, as she explains, "everything I say, how I speak, and what I do is filtered through White eyes" (p. 493). Thus, upon "implementing an 'approachable style' (Avalos-C'deBaca, 2002)," Rodriguez (2009) realizes "that students may misinterpret my teaching style as a weakness" and see her as "someone lacking the ability to control class" (pp. 493–494). One semester, "I tried opening up to my undergrad students, only to be ridiculed in my student evaluations" (p. 494). She understands her predicament: "I represent the 'oppressed,' and teaching about White supremacy and patriarchal forms of domination simply reinforces White students' fears of confronting their own White privilege and domination" (p. 494). Whites have "sincere fictions" preventing them "from questioning their own assumptions about race, recognizing the normative Whiteness on which these assumptions are based, and consequently hindering a deep understanding about structural racism and their own social responsibility to address it" (p. 494). "White students instead minimize the reality of racism" and "invest in racial denial" (p. 495).

Constantly having her knowledge questioned, Rodriguez (2009) feels positioned as "suspect—suspect for not knowing or at least not knowing what majority students want to hear" (p. 495). In her experience, "students also verbally challenge lecture material, assignments, and so forth by commonly engaging in *White talk*" (p. 495). White talk frees them from taking responsibility for racism and "can also serve as a means of resisting in the classroom," thereby "dismissing White privilege and recentering whiteness" (p. 495). In her experience, sometimes "remaining distant and using a traditional style of teaching (Briskin, 1990; Hoodfar, 1992; Shrewsbury, 1987) is beneficial, other times placing oneself as an instructor at the center (Jacobs, 2005) can be helpful in moving students into critical consciousness" (p. 496).

Rodriguez (2009) finds that many of the challenges she experiences "are embedded in White entitlement" (p. 496). She surmises that "the view that there is a social cost to being White" is coupled with "the perception that people of color are taking away the unearned rewards from Whites" (p. 496). She further explains, "This sense of entitlement is based on the myth of meritocracy espoused by White students" and "supports the idea that rewards are somehow *White* rewards to begin with" (pp. 497–498). Rodriguez has come to realize that her "professorial authority may make White students feel uncomfortable and resistant to accept someone like me as a professor," and thus she brings in "White colleagues to decrease White student resistance" (p. 498). She finds that in her work, she "must learn how to negotiate power in the classroom" especially given the paradox noted earlier: "Not having any presumed authority lends to the difficulty of controlling a classroom as well as disrupting dominant narratives often expressed by students" (pp. 498–499). Rodriguez does "dress the part every week," although it is sometimes "a poor attempt to gain respect from students" (p. 499).

In the case of female faculty of color, relinquishing authority is not an option; their authority is questioned before they even enter the classroom. Rodriguez (2009) observes that her attempts to exert authority under these conditions have "been partly responsible for the negative reactions of White students" (p. 499). So she works to strengthen her authority in "small ways": by "making my credentials known," by finding ways to "remind students of my position," and by "questioning their comments, attempting to make it a pedagogical moment for all" (p. 500). In attempting to survive an academy that seeks to "separate our cultural and linguistic identity from our professional identity," Rodriguez favors "recognizing that in order to change the system, we have to learn how to live within it" (p. 500). Autoethnography plays a role here, as Rodriguez explains, "By writing about my experiences, I hope to disrupt 'business as usual' in the White academy" (p. 501). In general, Rodriguez charges, "We must speak out against the normalized discourse that perpetuates inequality despite the fact that we may be alienated. We must actively support women of color colleagues in their teaching, research, and administrative duties as well as create spaces for students to challenge existing paradigms" (p. 501).

Rodriguez (2009) offers conclusions to her fellow professors of color: "We have to not hesitate to use authority when appropriate" in order to "challenge these racist assumptions" and "get used to not necessarily being seen as positive" (p. 501). Rodriguez ends with encouragement for female faculty of color, and seemingly for all faculty of color teaching as "other," to be "more interested in exploring their reasons for why they see the world as they do" and to "work through our feelings of frustration" both by challenging "students to think beyond their subjective social locations" and by holding steadfast to the notion "that hope is essential to the learning process" (p. 502).

Hughes

Hughes's (2008b) key metaphors, "mining and priming," signal his interest in this autoethnography.[1] However, the autoethnography is also replete with metaphors that speak to the phenomenon of interest observed in the previously analyzed autoethnographic texts (see Table 5.6). *Mining* refers to "the teacher's responsibility. . . . to pull knowledge out" of the students (p. 249). *Priming* refers to "putting something into students' minds," but in Hughes's usage priming is in the service of mining. In other words, you prime in order to draw out "well beyond the quantity and quality of that which was used for priming" (p. 249). In Hughes's account, these two tasks work together as a critical pedagogy to teach theory (note this difference from other articles on teaching about the "other" that "emphasize multiculturalism and race") (p. 253). Hughes is an African American scholar teaching largely White college students in education, and he describes himself as the "other" who works in and with a "body of resistance" comprising "white, urban grade-school practitioners" (pp. 246–247). He teaches critical social theory as theorizing about privilege and oppression to "build a foundation for critical praxis" (p. 247). In this work, he is "learning to be better prepared for

---

[1] To address the conflict of interest issue posed by Sherick Hughes's being the book author and the coauthor of this chapter, George Noblit did the first reading and analysis of this autoethnography, and then Hughes and Noblit worked in dialogue to infuse it into the meta-synthesis.

failure yet, to survive and to engage again a successful struggle for hope . . . at the risky intersection of racialization, conscientiousness, and resistance" (p. 248). His approach is broadly Freirean, a "pedagogy of hope and struggle" warning against "separating hope from action" (p. 249).

Hughes (2008b) centers his work as "the critical art and social science of teaching and learning," moving from "sculpting model units" to "scaffolding to paint a heightened portrait for all students" to "conscientious performance" (p. 250). Taken together, these concepts "can allow students to recognize and alleviate oppression of self and others while balancing life with the thoughts and actions that breathe hope" (p. 250), which is consistent with the requirements of being a progressive teacher. Hughes notes that he chooses critical reflexive autoethnography as his approach because of its "capacity to engage first person voice, and to embrace the conflict of writing against oneself as I find myself; entrenched in the complications of my position of teacher as 'other,' and because it can be seen as 'pedagogy'" (p. 252). As the "other" in the classroom, Hughes is told, "You don't look like a professor" (p. 252) regardless of his status as one. These classrooms are filled with "student bodies of resistance," either "benign" or "malignant"—"encompassing some degree of ignorance" (p. 254).

Hughes (2008b) offers a set of "white body–related narratives of struggle" (p. 255). "Silence as power–white body withdrawal behaviors" is about using silence to deflect engagement (p. 255). "Intimidated, anxious, and guilty–white body awareness behaviors" implicate both the course content and White guilt in avoiding engaging the course material (p. 255). "Colorblind–white body challenging behaviors" deny the salience of race and racism; these behaviors are related to "white body in denial assertion behaviors," which may acknowledge race but deny its significance (pp. 255–256). "Resistance is not to be ignored or underestimated," Hughes contends (p. 256). He identifies "white body support group solidarity behaviors" that resisted coursework, but benignly, while at times race was avoided and support sought. Hughes also recounts "white body-related narratives of hope" that are connected to his "mining and priming by a black 'other'" (p. 257). In addressing "humility in teaching and learning theory," Hughes expresses feelings of being "humbled" by thoughts of preexisting student "abilities" that led to his "enlisting, embracing, and cultivating" some students to provide leadership in the classroom and in the workplace (p. 257).

The "white student body sample narratives of hope" that follow link Hughes's (2008b) teaching efforts to the students' narratives (p. 259). Hughes worked with students to understand the distinctions between "reading the world versus reading the words" (p. 259). Hughes also links mining and priming about the students' "daily lives as practitioners" to "practicing and theorizing as knowing versus memorizing theory and rote methods for teaching and learning" (p. 260). The professor's uses of "student investigation of topics over extended periods" leading to "student presentations, debates, posters, etc." that students express are worthy of further dissemination and adaptation (p. 260). Hughes complies with Freire's warning against "bureaucratization of the mind" (p. 261), which ultimately involves his employing "moral resources" as principles for action. A major source of joy for Hughes seems to be when students

TABLE 5.6 ● Autoethnography of Interest: Hughes (2008)

Hughes, S. A. (2008). Teaching theory as "other" to White urban practitioners: Mining and priming Freirean critical pedagogy in resistant bodies. In J. Diem & R. J. Helfenbein (Eds.), *Unsettling beliefs: Teaching theory to teachers* (pp. 245–272). Greenwich, CT: Information Age.

Metaphors Identified	Pages	Metaphors Identified	Pages
Teaching critical social theory as "other" as mining and priming	249	Resistance as benign and malignant	256
Priming is in the service of mining	249	White body support group solidarity behaviors	257
Critical pedagogy to teach theory	246–247	White body narratives of struggle	255
Teaching as other urban grade school practitioners	246–247	White body narratives of hope	257
White student body of resistance	246–247	Humility in teaching and learning theory	257
Social theory as theorizing about privilege and oppression	246–247	Mining preexisting student abilities: enlisting, embracing, and cultivating some White students to provide leadership in the classroom and in the workplace	257
Social theory as a foundation for critical praxis	247	White student body sample narratives of hope	259
Teacher as learner and survivor: learning to be better prepared for failure, yet to survive and to engage again	247–248	Reading the world versus reading the words	259
Successful struggle for hope at the risky intersection of racialization, conscientiousness, and resistance	247–248	Practicing and theorizing as knowing versus memorizing theory and rote methods for teaching and learning	260
Professor as separating hope from action	249	Students as investigators into their own crafts and work with/as "other"	260
Pedagogy as sculpting model units, scaffolding to paint a heightened portrait for all students and conscientious performance	250	Bureaucratization of the mind: saving ourselves	261
Students as capable of recognizing and alleviating oppression of self and others	250	Employing "moral resources" as principles for action	261
Students as capable of balancing life	250	Reality "hit some white students very hard"	261

(Continued)

TABLE 5.6 ● (Continued)

Metaphors Identified	Pages	Metaphors Identified	Pages
Thoughts and actions can breathe hope	250	Understanding the challenges and promises of freedom and risk	261–262
Autoethnography as capacity to engage first-person voice and to embrace the conflict of writing against oneself	252	Detailed individual roles assigned to group members to encourage "open dialogue and resistance," which lead to students learning "how to change or where to start"	261–262
To Hughes: "You don't look like a professor"	252	Education is testimony	262
Student bodies of resistance as "benign" or "malignant ignorance"	254	Teaching social justice theory as "other" is risky and can be quite lonely	263
Silence as power–White body withdrawal behaviors	255	White colleagues' public support as crucial validation of faculty of color in predominantly White departments, colleges, and universities	263
Intimidated, anxious, and guilty–White body awareness behaviors	255	Autoethnography as a period of reconsideration	264
Colorblind–White body challenging behaviors	255–256	Autoethnography as a way to renew critical conscientiousness in our own lives	264
White body in denial assertion behaviors	255–256	Autoethnography as a way to "offer a pedagogy of theorizing" (Giroux, 1996) and practice from a target's perspective	264

articulate that the course has been useful to their development as professionals even if the reality of it "hit [them] very hard" (p. 261). In addressing "the challenges and promises of freedom and risk" (p. 261), Hughes furthers his mission of using groups arranged around "diversity" and assigning "detailed individual roles for group members" to encourage "open dialogue and resistance," which lead to students learning "how to change or where to start" (pp. 261–262). Finally, "education is testimony" as Hughes gives real-life examples of "current work with grade school students" to encourage student "personal accounts," with students "often times reflecting on things said, and stories shared in class" (p. 262).

While Hughes (2008b) focuses on what students experienced and learned from the "other" in this account, he concludes that his work "is risky and it can be quite lonely" (p. 263). Thus, the public support of a White colleague was "validating," and "such validation was crucial to fulfilling any social justice education mission and imperative for the retention of faculty of color at predominantly white departments, colleges, and universities" (p. 263). Furthermore, this autoethnography for Hughes encapsulates a "period of reconsideration" to "renew critical conscientiousness in our own lives" and "offer a pedagogy of theorizing (Giroux, 1996), and practice from a target's perspective" (p. 264).

Synthesis as Translation: A Reciprocal Analogy

The careful reading and identification of key metaphors in each of the autoethnographies highlights much of the difference across the texts. The authors are different, teach different courses, use autoethnography differently, and so on. Yet there is an analogy that pulls these studies together. As Turner (1980) suggests, we explain these in terms of how one would explain the different rules of games. In this case, the overall game is teaching difference to White students in higher education, but the rules differ across these accounts, not so much by the type of course being taught but more by who is the teacher of difference. Thus, we can express the synthesis. It is "as if" teaching difference has three sources of resistance. First is the larger society, where difference is stigmatized and where Whiteness, White supremacy, and color blindness are characteristic. Second, in the classroom itself the White students are "bodies of resistance" and, while different in views and backgrounds, act out the Whiteness that permeates the wider society. The students are more like actors of resistance and the society more like the context in these accounts, but these blend. There is also a third source of resistance—the academy itself. The academy is less analyzed here, but it is represented as both Whiteness and organizational oppressor, enforcing White superiority through its rules and denying the special case of teaching difference as well as teaching difference as a "marked" professor.

The teachers are *othered* through their difference from their students and the wider society, and this othering is played out through the students' presumptions. Being "marked" stigmatizes the teacher, and thus students challenge and insult both the competence and the authority of the teacher. There is also a known pedagogy for this kind of teaching that involves the engagement of the personal, the embodied, and the emotional. This pedagogy requires professors to use their bodies and personal experiences as ways for students to engage their experiences and emotions. Yet for professors of color this becomes a contradiction. Prejudged by Whiteness as not competent and of dubious authority, professors of color are read as weak—more evidence of lack of authority and competence. Professors of color use theory and content knowledge to combat their denigration, but this is only partial and violates the known pedagogy as well as their own beliefs about the true depth of prejudice and racism. The sole White professor living without the stigma of disability in these accounts was able to get personal, and her students made significant inroads into their Whiteness and their role in a racialized U.S. society. She had to work against herself and the presumed politeness of White women to accomplish this. She had doubts about how much was accomplished—a reflection largely consistent with the accounts of the "marked" professors. The accomplishment in all these cases was but partial (and maybe fleeting), which is troubling in that any hope for a successful pedagogy seems muted.

Yet, in the absence of comparison to other accounts of what and how students learn in higher education courses, the above conclusion may be too harsh. Each autoethnography provides strategies that seem to have potential and, while not fail-safe, may be the best that can be hoped for. It may be that those who teach difference in a society that enforces Whiteness must live with partial success and much pain and concern. Notably, these accounts hold out the possibility that nonmarked faculty could be effective at some level and under some conditions, and Pennington's account seems to offer confirmation on this point. Hughes's account seems to reflect a more positive view than some of the others, but it is focused on teaching theory as much as on teaching difference. Yet even this account offers resistance as a constant and success as partial. Embracing teaching difference as a struggle bound up in hope and resistance seems to be the testimony of these accounts.

As sobering as the above conclusion is, this synthesis suggests several lines of inquiry for future autoethnographies. To better contextualize this synthesis, we need more autoethnographies of teaching in higher education itself and of teaching various content by different types of instructors. It would also be interesting to have autoethnographies of students who have experienced these and other courses as well as autoethnographies of academic administrators charged with oversight of these and other courses. With all these data points, we could use MICA to compare and contextualize what we have found here. Ultimately, this example is intended to demonstrate the potential of the MICA method to synthesize autoethnographies in ways that can generate questions that have yet to be asked and lead to improved interpretations and deeper understandings of the central phenomenon of interest that is explored.

Concluding Thoughts

Since research using the MICA method, unlike meta-autoethnography, is secondary research, it is likely that the general format outlined above will often be used. The synthesizer in a MICA study is not speaking about her or his experiences but about what others have said about their experiences, and thus is a distanced author. Of course, first person can be used for what the MICA author is doing and thinking, and in general we recommend using pronouns that remind the reader that MICAs are humanly constructed by people with values, interests, and perspectives that affect what is of interest and what is to be said. We (Sherick Hughes and George Noblit) have presented a sample to demonstrate the MICA method because of what is important to us and those around us. We want everyone to remember this as they read it, and so should everyone applying the MICA method.

This statement made, however, autoethnographies are not like other forms of qualitative research in some key ways (e.g., Smagorinsky, 2011; Winograd, 2003) Further, even more standard ethnographic approaches are leading to other forms of expression. Narrative, poetry, music, performance, theater, video, audio, dialogue, and so on are all increasingly common at professional meetings, and studies using such approaches have become widely available for more general consumption online, in online peer-reviewed publications and elsewhere. Autoethnographies, as first- or third-person accounts, are often in narrative form, albeit with a range of structures. The challenge coming will be to push MICA to be more narrative than other forms of research synthesis and then to engage all the other forms of expression now used for qualitative research. In this, different autoethnographic accounts may become ideational or experiential characters, even antagonists. Lines of argument syntheses may become plotlines, and so on.

But this is about a future we hope will soon be upon us. Here our MICA application is bound to text—this is a book, after all. We write our synthesis in the third person because we are jointly writing this chapter and applying the MICA method. We share an interest in teaching race to White students in higher education and in preparing students from our school to do so as well. The studies we have synthesized will help us understand our work and interests better and will inform our work with our colleagues and doctoral students who teach race to Whites. It is as personal as it is professional with both of us—even though we are quite different people. We want to learn from the experiences of others, and the MICA method is one way for us to do this together.

Group Activity

Purpose: Involve students in preliminary thinking about synthesizing autoethnographies and recording their ideas about two or three phenomena of interest.

Activity: Journaling; justification of selected phenomena of interest and potential keywords to search.

Evaluation: Determine whether selected phenomena of interest are defensible for an academic audience and if the keywords are plausible.

Individual Activity

Purpose: Expose students to the MICA method.

Activity: Think-pair-share in which students first work alone using a relevant library search engine to search keywords to locate autoethnographies with the central phenomena of interest, and then work with other students in groups to unpack and identify relevant issues pertaining to the search and to funnel down the studies located to a manageable group (three to five) for synthesis using the MICA method.

Evaluation: Determine whether students understand how to use the search engine to locate studies that share one central phenomenon of interest.

Note for instructor: Students are sometimes shy, or even reticent, about participating, so prepare to change plans if necessary.

Sites for Students to Consider

Barnett-Page, E., & Thomas, J. Methods for the synthesis of qualitative research: A critical review. ESRC National Centre for Research Methods. http://eprints.ncrm .ac.uk/690/1/0109%2520Qualitative%2520synthesis%2520methods%2520paper%2520N CRM.pdf

Can qualitative metasynthesis make a contribution to evidence-based practice? Issues and challenges in an era of research (PowerPoint presentation). http://www.powershow.com/ view4/485739-ZGVkY/Can_Qualitative_Metasynthesis_Make_a_Contribution_to_Evidence -Based_Practice__Issues_and_Challenges_in_an_Era_of_Research_Integration_powerpoint_ ppt_presentation

The Future of Autoethnography

A Prism of Possibility

PART III

I
n this final part of the book, we anticipate the future of autoethnography based on past and current trends related to this qualitative genre in educational research. Chapter 6, "The Possibility of Autoethnography as Critically Reflexive Action Research," discusses the possibilities of moving theory into practice through the application of autoethnography as critically reflexive action research, or CRAR, using an "epistemologies of practice approach" (Weil, 1998, p. 37). This move may not only attract quantitative educational researchers but also necessitate their becoming autoethnographers each time they initiate social science educational research on marginalized populations. Promising examples of autoethnography as CRAR are referenced in this chapter.

The final chapter of the textbook, Chapter 7, "Anticipating the Future of Autoethnography as Critical Social Research," discusses the continued growth of autoethnography in education and in the educational research of other social sciences. Technological advancements such as social media provide some rich possibilities for conducting autoethnographies and disseminating autoethnographic findings. In light of these advancements, the chapter discusses (a) taking risks in autoethnography, (b) exploring qualitative theses and dissertations, (c) determining "good enough" autoethnography, (d) access to and availability of data, (e) politics and autoethnography, (f) the sustained growth of autoethnography as well as continued skepticism toward the genre, (g) social media and autoethnography, (h) new syntheses of ideas, and (i) the increasing acceptance of autoethnography. The chapter also includes a list of highly selective peer-reviewed journals with a qualitative focus that publish autoethnographies as well as a list of scholarly publishers that publish autoethnographic work. Part III is followed by appendixes that include a sample autoethnography assignment, a sample syllabus, and samples of autoethnographic work by undergraduate students.

6

The Possibility of Autoethnography as Critically Reflexive Action Research

istockphoto.com

●
Focus Your Reading

- Action research is a type of applied critical social research that aims to address perceived problematic situations in given cultural contexts through a process of collaboration in which both researchers and the researched initiate and evaluate interventions. Action research is intended to be educational and empowering for all who choose to participate.

- Autoethnography may take the form of action research. In fact, some autoethnography scholarship appears to take the specific form of critically reflexive action research, or CRAR; however, the authors do not name CRAR because this hybrid possibility has only recently begun to be introduced to the autoethnographic research community.

- Although CRAR and autoethnography were initiated separately and have different histories, the application of autoethnography as CRAR can be a promising advance in critical social research, as evidence from several autoethnographies published in the past decade suggests.

Since critically reflexive action research, or CRAR, is one type of action research, it seems most logical to begin this chapter with a brief review of action research. **Action research** is a type of applied critical social research that aims to address perceived problematic situations in given cultural contexts through a process of collaboration in which researchers and the researched initiate and evaluate interventions. Such research is intended to be educational and empowering for all who choose to participate. Unlike traditional evaluation research, action research does not attempt to measure the influence of interventions without the active collaboration of the research participants. Action research has two integral features: (a) the cyclical process and (b) the research partnership (Newton, 2006). An action research cycle begins with the analysis of a social situation or the identification of a problem; this is usually followed by the planning, formulation, reflection, and evaluation of a proposed or available intervention (Newton, 2006). With action research, veteran educators, through professional development, may change the way they carry out some aspect of professional practice in relation to youth of color. For example, U.S. educational leaders who experience professional development in anti-racism may begin contributing to changes in documented inequitable responses to the emotions and behavior of Black male students and thereby decrease the school-to-prison pipeline problem (a problem acknowledged in 2010 by the U.S. Departments of Justice and Education).

It is commonly understood among qualitative researchers that autoethnography may take the form of action research (Herr & Anderson, 2005). In fact, some

> ### Action Research
>
> Action research is focused on the analysis of a social issue with the goal of planning, formulation, reflection, and evaluation of interventions. It relies on two elements:
>
> 1. The cyclical process
>
> 2. The research partnership

autoethnography scholarship appears to take the specific form of CRAR; however, the authors do not name CRAR, most likely because this hybrid possibility has only recently been introduced to the research community. Although CRAR and autoethnography were initiated separately and have different histories, the application of autoethnography as CRAR could make a promising contribution to research, as evidence from several autoethnographies published during the past decade suggests. This chapter presents an argument for the possibilities of applying autoethnography as CRAR and demonstrates how to apply CRAR as an analytic tool as well as how to produce an autoethnography as CRAR. We begin with an in-depth look at the origins and elements of Susan Weil's (1998) CRAR method and an argument for the possibilities of applying autoethnography explicitly as CRAR. We then present an analysis of several autoethnographies from the past decade that exemplify the seven cyclical processes of CRAR, although the authors do not explicitly name CRAR, as they had not yet been introduced to this method. We conclude the chapter with thoughts on the future possibilities of educational research that applies autoethnography explicitly as CRAR.

The Origins and Elements of CRAR

The late Donald Schon is commonly considered to be one of the key architects responsible for the blueprints for *action research, reflexivity,* and *self-study* to improve one's professional practice. Susan Weil was a student and friend of Schon, and she was inspired by his tutelage to develop what came to be known as critically reflexive action research. Through a CRAR lens, Weil (1998) explains that public service workers (e.g., teachers and teacher educators) must work simultaneously with multiple responsibilities and accountabilities. Although her work is based in the United Kingdom, it offers a picture that mirrors the current U.S. cultural and socioeconomic context in that it both informs and is informed by complexities and dilemmas often linked to ideology, the political economy, P–12 schooling, and higher education. Weil developed CRAR over years of working with such complexities and dilemmas within contexts of multiple and conflicting accountabilities, including the following:

- Developing and providing distinctive and effective services that meet multiple and shifting expectations of quality
- Delivering social outcomes that have meaning and impact in communities, such as reduced crime or improved health
- Meeting demands to achieve high levels of comparative performance, despite the distorting effects of certain kinds of national performance indicators (Weil, 1998, p. 41)

Three interdependent elements provide the foundation for CRAR work: epistemologies of practice, on-site CRAR/off-site CRAR, and the seven key cyclical processes of CRAR. It is important to understand these elements before considering the possibilities for applying autoethnography as CRAR. While these elements are applied interdependently, we detail them separately in this chapter to enable you to grasp each concept in depth before you attempt to consider how they might work together in your autoethnographic educational research.

Epistemologies of Practice

An understanding of the notion of epistemologies of practice is dependent on an understanding of epistemology. Epistemology is a field of philosophy concerned with the possibility, nature, sources, and limits of human knowledge (Sumner, 2006). Scholars of epistemology also ask whether or how we can have knowledge of reality. While it is uncommon within many spheres of influence for novice critical social researchers to hear, "Let your epistemology determine the methodology," it is quite common for them to be told, "Let your central research question(s) determine the methodology." Yet the former message may be just as, if not more, important for novice critical social researchers to hear. Why? Historically, there have been clear lines of demarcation separating not only critical social researchers but also educational researchers along epistemological lines. The polar extremes of the epistemological spectrum are objectivism on one end and subjectivism on the other. Whereas objectivism asserts that there is an objective reality to be captured, measured, and tested, subjectivism asserts that reality is a human-negotiated (Sumner, 2006) and thereby subjective space that cannot be captured by one with implications for all, but can be studied, critiqued, and appropriated as a systematic social construction with implications for some. The approach known as epistemologies of practice challenges autoethnographers to step outside their traditional comfort zones to consider a comprehensive and yet flexible perspective that can be described as detailed in the following 10 points (Weil, 1998, pp. 42–43):

1. Epistemologies of practice promotes an approach to research that challenges our taken-for-granted knowledge and exposes our tacit assumptions and worldviews, which can vary widely from that which we espouse.

2. Epistemologies of practice renders the distinction between theory and practice irrelevant by focusing our learning within and on situations of action. For example, within classrooms, curriculum, instruction, and "implementation are not polarized as separate processes but can become integrated ongoing cycles of strategic learning."

3. Epistemologies of practice involves exploration through action questions such as "What counts here as legitimate knowing, thinking, and deciding? What are the limitations and other characteristics of these processes of knowing, thinking, and deciding?"

4. Epistemologies of practice questions the soundness of our action choices in relation to different dilemmas.

5. Epistemologies of practice invites notions of multiple authorship, and multiple subjectivities are no longer managed out. Instead, they are allowed to emerge, as sources of innovation and novel response to interaction with the environment, within mutually clarified parameters and anchored in shared values.

6. Epistemologies of practice promotes learning not as something people do as separate from their work or their lives; instead, it focuses on the complex ways in which learning, as both enabling and disabling, influences a system's capacity to thrive in an ever-changing situation.

7. Epistemologies of practice enables us to examine the appropriateness of assumptions deriving from different paradigms of thought and the influence of those assumptions on our choices of action and inquiry, our languages, and our metaphors.

8. Epistemologies of practice is based on an alternative, emergent worldview that sees us as implicated and embedded in the realities we are creating, including through our rhetoric. It shifts the emphasis from causes, effects, and linear change to seeing people as engaged, fallible "change agents" and organizations as living systems that are continuously learning and changing, coevolving through dynamic interactions within their environment.

9. Epistemologies of practice focuses on how epistemologies are "lived" out in the behaviors and choices of people who see themselves as either "managing" learning and change or, alternatively, "working with learning and change."

10. Epistemologies of practice gives rise to different emphases and choices in action (i.e., objectivism versus subjectivism).

Relevance to Autoethnography in Educational Research

One advantage of a marriage between the philosophical concept of epistemology and the "real-world" experience of practice is that its offspring, epistemologies of practice, provides an academically defensible justification for thinking across the traditional epistemological divide between objectivism and subjectivism. Another advantage of this marriage of philosophy to practice is that it allows educational researchers to initiate their studies with a central phenomenon of interest and relevant central research questions, as opposed to having their studies driven by whatever side of the epistemological spectrum they may find most comforting. Moreover, the advent of epistemologies of practice challenges traditional approaches to gaining new knowledge. These challenges are crucial for the growth of autoethnography in educational research within the social sciences because they justify autoethnography's applicability across the epistemological spectrum toward advancing hybridity in multiple disciplines (e.g., K–12 education, nursing education, physical therapy education, medical education, and sociology and anthropology of education).

Off-Site CRAR Versus On-Site CRAR

Her professional experiences with organizations in the United Kingdom influenced Weil (1998) to develop the notion of epistemologies of practice and, thereby, to explore theory in and out of practice (pp. 45, 47). What emerged from this exploration was another important element of CRAR: how it operates *off-site* versus *on-site* (see Figure 6.1). *Off-site CRAR* connects a range of people to engage the key cyclical processes of CRAR inquiry. It also involves meetings that should occur regularly (e.g., monthly, biannually) over an extended period of time. Weil references this period as a crucial time of shaping the CRAR learning network. Whereas off-site CRAR can stimulate and support *on-site CRAR,* the latter is inquiry undertaken in collaboration with colleagues and others (such as educators) within one's own organizational system (p. 46).

Relevance to Autoethnography in Educational Research

For educators, off-site CRAR may involve weekly coursework in autoethnography at a local university, with one-on-one dialogues and relationships with peers and

FIGURE 6.1 ● CRAR as Interweaving Cycles of Social/Organizational Learning

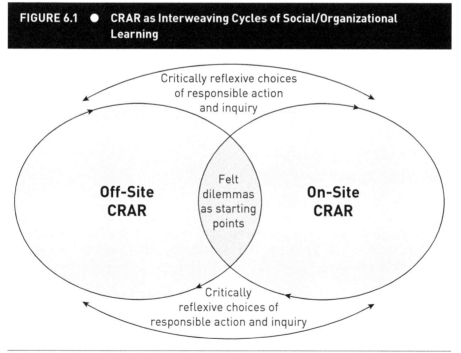

Source: Weil, S. (1998). "Rhetorics and Realities in Public Service Organisations: Systemic Pactice and Organisational Learning as Critically Reflexive Action Research (CRAR)." *Systemic Practice and Action Research, 11*(1), 37–62. Reprinted with permission of Springer.

professors thinking critically and reflexively about their K–16 teaching experiences from various institutions and multiple grade levels (see Figure 6.1). On-site CRAR could also work for educators involved in teams, inquiry groups, and the like within their own schools, departments, and units. It can also involve several of the types of autoethnographies mentioned in Chapter 1. For example, an individual educator/ educational researcher may engage *racial autoethnography* and share with others as part of both on-site and off-site CRAR efforts to change student outcomes of a race-based issue, like the disproportionate placement of Black and Latino youth in special education. In another example, two or more educators/educational researchers may engage methods such as *co-constructed narrative* and *critical co-constructed autoethnography* as part of on-site CRAR efforts within one institution or off-site CRAR efforts across institutions. The prospect of engaging on-site/off-site CRAR as part of an autoethnography affords participants another justification for think-pair-share exercises, which can be particularly useful for autoethnographies sharing similar phenomena of interest.

Seven Key Cyclical Processes of CRAR

The more philosophical first and second elements of CRAR (epistemologies of practice and on-site/off-site CRAR, respectively) come to life together in the practical application of CRAR's third element, the seven key cyclical processes (KCPs):

1. Appreciating starting problems/dilemmas

2. Focusing/framing inquiry cycle in context

3. Broadening/deepening understandings of inquiry focus/question

4. Reframing/refocusing inquiry

5. Planning for insightful actions

6. Critical reflection in/on actions

7. Communicating/learning/checking outcomes

The conceptualization of these processes is detailed below, prior to our discussion of published cases of autoethnography that inadvertently demonstrate the seven KCPs of CRAR (see Figure 6.2).

1. Appreciating Starting Problems/Dilemmas—On-Site and Off-Site

Unlike traditional action research, which focuses on identifying the problem(s) for linear problem solving, CRAR involves the appreciation of a range of possible starting dilemmas and questions approached through a particular CRAR learning network process. All members, at the beginning of a monthly session, are invited to identify a current "dilemma" on which they would like to work. All the dilemmas named are recorded on a flip chart. Each situation is clarified, and members vote for the two

FIGURE 6.2 ● Seven Key Cyclical Processes of CRAR

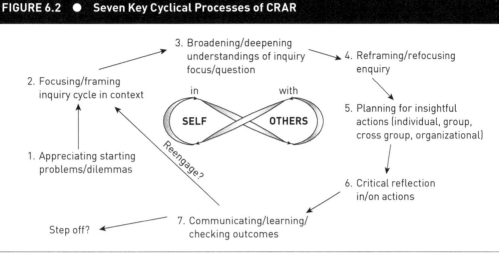

Source: Weil, S. (1998). "Rhetorics and Realities in Public Service Organisations: Systemic Pactice and Organisational Learning as Critically Reflexive Action Research (CRAR)." *Systemic Practice and Action Research, 11*(1), 37–62. Reprinted with permission of Springer.

dilemmas with which they can currently identify, in terms of challenges in their own roles (Weil, 1998). For teachers and teacher educators, the university is a shared center for on-site and off-site CRAR. In essence, off-site CRAR provides an opportunity to rehearse insightful action (Weil, 1998).

For example, educators/educational researchers may take back to their K–12 class-rooms and teams promising strategies that they are learning from autoethnography through off-site CRAR encounters and redefining roles with peers at the university who represent various schools and who teach various grade levels and subjects. In another example, educators/educational researchers learning from autoethnography through off-site CRAR encounters on committees or teams and at conferences dedicated to education research may take promising strategies for addressing dilemmas of theory and practice back to their on-site spaces. The university classroom is interesting as a potential hybrid space because it can be rendered as an on-site CRAR space for teacher educators and yet it can be an off-site CRAR space for teachers, both groups of educators hoping to inform and/or be informed by their crafts.

2. Focusing/Framing Inquiry Cycle in Context

This process takes place during the time after the dilemma selection process as group members try to understand the dilemmas within the circumstances and culture of a particular organization. For example, co-constructed narrative group members may be asked, initially, to clarify things that appear to be important for attuning to a dilemma situation. Questioning in the form of a cycle and contextualized form that includes focusing/framing inquiry can help group members to understand a "felt dilemma" more systemically (Weil, 1998).

3. Broadening/Deepening Understandings of Inquiry Focus/Question

To begin to broaden and deepen understanding of a dilemma in systemic terms, Weil (1998) applies another layer of inquiry at this stage to support group members in becoming more reflexive about what is emerging. Self-selected individuals may be called upon to brief several people in the group to attend to things that they see as important here. One may be asked to attend to issues of power. Another may be delegated to record key general issues throughout on an electronic whiteboard. One person may be invited to listen as the head administrator. Another may be asked to attend to metaphors and language and to "blindnesses" and contradictions between members' own espoused epistemologies of practice and what is being revealed in this situation of action. This phase can be prompted by previous autoethnographic work in a group on different emphases for change. In short, the group wants to understand better how members and issues may be systemically restricting choices of action and inquiry.

This move would give members different data sources to guide choices about on-site CRAR that they might initiate within their own organizations. In the university classroom, the group members could role play to simulate the various dilemmas faced by peers en route to CRAR. A CRAR group may include someone taking a turn in the "dilemma seat," someone playing the role of the "boss" or lead administrator unwilling or unable to acknowledge the dilemma, someone sitting alongside the person in the dilemma seat as an advocate, and a lead facilitator, who holds the bulk of the responsibility for facilitating reflections. The group is charged to support collaborative decision making and choices. The lead facilitator applies the CRAR method as the inquiries related to a given dilemma unfold, stopping or redirecting any line of inquiry that the advocate considers unproductive or inappropriate. The lead facilitator and group members help to explore the situation through a line of questioning that broadens and deepens understanding about the given dilemma. The lead facilitator of the group then stops the process and invites reflections. This, in turn, models reflection in and on action and processes of working with what has emerged as the basis for subsequent action and inquiry. The member playing the role of lead facilitator could also check out dimensions of effectiveness in the role from the vantage point of other members—a process that also models reflexive practice.

These cycles of multilayered inquiry generate insight into systemic patterns and processes and hypotheses about enabling and disabling effects on group members (Weil, 1998). For example, some autoethnographers may recognize how they have absorbed epistemologies of practice that are incongruent with their values, roles as formally defined, and emergent needs in the organization. In other words, they may begin to feel that they have become "unreflexively" and inappropriately stuck in their roles. Although work on "future vision" has essentially involved only the top, and communication has largely been a one-way, top-down affair, concerned with getting the message across, a preferred "epistemology of practice" is oriented toward processes of collaborative envisaging and participation (Weil, 1998).

4. Reframing/Refocusing Inquiry

This process, which involves "holding the systemic picture" and understanding enabling and disabling patterns—while under pressure to act—often requires a number of cycles of inquiry before the shift to insightful action becomes meaningful. Weil (1998) suggests that reflecting from yet another angle as part of the reframing and refocusing process is crucial. It can force group members to become more reflexive about the limitations of their own constructions, and what contributed to these, within that particular context—and the unintended systemic effects these might have. Throughout this process, educators/educational researchers, whether applying CRAR in a role-playing activity or in an on-site critical team meeting, should make no pretense at stimulating any single reality; instead, they should begin to make manifest some of the complex realities of their classrooms through autoethnography. By sharing their autoethnographies, educators may begin to recognize the contradictions and disjunctions that they are creating within the classroom, particularly in the context of their espoused values in relation to K–12 school and university purposes (Weil, 1998).

5. Planning for Insightful Actions

The process of planning for insightful actions involves a "private conversation" with an advocate to help group members consider what choices are being revealed (Weil, 1998). At this stage, the desire to "pull back" to the status quo can be overwhelming (Weil, 1998). Insight in itself does not necessarily lead to more insightful action and choice, because the real challenges lie in seeing and acting differently as contradictions between rhetorics and realities become clearer (Weil, 1998). For educators/ educational researchers, the university can be a center that serves as an important off-site rehearsal space for applying and sharing autoethnography in order to empathize and work through ambivalence and see how all individuals potentially mute their own and others' insight and wisdom. Group members' entire view of the situation may be turned upside down at this stage (Weil, 1998). Without this process, contradictions between espoused and expressed values may intensify, thereby further disabling possibilities for learning, genuine communication, and inquiry. Cynicism may also increase without meaningful planning for insightful, plausible on-site actions with an advocate, thereby damaging perceptions of CRAR's capacity to fulfill its role.

Low levels of participation and high levels of cynicism and resistance are equally likely to reduce a school or university's capacity to deal with uncertainty and unpredictable developments (Weil, 1998). Therefore, at this stage of the process described above, the lead facilitator helps to dissuade perceptions of the person identifying the problem and sitting in the "dilemma seat" as engaging a lone act of collusion, which could have far-reaching systemic consequences (Weil, 1998). Rather than "solving the problem" as originally defined, the facilitator can work with teachers and teacher educators to reframe strategic planning participation on the part of colleagues when engaging a dilemma (Weil, 1998). Questions that may emerge for educators/educational researchers at this stage include the following:

- How can I redefine the boundaries of my role and of my colleagues' involvement in the strategic planning process to address the dilemma(s)?
- How can I gain insight and convey that insight into the self-reinforcing nature of dominant epistemologies of practice and any unintended disabling effects of our current practice?
- How can I model CRAR in a way that promotes the group's/team's/classroom's capacity to become more critically reflexive about their own choices of responsible action and without reducing this strategic planning exercise to the level of merely another meaningless task with "busywork"? (Weil, 1998, pp. 51–52)

6. Critical Reflection in/on Actions

In this stage group members can experiment with making explicit their own hypotheses about disabling patterns and competing epistemologies at play in this situation. Whether through off-site or on-site CRAR action, this part of the cyclical processes of CRAR may in fact lead participants to rehearse ways of sustaining critical reflection in and on action within their own on-site settings (Weil, 1998). Autoethnographers may realize the importance of a stance as co-inquirer and co-learner in this situation, rather than as all-knowing change agent. Although there are likely to be initial concerns among some participants regarding trust and vulnerability, Weil (1998, pp. 51–52) suggests that group members keep an "ear to the ground" to stimulate constructive risk taking.

7. Communicating/Learning/Checking Outcomes

The process of communicating, learning, and checking outcomes provides insight into how dominant epistemologies of practice had in fact been restricting how group members made use of their own differences within the organization. At this stage, they can share the ways in which they intend to use CRAR-type processes to interrupt these "stucknesses" within their own organizations. Individual autoethnographers may envisage ideas for action inquiry that will have meaning and relevance in their own environments, including possibilities for interweaving off-site and on-site CRAR for their organizations. For example, they may recognize how some processes used as part of the learning network could provide the basis for away day work (see also Weil, 1998), as long as this was not approached as a "quick-fix solution" but, rather, as part of continuing inquiry embedded in action. This stage involves communicating insights about collaborative inquiry generated in terms of challenges reminiscent of those faced in many public service organizational contexts. Autoethnographers may also benefit from other insights that their stories might generate. In Weil's (1998) example, "several . . . group members spoke at length about how they had realized their own complicity in some of their isolation in their organizational development roles and the more critically reflexive possibilities for action and enquiry that had been stimulated by Tessa's work dilemma" (p. 53).

As Weil (1998, p. 53) notes, this seventh stage is essential for group members' exploration of the meaning and relevance of off-site CRAR for working with dilemmas on-site. At one level, off-site CRAR, which uses principles of critical learning theater and dialectical inquiry to create a complex improvisational environment, can feel quite detached from anything that learning network members might attempt in their own organizations. These processes surface an overabundance of reality and of systemic patterns that often remain "un-discussable" within organizations. At the same time, the failure to recognize these, and to learn from the contradictions and disjunctions at play, is often at the root of deep organizational "stucknesses." Too often organizations then attempt restructuring as the solution to challenges that may be more appropriately seen as challenges of organizational learning.

This stage can enable group members to generate insight from individual and co-constructed autoethnographies concerning how the key processes of the CRAR cycle might be approached within the circumstances and cultures of their own organizations. Off-site CRAR can then support on-site CRAR as it emerges. Off-site CRAR, over the course of a learning network's existence, can also give group members experiential understanding of what it means to build collective capacity for learning. They can come to recognize how individual learning is integral to this but by no means sufficient to maintain the system's capacity to learn and thrive through dynamic and continuous cycles of action inquiry (Weil, 1998, p. 53).

Selection Process for Autoethnography Literature to Consider as CRAR

Referring to the key processes enumerated above, Weil (1998) notes that not only can "multilayered tracking of the 'messiness' of such processes enhance our own reflexive understanding of the impact of CRAR as organizational learning and systemic practice, but also it enables us to address dimensions of quality, ethics, and trustworthiness in post-positivist research" (p. 54). In this section we track the rigor and yet the messiness of a particular literature review selection process that took place in 2012. The purpose of the process was initially to locate examples of autoethnography in education and educational research in the United States. Four doctoral students in Hughes's advanced qualitative research methods course volunteered to take part in the process.[1] The student team represented differences in race/ethnicity, class, and gender identification; specialties and areas of expertise within the teaching profession; and experiences with educational research.

---

[1] Hughes is the sole author of this chapter; however, while matriculating in 2012 as doctoral students in Hughes's qualitative research course at the University of Maryland, Dawn Jacobs, Angela Lawrence, Tamyka Morant, and Dawn Smith volunteered and contributed to the literature selection and analysis process.

During the course of our meetings, our diverse perspectives and experiences with teaching, teacher education, and autoethnography research provided a challenging yet invaluable intellectual asset for developing rigorous procedures to identify autoethnographic cases of CRAR. Once our diverse team was assembled, we first used four common academic library search engines—JSTOR, Project Muse, Social Sciences Citation Index, and Web of Science—with the keywords "autoethnography" and "education." JSTOR had the most hits (120) using these two keywords. When we compared the results from the four search engines, we noticed that the other databases had no items beyond those returned by JSTOR; all of their items overlapped with those from JSTOR using these keywords.

Second, we found that most of the 120 articles were well beyond the scope of our research, so we searched in JSTOR again using the keywords "autoethnography," "teaching," and "teacher education." This search garnered 63 citations. In an effort to double-check our work up to this point, we ran a Google Scholar search using the terms "autoethnography," "teaching," and "teacher education"; this led to us reading more than 800 abstracts of scholarship. Most of the "new" research found through this search was international in scope, and so irrelevant for our purposes, as we were focusing on autoethnography in teaching and teacher education within the United States. The remaining abstracts included and repeated the articles found in our original search of the four common college/university library search engines.

Third, we revisited the scope and focus of our research and found that we needed to develop a revised final set of funneling criteria that included only publications that represented (a) research based in the United States, (b) peer-reviewed journal articles, and (c) research articles, but not reviews or editorials about research. At this point approximately 54 articles remained. We then developed a checklist tool to help further reduce the list to the articles actually implementing autoethnography as CRAR, with signs of epistemologies of practice, on-site and off-site CRAR, and the seven cyclical processes. Our critical dialogues in class were key at this point, because we were aware that consensus would increase the credibility of our selection process. Our discussions also led us to the crucial decision that any autoethnography with signs of epistemologies of practice and on-site/off-site CRAR could remain on our list for further analysis if we found defensible signs to support the presence of at least four of the seven key cyclical processes. Each of us used the checklist to review approximately 13 articles individually. We then met to discuss the fact that, given our funneling criteria, only 12 peer-reviewed research articles remained. We member checked and reached consensus about the relevance of the remaining 12 cases before pursuing further review. Any article authored by a member of the team was analyzed by an elected member, so the author would not have the bias of analyzing her or his own work. Then we each selected 2 or 3 of the 12 articles to review again in more depth.

This chapter will discuss only 2 of those 12 autoethnography cases, because they exceed the criteria noted above by applying epistemologies of practice, on-site CRAR and off-site CRAR, and all seven KCPs. These autoethnographies not only represent all seven KCPs but also have the clearest, most defensible examples of those processes.

Moreover, the cases detailed below provide evidence of how autoethnography can be used as CRAR. Each case is intended to be "illustrative, but by no means definitive of CRAR possibilities. Nor, are they meant to represent a prescriptive methodology" (Weil, 1998, p. 43).

Finding Autoethnographies Demonstrating CRAR

As per our review, the authors of the autoethnographies selected applied autoethnographic research to improve professional instructional practices and the overall teaching and learning environment. The cases highlighted below—Hughes (2008a) and Laubscher and Powell (2003)—represent the multiple and dynamic ways in which autoethnography can be applied as CRAR in critical social research, with a particular focus on educational research. Educational research is considered here certainly because it is our disciplinary home, and because autoethnography has seen steady growth in the discipline during the past decade and could be conceptualized broadly as an umbrella of educational research that covers multiple disciplines with a focus on, teaching, student learning, teacher education, and classroom dynamics. However, you can and should select other disciplines and areas of focus for your own autoethnography searches.

Upon analyzing each case, we found that the application of the seven key cyclical processes of CRAR was evident, although the authors did not name CRAR, likely because the method had not been introduced to them as an alternative possibility for their educational research. After completing the review and analyses, we returned to the two cases to note their particular strengths in addressing the three major elements of CRAR: epistemologies of practice, on-site/off-site CRAR, and the seven key cyclical processes. Connections to these elements are indicated in Table 6.1. One of the two articles highlighted here may seem familiar to you, because it also appeared in Chapter 5 as part of the discussion of the MICA method. The repetition is pure coincidence, however; the two analyses were completed with different teams and several years apart.

Applying the CRAR Checklist/Rubric to Laubscher and Powell

Critically reflexive autoethnographies offer experiential tellings of the authors' stories—in this case, stories of exploration into the often uncharted territory of research on professors who teach about difference and are themselves considered "different" or "other" (Laubscher & Powell, 2003, pp. 203, 206). Both Laubscher and Powell (2003) "teach (or have taught) in psychology departments at predominantly White universities in the midwestern and eastern United States" (p. 203). Their article focuses on their experiences of teaching courses in critical multiculturalism within graduate-level counseling and clinical psychology departments. Examples of their

TABLE 6.1 ● **Sample Checklist/Rubric for Applications of Autoethnography as CRAR**

Auto ethnography	Epistemolo- gies of Practice	On-Site and Off-Site CRAR	Elements of CRAR						
			1. Appreciating/ Starting Problems/ Dilemmas	2. Focusing/ Framing Inquiry Cycle in Context	3. Broadening/ Deepening Under- standings of Inquiry Focus/ Question	4. Reframing/ Refocusing Inquiry	5. Planning for Insightful Actions	6. Critical Reflection in/on Actions	7. Communi- cating Learning/ Checking Outcomes
Laubscher & Powell (2003)	X	X	X	X	X	X	X	X	X
Hughes (2008a)	X	X	X	X	X	X	X	X	X

course titles include "Culture and Psychology," "The Social and Cultural Foundations of Psychology," "The Psychology of Difference and Diversity," and "Phenomenology and Race" (p. 204). *Epistemologies of practice* are evident in Laubscher and Powell's autoethnography for at least 10 reasons:

1. Laubscher and Powell use autoethnography to challenge taken-for-granted knowledge and to expose tacit assumptions.

2. Laubscher and Powell render the distinction between theory and practice irrelevant by focusing our learning within their psychology classroom. For example, they clearly came to view their classroom as a space for co-instructors who became integrated together through ongoing cycles of strategic learning; they did not see themselves as two teachers working through separate processes.

3. Laubscher and Powell posit exploration in action by exploring how they as professors are "marked" by difference and what those markings do to influence their experiences of teaching about difference.

4. Laubscher and Powell move forward by involving epistemologies of practice that question the soundness of our action choices in relation to different dilemmas.

5. The use of epistemologies of practice invites notions of multiple authorship, and multiple subjectivities are no longer managed out. Through Laubscher and Powell's coauthored autoethnography, the uniqueness and yet unity of their experiences are allowed to emerge, as sources of innovation and novel response to interaction with the environment, within mutually clarified parameters and anchored in shared values.

6. Such coauthorship also promotes learning as something that is not separate from people's work or their lives. Laubscher and Powell's focus is on the complex ways in which learning is both enabling and disabling and how it may influence a system's capacity to thrive in the ever-changing cultural context of the United States. Their coauthored autoethnography enables us to examine the appropriateness of assumptions deriving from different paradigms of thought and the influence of those assumptions on our choices of action and inquiry, our languages, and our metaphors.

7. Epistemologies of practice is based on a worldview alluded to by Laubscher and Powell that sees people as implicated and embedded in the realities they are creating, including through rhetoric.

8. Laubscher and Powell's coauthored autoethnography adds an alternative emergent worldview that shifts the emphasis from causes, effects, and linear change to seeing people, including the authors themselves and their students, as engaged, fallible change agents.

9. Laubscher and Powell use epistemologies of practice to begin "working with learning and change" along with their students.

10. Laubscher and Powell's inadvertent use of epistemologies of practice is evident in the way their work gives rise to different emphases and choices in action.

Signs of On-Site and Off-Site CRAR

Laubscher and Powell (2003) also demonstrate the process of on-site and off-site CRAR. During on-site CRAR, the professors engaged students in critical thinking and critical dialogues in the classroom. During off-site CRAR, the professors interacted with each other to discuss any blind spots, missteps, and miscalculations that occurred as they formed their senses of themselves as the embodiment of marginalization.

Signs of the Seven KCPs

While some autoethnographies involve all seven of the key cyclical processes of CRAR, others, like Laubscher and Powell's (2003), are stronger in some elements than others. Their article reflects Process 1, appreciating starting problems/dilemmas, in their agreement to work together to tackle a gap "where the literature is decidedly silent in cases where the learner's experience intersects with a teacher who is marked as 'different' or 'other'" (p. 205). The authors see an opportunity in this gap in the literature for them to start the process of addressing problems/dilemmas that force them to "reflect on the ways our experiences as academics (primarily in the classroom, but also in the broader institution) are mediated by the ways we are both marked as, or identify ourselves as, different" (p. 205). However, they remind us, "it is not without some effort and discomfort that we describe our experiences and identifications" (p. 210).

With Process 2, Laubscher and Powell (2003) focus/frame their inquiry cycle in context. They explain how "describing ourselves in written form demands a new naming dynamic that is particularly salient to the thrust of our argument" (p. 209). They further explain the need to focus their inquiry cycle in the context of their physical bodies: "When we walk into our classrooms we are immediately identified by gender and the hue of our skin and the shape of our bodies. . . . The written form erases these marks of difference, hence our need to mention them" (p. 209). Similar to Process 3 of the cyclical processes of CRAR, Laubscher and Powell continue broadening/deepening understandings of their inquiry/focus/question by reflecting off-site on their shared and different experiences of privilege and oppression. Both of them reflect on shared experiences of working-class backgrounds, lives as critical feminists, and lives as heterosexual queer activists with Protestant Christian backgrounds (pp. 206–207). Additionally, Laubscher reflects on his different experiences of marginalization as a Black South African man and "foreigner," while Powell reflects on her experiences of being an Appalachian woman described as "deformed" or "disabled" due to her being born with fully functioning yet overgrown hands due to a genetic condition (pp. 206, 208). Laubscher acknowledges his experiences of male privilege, while both discuss recognizing their shared privilege based in socialization, heterosexism, and religion.

Process 3 is demonstrated in an on-site classroom example. Powell describes an encounter where she served as a "lead facilitator" in her own class when a White student repeatedly responded to an African American female student's narrative on the last day of class with the assertion that "we all deal with" the burden of being judged unfairly during job interviews (Laubscher & Powell, 2003, p. 219). Powell intervened calmly and nondefensively "even though she felt disappointed and exhausted" (p. 219). She noted that "race and physical difference are not equivalent in shaping [their experiences], but acknowledged that she could use her experience with marginalization as an entry to understanding and connecting with the African American woman's experience" (p. 219). While the African American woman seemed relieved and validated, the White woman and other students were mostly quiet, though some nodded to suggest an understanding during Powell's intervention. Reconnecting off-site offers researchers a way for them to problematize what they have learned. For example, off-site they can discuss privately how "such interventions can feel supportive to some and distancing to others, as it might challenge their worldview or self-image" (p. 219).

Laubscher and Powell (2003) engage Process 4 by reframing and refocusing inquiry through a call on "other faculty to examine difference in their courses, and to challenge the notion that diversity is a bounded body of knowledge, appropriately fixed in a particular course" (p. 221). The authors contend that "teaching about diversity is not without significant cost and burden to instructors marked as different. We expend tremendous energy attempting to both facilitate students' self-exploration and understanding and manage our own reactions" (p. 220). They explain that this work does not suggest, however, "that only faculty who are marked as different can effectively teach about difference, or that such faculty are automatically qualified to teach such courses" (p. 220).

Laubscher and Powell (2003) work to engage the planning for insightful actions of Process 5 by describing the particular challenge of how to structure learning so that students engage with the material both affectively and bodily (p. 215). They further state a desire to leave students with more, and note that they are beginning to plan for their students' experiences of "shame, guilt, anger, and even paralyzing hopelessness." Such emotions "may be necessary way stations, inasmuch as students come to learn from them what their identifications and bodily presence signify to others, but they are not the destination" (p. 220).

Insightfully, Laubscher and Powell (2003) "challenge students to select their sites of active struggle—a position that we believe is made possible by the fact that we don't only teach what it is like to be Black, queer, or disabled, but also what it is like to be White, straight, or nondisabled in a diverse world" (p. 220). They further cross-check their plans to act on-site in ways intended to "encourage students to recognize and explore [their] emotional way stations, but also move beyond them" (p. 220). The authors engage Process 6 of the KCPs by critically reflecting on their actions with students, because "students play a significant role in this process, as their openness and willingness to engage in such dialogue is crucial" (p. 215). They later write that "students are challenged to consider that social activism is not simply about working for the other, but perhaps more importantly about freeing themselves from the constraints of bias, prejudice, and unthinking collusive relations to oppressive practices" (p. 220). They observe that "purposeful political activity is necessary outside of the classroom to ensure the loftiest of ideals of education in a democratic society" (p. 218).

Laubscher and Powell (2003) discuss the tension between challenging students to explore biases and not being able to act in ways to force or enforce such exploration. They explain that "even if students leave our classrooms with the same biases . . . they entered with, we hope that they also leave with a different model of . . . engagement . . . that emphasizes continued dialogue, openness to complexity, affect, respect, honesty, and a committed search for a truth that resists emotional foreclosure" (p. 218). Ultimately, the authors critically reflect in/on the influence of their actions on students, "What form this action will take differs from student to student. . . . When students leave our classes . . . their classroom experiences [at least] prevent them from saying, 'We didn't know'" (pp. 220–221).

The final step of the cyclical processes of CRAR promotes communicating/learning/checking outcomes. Laubscher and Powell (2003) engage Process 7 by communicating with readers through the publication of their article in the highly visible *Harvard Educational Review*. They place the burden back on the readers (i.e., other teachers and teacher educators) to begin examining how issues of difference affect American society's institutions in their concluding remarks:

> We conclude by revisiting the title of this article, which serves as a metaphor for much of what we have argued. We chose the title for its ambiguity. First, it alludes to skin, and our arguments of othering have presented the importance of body and skin color in the process of othering the teacher who is considered different. Further, to skin a drum may mean to "take off," to subject one's insides to a painful scrutinizing gaze. But to skin a drum may also mean to "put on," to be the drum maker who gives the drum its substance, its voice. This particular kind of voice, produced by pounding and hammering on the skin that gives it form, is painful, but also powerful. We hope that readers, like our students, will not only appreciate the many ways to skin a drum, but perhaps also be moved to recognize the rise and fall of their own beats within the drumming circle. (pp. 221–222)

Applying the CRAR Checklist/Rubric to Hughes

In his investigation of methods of college teaching, Hughes (2008a) notably acts as a participant observer while engaging graduate student teachers in a critically reflexive autoethnography. Again, the central theme of this chapter is whether autoethnography can work as CRAR. Additional evidence from Hughes (2008a) suggests that it can, given Hughes's application of epistemologies of practice, on-site and off-site CRAR, and the seven cyclical processes, as detailed below. First, epistemologies of practice are evident in Hughes's (2008a) autoethnography for at least 10 reasons:

1. Hughes uses autoethnography to challenge taken-for-granted knowledge and expose tacit assumptions.

2. Hughes renders the distinction between theory and practice irrelevant by focusing our learning and unlearning on implicit bias in the classroom. For example, he clearly came to view the graduate classroom as a space for the experienced teachers to be creative in engaging the mundane yet at times overwhelming issues of K–12 classroom management.

3. Hughes posits exploration in action by exploring how professors are "marked" by difference and what those markings do to influence their experiences of teaching about difference.

4. Hughes moves forward by using epistemologies of practice that question the soundness of our action choices in relation to different dilemmas.

5. The use of epistemologies of practice invites notions of multiple authorship, and multiple subjectivities are no longer managed out. Whereas Laubscher and Powell (2003) coauthored autoethnography as colleagues, Hughes invited Maggie to be a coauthor of sorts through a genuine member-checking process that ultimately forced him to rewrite the manuscript that was later published.

6. Hughes's autoethnography invites readers to examine the appropriateness of assumptions deriving from different paradigms of thought and the influence of those assumptions on our choices of action and inquiry, our languages, and our metaphors.

7. Epistemologies of practice is based on a worldview that sees us as implicated and embedded in the realities we are creating, including through our rhetoric. Hughes was clear in his effort to seek the social construction of Maggie while also considering any part he played in a faulty "savior" narrative.

8. Autoethnography is a genre that gives Hughes the tools he needs to invite interested graduate students to participate in an alternative emergent worldview that shifts the emphasis from causes, effects, and linear change to seeing people, including himself and his students, as engaged, fallible change agents.

9. Hughes used epistemologies of practice to begin "*working with* learning and change" as opposed to *working for* or *working to manage* learning and change alongside his students.

10. Hughes's inadvertent use of epistemologies of practice gives rise to different emphases and choices in action.

Signs of On-Site and Off-Site CRAR

There are clear signs of the second element of CRAR, on-site and off-site CRAR, in Hughes's (2008a) autoethnography. During on-site CRAR, the professor engaged students in critical thinking and critical dialogues in the classroom. During off-site CRAR, students interacted with the professor off campus and with each other outside of class to discuss any blind spots, missteps, and miscalculations that occurred as they formed their senses of themselves as the embodiment of marginalization. Reconnecting off-site can also offer a way for autoethnographers to problematize what they are learning. For example, off-site they can discuss privately their differing responses to the discussions that have taken place on-site (Hughes & Willink, 2015).

Signs of the Seven KCPs

The seven cyclical processes of CRAR are evident in Hughes's (2008a) autoethnography. The identification of the problem and placement of the issue in a classroom context clearly highlight Process 1 and Process 2 of the CRAR cycle. The researcher moves to the third stage of CRAR by selecting Maggie as the primary participant from 25 students in the class. He explains that he focuses on her experiences because she is "an archetypal case of change in my graduate courses full of students whose voices speak to white middle-class, female teachers finding themselves in the challenging position of both teaching and learning daily as an 'other'" (p. 78). This broadening of the problem strengthens the exploration because Hughes is able to observe and describe the epistemology in action through Maggie's experiences. He continuously broadens and reframes the question in Process 3 for deeper knowledge and understanding of the problem with his students in a graduate teacher education course. Process 4 is evident as Maggie decides to explore the origination of prejudice in her life and continuously changes and develops her initial inquiry. As she recounts her journey, the author provides direct quotes from himself and Maggie, highlighting the triangulation of the data.

Furthermore, Process 5 of the cycle, "planning for insightful actions" is particularly evident in the description of an incident that occurred in the course. As Hughes (2008a) recounts, one day during class Maggie asked, "'What's the matter, aren't you prepared?' I immediately responded, 'That's an interesting question, which leads me to ask 'Why do so many White people suggest that I'm not prepared to do my job?''" (p. 84). Hughes also discloses the varying interpretations of the incident among himself, Maggie, and other classmates. More important, the autoethnography adheres to Process 6 in that the dissonance is recognized, described, and addressed, highlighting the "critical reflection." Following reflection, the author concludes that autoethnography can be a tool to discuss issues of class, race, and gender, thereby functioning as critical race pedagogy. By challenging graduate students to pose and answer difficult questions regarding varying constructs, he encourages them to become "more transformative caring agents" (p. 91). Process 7 of the cycle, communicating and learning from the outcomes of the research, is fulfilled in the Hughes (2008a) example by direct quotes from Maggie describing her transformation and confirming the author's narratives provided by the author. The alignment with CRAR throughout this study clearly depicts and validates the presence of this process.

Concluding Thoughts: Toward Communicative Competence and Communicative Praxis

The researchers in both of the cases analyzed above demonstrate various ways in which autoethnography can be used as a CRAR tool to improve classroom environments for teachers and learners. Both cases reveal educators/educational researchers applying autoethnography as action research for "change," and more distinctly as CRAR toward communicative competence (Bowers, 1984) and communicative praxis (Wildemeersch & Jansen, 1992). A diverse array of research suggests that "action research appears to lead to understanding improvement, empowerment, and even transformation" (Rogers, Noblit, & Ferrell, 1990, p. 181). The growing burden of school reform on teachers "also . . . does not acknowledge the many structural features of school systems that constrain bottom-up, inside-out reform" (Rogers et al., 1990, p. 181). Rather than a less plausibly successful, and often paternalistic, push for linear change through individual action research per se, the evidence in this chapter supports the application of autoethnography as CRAR, precisely because of its links to collective action, communicative competence, and communicative praxis. With communicative competence, one has the "ability to read or decode the taken-for-granted assumptions and conceptual categories that underlie the individual's world or experience" (Bowers, 1984, p. 2).

One challenge of applying autoethnography as CRAR, even when seeking communicative competence or communicative praxis, is that our self-studies are "unlikely to change our classrooms in ways we might have wished initially, because our students and our 'selves' are now better able to create the classrooms as we would wish them to be" (Rogers et al., 1990, p. 183). The determinism of action leading to linear change is challenged by the application of this method as well. Thus, we should remain cognizant of the fact that with communicative competence and communicative praxis, we are "empowered to both change and stay the same, negotiate these meanings with other[s]" (Rogers et al., 1990, p. 183). Moreover, educators applying autoethnography as off-site CRAR may engage honest, thoughtful, serious dialogues with relevant teaching assistants and other co-teachers about what actions to take and what actions not to take. In the Hughes (2008a) example, Maggie, a graduate student in the course, became the co-teacher during and after the course.

A second challenge of applying autoethnography as CRAR in the real world of K–16 education is that each case of autoethnography seems to describe the messiness and uncertainty of "change" as autoethnographers work toward a high level of communicative competence. Yet "being communicatively competent does not mean that teachers [students, parents, or administrators] will inevitably adopt critical social science perspectives or transform their identities" (Rogers et al., 1990, p. 183). More likely to emerge from the application of autoethnography research as CRAR are communicatively competent educators with the tools for developing a critical "voice and a chance to participate in the discussions about what to change or what not to change in their classrooms" and schools (Rogers et al., 1990, p. 183). Still, in light of these challenges and the illustrative cases, we contend that the prospects of an applied autoethnography as CRAR are good, and the evidence suggests that this method is a viable and promising alternative in critical social research that until now has remained unnamed.

Concluding Thoughts

Autoethnography can take on many forms in a broad array of readings from fiction and poetry to more (Duncan, 2004) or less (Holt, 2003) traditional social science approaches. Research focused on improving the craft of educators/educational researchers can involve "a form of action research . . . called autoethnography" (Herr & Anderson, 2005, p. 25). A growing body of education research around the globe involves teachers and teacher educators engaging the social science form of autoethnography as "a writing genre in which the researcher 'becomes' the phenomenon under investigation" (Duarte, 2007, p. 1). Further inspection reveals that this particular research applies autoethnography in a manner that may seem quite different to readers expecting a more traditional action research (Corey, 1953) or participatory action research (Fals Borda, 2006) methods. As we found in our literature review, educators/educational researchers who apply autoethnography closely reflect a type of action research developed by Weil (1998) that has yet to be discussed in education scholarship: critically reflexive action research. Through CRAR, educators and educational researchers seem to act not only on seven cyclical processes of critical reflexivity but also on the big critical self-reflexive questions, such as: How might I be part of the problem that I am having with this educational organization? How might I begin to alter my outlook on teaching and learning and force myself to reflect more critically on why I respond the way I do, while looking at my pedagogical practices anew (Duarte, 2007)? Additional CRAR research questions might ask, "What counts here as legitimate knowing, thinking and deciding? What are the limitations and other characteristics of these processes of knowing, thinking and deciding?" (Weil, 1998, p. 42).

Unlike traditional action research and participatory action research, autoethnography as CRAR is not merely about promoting change, problem solving, empowerment, or transformation but also about building an internal and external social infrastructure where the "capacity to work with shifting sands, ambiguity, and uncertainty can be cogenerated" (Weil, 1998, p. 58). We have explored how autoethnography as CRAR centers not the method but the teachers and teacher educators as agents developing communicative competence (Bowers, 1984) and communicative praxis (Wildemeersch & Jansen, 1992), "which in turn gives [them] a voice and a chance to participate in the discussions about what to change or what not to change in their classrooms" (Rogers et al., 1990, p. 183). Evidence suggests that the possibilities of applying autoethnography as CRAR explicitly are quite promising for the development of defensible, credible, critical social research.

Group Activity

Purpose: Involve students in preliminary thinking about developing autoethnography as CRAR and recording their ideas about plausible and useful CRAR projects.

Activity: Journaling; justification for developing autoethnography as CRAR and defense of why a selected CRAR project is "plausible" and "useful."

Evaluation: Determine whether selected autoethnography as CRAR projects are defensible for an academic audience.

Individual Activity

Purpose: Expose students to autoethnography as CRAR.

Activity: Think-pair-share in which students first work alone to develop initial drafts of their own "autoethnography as CRAR" projects and then work with other students in groups to unpack and identify relevant issues pertaining to their individual plans to engage the seven cyclical processes of CRAR through autoethnography.

Evaluation: Use the CRAR rubric to determine whether student drafts of plans to engage autoethnography and the seven cyclical processes of CRAR are plausible and defensible to an academic audience.

Note for instructor: Students are sometimes shy, or even reticent, about participating, so be prepared to participate and share your own ideas for autoethnography as CRAR.

Site for Students to Consider

Hopkinson, C. (2015). Using poetry in a critically reflexive action research co-inquiry with nurses. *Action Research, 13*(1), 30–47. http://arj.sagepub.com/content/13/1/30.full.pdf

Weil, S. (1998). Rhetorics and realities in public service organizations: Systemic practice and organizational learning *as* critically reflexive action research (CRAR). *Systemic Practice and Action Research, 11*(1), 37–62. http://link.springer.com/article/10.1023/A:1022912921692

7

Anticipating the Future of Autoethnography as Critical Social Research

istockphoto.com

●
Focus Your Reading

- Autoethnography continues to grow in the critical social research literature; however, some ethnography scholars argue that the method should assume a more traditional qualitative direction.

- Social media and supporting technologies are opening possibilities for autoethnography.

- Autoethnographic writing, performances, presentations, and professional development at major academic research associations continue to increase. Autoethnography is finding additional academic spaces with the growth of interest in mixed methodologies and interdisciplinary research.

- The future of autoethnography will depend on how scholars of the approach begin addressing key gaps in its application, including epistemology, clarity, transparency, and evaluation.

- Many highly selective academic journals of critical social research publish autoethnography articles, and most of them also publish quantitative research, thereby extending the potential reach and respectability of the genre.

Growth and Creativity, Yet Sustained Skepticism and Criticism

Growth and Creativity in Autoethnography

Autoethnographic processes and products can take on multiple forms, including, but not limited to, memoirs, personal essays, short stories, journals, scripts, and poetry. The sustained growth of autoethnography as a possibility of critical social research remains contingent on the creativity of researchers and the leaders of international publication venues for qualitative and quantitative research. In addition to the 20 established iterations of autoethnography described in Chapter 1, we anticipate that lesser-known and less frequently published forms of autoethnography will continue to grow and inform researchers' work internationally. Among those iterations is the application of autoethnography as narrative inquiry to study intercultural communication in higher education (e.g., Trahar, 2009). The following three additional creative directions in autoethnography are less established, but they offer some promising possibilities for the future of the genre as critical social research:

- Autoethnography and the arts
- Autoethnography and mental and physical health/well-being
- Autoethnography in/as coursework

Autoethnography and the Arts

The arts in synthesis with autoethnography have led to some interesting research in small but growing new forms of the genre, such as *visual autoethnography* (Smith-Shank & Keifer-Boyd, 2007). As mentioned in Chapter 1, there are audiovisual forms of autoethnography that tend to extend beyond the realm of those accepted by academic (peer-reviewed and non-peer-reviewed) publications. Still, it would be neglectful to dismiss signs of the future for academic publications in this area. For example, visual autoethnography extends from the inclusion of digital photos and graphics to the use of technology for digital literacy and digital storytelling projects. An exemplar of such work is Eldridge's (2012) collaged critical reflection on art teaching in the *Journal of Social Theory in Art Education,* which is based in social justice and visual culture theory. Another new form of autoethnography gaining traction for the future of autoethnographic work in academic publications is musical autoethnography, which originated in Australia. Autoethnography pioneer Carolyn Ellis and Australian scholar Brydie-Leigh Bartleet introduce musical autoethnography in a coedited book format in which individual chapters are written through the eyes, ears, emotions, experiences, and stories of music and autoethnography practitioners, with the goal of telling and demonstrating how autoethnography can extend musicians' critical awareness of their praxis and, in turn, how musicians can augment the creative possibilities of autoethnography in the arts (Bartleet & Ellis, 2009). The influence of this work on a Sri Lankan immigrant to Australia, Rohan Nethsinghe (2012), is unmistakable.

Paying homage to the work of Bartleet and Ellis (2009) early in his music-based autoethnography published in the *Qualitative Report,* Nethsinghe (2012) applies autoethnographic method to investigate his own musical background, including the different modes of music education he received. From this genre, it was possible for Nethsinghe, then a doctoral candidate in music education at Monash University, to reconstruct that "my interests along with the methods of interpretations I practice in the field of multicultural music are influenced by and formulated through my appreciation and understandings of and beliefs gained from education" and "shaped by the social context, cultural placing, and life experiences" (p. 1). His autoethnography gleans information from personal journals, photographs, performance programs, records of achievements including certificates and newspaper articles, and information collected by talking to family members. Similar to Hughes's doctoral students who contributed to Chapter 3 of this textbook, Nethsinghe describes the process of autoethnography as "one of the most difficult tasks that I have encountered, as I felt uncomfortable" and sensed that it was culturally inappropriate to begin "articulating my personal achievements," while conversely feeling that "it was also hard to discuss some conflicts I faced as a school student" (p. 3). Moreover, he concludes, as did Hughes's doctoral students, that the findings of his autoethnographic study "at the end . . . provided me with some valuable insights about what shaped my professional practice and beliefs" (p. 3).

Autoethnography and the Arts

Autoethnographers are using multiple forms of representation (e.g., music, art) beyond journal articles and texts to bring their work into other realms.

Autoethnography and Mental and Physical Health/Well-Being

Through psychology, psychiatry, and social work research as well as nursing research, autoethnography is beginning to extend other fields toward developing strong possibilities for its interdisciplinary contributions to critical social research. *Transpersonal psychology* was born in the 1960s out of the humanistic psychology research of Abraham Maslow. The goals of transpersonal psychology and autoethnography are linked through their concern for meta-thinking, critical consciousness, and self-discovery en route to transformation from an undesirable mental/physical space to mental health and well-being. For example, Raab (2013) finds the link between transpersonal psychology and autoethnography to be organic, because both of them highlight experiential data, "which can be easily documented in autoethnographical format." Such a format "can be therapeutic and healing in that the information presented by the autoethnographer involves self-discovery, self-awareness, and a sense of empowerment" (p. 2).

Similarly, *vocational psychology* and autoethnography share the goal of appreciating how lives are informed by issues of consciousness and social class. However, autoethnography's role in vocational education differs from its role in transpersonal psychology. Peter McIlveen (2008) of the University of Queensland, Australia, notes that in vocational psychology, autoethnography is presented as a potential vehicle to improve vocational psychologists' own class consciousness, and it is intended to improve their capacity to grasp social class in their own research and practice. McIlveen concludes that it takes a step further to recommend that autoethnography be used for research, training, and professional development for vocational psychologists.

Brenda A. LeFrançois (2013) extends autoethnography to explore the *psychiatrization* of children and how she was complicit in perpetuating First Nations genocide through "benevolent" institutions, such as child protection and psychiatry, institutions that, she argues, too often produce "mental illness" through the psychiatrization of the people they are meant to support (p. 108). In her article in the journal *Decolonization: Indigeneity, Education & Society,* LeFrançois applies autoethnography to offer an example of the ways in which a child welfare organization can be both sanist and racist in its organizing principles and in its interpretations of the needs and desires of indigenous peoples. Her autoethnographic narrative also provides an example of how an autoethnographer's own shifting complicity within the relations of power can occur (in her case, in a particular "benevolent" child protection agency). LeFrançois, in sum, offers "a narrative that uses autoethnographic knowledge and queers my lived experience in order to unwrap and make visible the normalizing connections between psychiatrization, colonialism, racialization, and adultism" (p. 108). Similarly, Shahram Khosravi applies autoethnography in his book *"Illegal" Traveller: An Auto-Ethnography of Borders* (2010) in a manner that effectively challenges the notion that we live in a world without borders. Traveling from Iran to Sweden, Khosravi offers a critically reflexive

Autoethnography and Well-Being

Autoethnographers in health-related fields are exploring how understanding the self and identity plays a role in health care.

account of his personal experience as an "illegal traveler," largely by exposing the inequitable and inhumane racial dimensions of crossing borders, why and how people like him risk their lives do so "successfully," and what happens to those border crossers during and after their journeys, including how they reflect upon and make sense of the experience toward healing.

During the past decade, we have witnessed the slow but steady growth of autoethnography in nursing research in both *psychiatric mental health nursing* (e.g., Foster, McAllister, & O'Brien, 2006; Sealy, 2012) and nursing in general (Peterson, 2015). Nursing researchers are finding the subjective lens of autoethnography to be a useful qualitative methodology that can offer insights and opportunities for exploring the influence of nurses' personal and professional cultural identities on their practice. In the *International Journal of Mental Health Nursing,* Foster et al. (2006) detail their study of a psychiatric mental health nurse's application of autoethnography for exploring the experiences of being an adult child of a parent with a psychosis. As a qualitative research method, the authors find "autoethnography is useful for making connections between researcher and participant, deepening interpretive analysis of both common and differing experiences, and producing knowledge drawn from compassionate understanding and rigorous reflection" (p. 44). Citing Foster et al. (2006), Patricia Ann Sealy (2012) describes her application of autoethnography as part of an overall mental, physical, and metaphysical approach to healing from breast cancer.

The specific purposes of Sealy's (2012) autoethnography, published in the *Clinical Journal of Oncology Nursing,* are to increase nurses' understanding of the primary cultural implications of "unresolved emotional issues from the past complicating current treatment and recovery for locally advanced breast cancer" and to inform nurses that "reflective journaling and meditation can provide an opportunity to 'socially construct' past psychological injury" (p. 38). It was the way in which autoethnography moved Sealy to pursue critical, reflexive reconstructions of her past, including reexperiencing childhood wounds (e.g., losing her mother at age 5 after her father abandoned the family), that impressed her enough to share the process, product, and possibility of the method with others. Her autoethnography reframes mental health providers as both healers and in need of healing, and it challenges the mutual exclusivity of mental and physical health. Moreover, autoethnography became a process through which Sealy could gain insight into her duality as nurturing mother providing comfort and support for her family while battling breast cancer and as nurturing mother in need of help for the wounded child within her who still longed for the comfort and support of the mother she had lost at such a young and vulnerable age. The combined autoethnography reflective journaling/meditation approach "empowered" Sealy "toward self-acceptance and self-worth" and "finding meaning in suffering" to "heal pain and free energy for the pursuit of justice, peace and joy" (p. 38).

Similarly, in the *Journal of Research in Nursing,* Jane Wright (2008) evaluates positively the validity of autoethnography with reference to nursing and nurse education, concluding that "autoethnography is a useful research tool, which provides personal insights, which can provide meaning to others. This is particularly true when creative methods of expression are harnessed" (p. 338). Her autoethnographic contribution began with her application of critical reflexivity on her creative identity as a female nurse and lifelong learner from a White, middle-class Northern Irish background. Peterson (2015) implies in the *Journal of Advanced Nursing* that autoethnography can invite and move nurses to share stories that would otherwise not be heard and that, as a process, autoethnography supports nurses to be courageous in a different way by "laying bare of the self to gain new cultural understandings"; further, "it offers the potential for nurses to learn from the experiences and reflections of other nurses" (p. 226).

There are even signs of autoethnography extending beyond nursing research to more specific research concerning rehabilitation for alcoholism and drug abuse. Elizabeth Ettorre (2013) found that doing reflexivity via autoethnography with women who were drug users has some cathartic and healing influences. Unfortunately, there is a dual stigma attached to alcoholism and drug abuse that only adds difficulty to the healing process. The stigmatized alcoholic/drugged self is too often rendered not quite human and dangerous (Goffman, 1963), and that stigmatized self "may suffer from the imposition of a double, contradictory identity: ' . . . perceived as being sick, as suffering from an illness or a disease, but lacking willpower and self-will' (Denzin, 1995, p. 3)" (Grant, 2010, p. 577). In the *Journal of Psychiatric and Mental Health Nursing*, Grant (2010) confronts this dual stigma in depth through an autoethnography based on his battle with alcoholism over two decades. His approach to autoethnography involves "literary devices, including poetry, [and] time changes to tell the story" of his lived experiences of feeling increasingly stigmatized and treated as other by members of what he calls "the humanistic counselling and therapy fraternity" (p. 377). In the end, Grant's autoethnography provides insight into the development of selfhood in society, including the ways in which alcoholic selves can become stigmatized and "othered" (p. 377). Grant invites his readers to contribute toward ending "us–them" divisions. His concluding thoughts have a more specific message for the mental health nursing community that builds on his previous applications of the genre (e.g., Short, Grant, & Clarke, 2007) to decrease the mental health difficulties associated with alcoholism: "It would be of great historical significance if more mental health nurses, nurse therapists and mental health nurse academics engaged with autoethnographies of suffering or did autoethnographic work around their own mental health difficulties" (p. 582). Furthermore, Grant envisions a future of writing autoethnography in this field that "would contribute towards destigmatiz[ing] these difficulties and would document and communicate crucial experiences, including the firsthand experience of being on the receiving end of unsympathetic services" (582). A decade of evidence from Foster et al. (2006) and Grant (2010) to Sealy (2012) and Peterson (2015) suggests a future for autoethnography as an evolving, flexible, applicable, and yet rigorous ethnographic option for critical social researchers in the areas of physical and mental health and well-being.

Autoethnography in/as Coursework

Autoethnography in High School. Some promising advances in autoethnography coursework are emerging at the high school, undergraduate, and graduate levels. There seems to be a particularly astute move toward using autoethnography to teach critical literacy skills. Camangian (2010) uses autoethnography to teach critical literacy in an urban high school, which he calls SHS, in the Slauson District of South Los Angeles. SHS had the highest Black student population (66.1%) in Los Angeles for a large comprehensive campus. The 2005–2006 school year began with a series of gang-related shootings near SHS and the murder of a recent graduate, who was shot at point-blank range. SHS had a statewide academic ranking in the lowest percentile, and for six years in a row it did not meet the adequate yearly progress criteria required under the U.S. No Child Left Behind mandates. In fact, SHS lost its accreditation by the Pacific Union of Schools and Colleges, which led to more than 100 parents withdrawing more than 600 students from the school, yet little to no discussion occurred about this social context with the children until Camangian decided to bring autoethnography into his high school English course. The triumph is recorded in his article in the journal *Research in the Teaching of English.* Camangian (2010) explains that he found that autoethnography not only met the 11th- and 12th-grade English/Language Arts Learning Standards for the California State Board of Education, but it also "increased students' sense of self and positionality in the world, mediated differences, and fostered compassionate classroom community" (p. 187). In fact, "beginning the year with autoethnographies urged students to intellectually analyze their own perceptions and practices while the oral communication cultivated understanding across perceived differences" (p. 187).

Autoethnography at the Undergraduate Level. Jenn Stewart (2013), a visiting assistant professor of English at Indiana University–Purdue University Fort Wayne, provides another connection between autoethnography and literacy through her description of an undergraduate-level assignment for a course in digital literacies, available online (http://www.scribd.com/doc/168753294/Literacy -Autoethnography). The stated purpose of the digital literacies/autoethnography assignment is for students to (a) better understand how they might situate themselves within the context of digital literacies by producing a literacy autoethnography, (b) apply autoethnography as a way of systematically analyzing their use of digital tools, or how these tools manifest in their everyday lives, and (c) connect the data collected via autoethnography to their existing beliefs about digital literacy, with a specific focus on the question "Do your findings challenge, reinforce, or confound your assumptions?"

> ### Autoethnography and Coursework
>
> Autoethnographers are bringing ideas of understanding and enhancing educational contexts to courses at the high school and university levels in order to address critical issues.

Another promising application of autoethnography in the undergraduate classroom is highlighted by Shudak (2015). South Dakota Indian Studies is one of two courses required by the state of South Dakota as part of the qualifications for teacher certification. While indigenous students constitute 10% of the state's population and a noticeable presence in each school district, 95% of the teachers are White, with cultural worldviews that tend to produce an identifiable mismatch. To address this cultural mismatch, the Oceti Sakowin developed a standards report for the purposes of intervention and prevention of any dire consequences for indigenous students. Shudak notes that the use of the name Oceti Sakowin is a critical conscientious "departure from the historically pejorative term *Sioux,* an English adaptation of a French corruption of an Ojibwa term . . . , which essentially means little snakes, devils, or demons" (p. 86). In conjunction with the Oceti Sakowin standards, as of 2012, all candidates who want to teach in South Dakota must show transcripts proving that they have taken an approved Indian studies course. Shudak engaged autoethnography and found it to be a useful tool for White undergraduate preservice teachers seeking to inquire into culture through resonances (similar to critical incidents, resonances are resounding differences and similarities that must be unveiled if harmonious, nondominant intercultural relations are to form and be sustained). Autoethnography was applied as a method of inquiry for Shudak's students, with the goal of finding concepts rooted in their cultures in order to find resonances with concepts rooted in the Oceti Sakowin culture. The students reached that goal and began to understand the "other" and the "self" in deep, powerful, and profound ways. Three "autoethnographically rooted" assignments were integral to achieving this goal: (a) Re-Presentation of the Self, (b) Re-Presentation of the Other, and (c) 5 Things. Shudak's student prompts for the first two of these assignments are presented below, followed by his description of the third.

RE-PRESENTATION OF THE SELF

Prompt 1: An understanding of autoethnography is that it is a type of study and writing that inquires into the self as the self is part of a larger context. In a few sentences, begin to re-present to yourself what you think is the larger context that encapsulates the individual self. What is in this context? What does it look/feel like? Who's there? What's there? Of course you can't add everything. I'd like you to limit yourself to about 150 words. Please be more matter of fact and descriptive than creative with your writing.

Prompt 2: Re-read your response to the first prompt. In terms of a larger context, what did you leave out and why?

Prompt 3: Prompt 1 asked you to focus on a larger encapsulating social context. For this prompt, focus on the self more narrowly. What do you think represents you as a self? There might be some overlap with the first prompt.

Prompt 4: How might your responses to prompts 1 and 3 sound differently would you have done this assignment five years ago? Why?

(Shudak, 2015, p. 93)

RE-PRESENTATION OF THE OTHER

Prompt 1: The first assignment asked you to think about your larger context as a way of helping you think about what makes you, you. This assignment asks you to identify what makes the Oceti Sakowin who they are. Identify 3 specific cultural "things" from the readings that you think re-present the Oceti Sakowin. Follow the example: Colors are extremely important to this group of people. There are four that stand out. Black is a representation of the West, where the Thunder beings and weather come from; White is a representation of the North, where the cold white winds come from; Red represents the East, the place of the rising star; and, Yellow is a representation of the South, where the summer and power to grow come from.

Prompt 2: This prompt asks you to dig deeply within to figure out why you chose those cultural concepts or "things" found in prompt 1. Write a couple sentences defending your choice, but defending it in a way that indicates how your chosen concepts "resonate" with you. Follow the example: In Catholicism, colors are quite meaningful to the mass, such that the altar is at times adorned with different colors during the different times of the liturgical calendar coinciding with certain celebrations. A few examples follow. White is used during Christmas and Easter and during feasts and ceremonies like nuptial ceremonies. It means light, innocence, purity, triumph, and glory. Red is used for the Lord's Passion, Palm Sunday, and Pentecost. It means the Passion, blood, fire, martyrdom, and God's love. Black is used on All Souls Day, for the dead, and for mourning in general. Black means mourning and sorrow. Though there are a few others, the ones above are in resonance with the Lakota concepts from prompt 1, and resonate with me personally.

(Shudak, 2015, p. 94)

5 THINGS

The third assignment . . . gives meaning to the other two assignments. This assignment is generally sandwiched between the previous two and is an accompaniment to several different kinds of readings and sources. . . .

. . . Each student is required to identify five "things" from the reading she/he thought was quite interesting. . . . Some of those "things" [are to] be explicitly cultural, but they can also be a point made by an author or a turn of phrase that caught [the student's] attention. Not only are the students to identify a "thing," they are to respond to that "thing." . . . Each response [should] be an explanation of why the identified "thing" was interesting, or, it can literally be a response, visceral, intellectual, or otherwise, to something in the text. . . . [This assignment] is a quick and simple way to get the students interacting with the texts, leads to quite a bit of discussion, and, when the assignment occurs later in the semester, resonance seems to be a natural outgrowth.

(Shudak, 2015, pp. 94–95)

Mini-Autoethnography at the Undergraduate Level. One of Hughes's own undergraduate courses, titled Cultural Competence, Leadership and You, includes what he calls a mini-autoethnography. This course, which is offered to undergraduate education minors at the University of North Carolina at Chapel Hill, has the goal of students becoming leaders who understand that transformative leadership begins with critical self-reflection. The work is referred to as a mini-autoethnography because it involves all of the previously detailed elements of autoethnography, except that the depth of writing required is about one-third of what would be expected of a typical published autoethnography. While the course is not required for education minors, it tends to fill up rather quickly with 30 students, largely because it is open to all undergraduate students and it counts as an elective for global studies and social and behavioral sciences. Students in the course also conduct oral history interviews with leaders of campus organizations that were founded historically by students from marginalized and underrepresented populations. Due to the sensitive nature of racial, ethnic, and cultural relations on campus, students are nudged to take the autoethnography very seriously. The evidence of the gravity of this assignment is that it serves as the midterm examination for students in the course. Coincidentally, prompts similar to those used in Shudak's (2015) assignments presented above are integral to the course, as are opportunities for students to read the mini-autoethnographies of previous students who earned exemplary midterm scores (with written permission from the students whose mini-autoethnographies are shared). Samples of exemplary work from the mini-autoethnography assignment are available in Appendix B.

In another capacity, Hughes spent two summers teaching autoethnography to undergraduate students in a 10-week intensive program called the Moore Undergraduate Research Apprenticeship Program (MURAP) at the University of North Carolina at Chapel Hill (UNC). The UNC–MURAP students are, quite simply, driven and brilliant, and Hughes often found that they taught him more about autoethnography as a process, product, and possibility than he was teaching them. MURAP is designed primarily to recruit and mentor top-notch undergraduates of color from throughout the United States to pursue doctoral degrees. Much like Camangian (2010), Stewart (2013), and Shudak (2015), Hughes found autoethnography to be an accessible and educative form of critical social research for these students, enabling them to challenge their own taken-for-granted knowledge and complicity and to seek renewal by analyzing their own perceptions and practices. In fact, Hughes recently recruited and funded one of his former MURAP apprentices to pursue her doctoral work with him at UNC beginning in the fall semester of 2015.

Autoethnography at the Doctoral Level. Students in Hughes's doctoral-level autoethnography course practice thinking of autoethnography as described in Chapter 3. It is both process and product, both art and science, a reflexive research practice that uses the lens of the self (auto) to study, represent, and write (graphy) about people in relation to cultural groups/contexts (ethno). This course also introduces doctoral students to the methodological and theoretical roots of autoethnography, and then guides them in becoming autoethnographic researchers. (See Appendix D for a sample syllabus and review Chapter 3 for an example of doctoral student autoethnography work.) It focuses on both the theory and the practice of autoethnography, or "reading" significant patterns in everyday experience and connecting those patterns to the self and to broader social concerns. At the end of the course, students are expected to be able to do the following:

- Summarize the emergence of autoethnography from its epistemological and methodological roots.
- Critically analyze contemporary examples of autoethnography.
- Evaluate the scholarly and artistic merits of autoethnographic writing.
- Conduct autoethnographic data collection via the principles of assemblage.
- Write an autoethnographic manuscript draft for conference and/or journal submissions.

Because it would be impossible to teach everything about the theoretical underpinnings and method of autoethnography before having students start their own independent research, most of the semester involves a combination of reading models of autoethnography, reading the few existing methodological "how-to" works, doing writing exercises, and creating independent autoethnographic projects. The growth of autoethnography coursework nationally and internationally at the high school, undergraduate, and graduate levels provides a refreshing glimpse of the future, if these students continue to add autoethnography to their critical social research repertoires.

Skepticism About and Criticism of Autoethnography

Although autoethnography continues to grow in critical social research, skepticism still looms among some qualitative scholars who seemingly view themselves as guardians of the ethnographic tradition. Some of these scholars argue that autoethnography should assume a more traditional qualitative direction. Others scoff at the notion of autoethnography as an empirical research endeavor to be pursued in the future. As discussed in Chapter 1, qualitative scholars in the former group call for the removal of all autoethnography from the lexicons of critical social research (e.g., Delamont, 2009). Those in the latter group call for the removal only of evocative autoethnography, the style made popular by Carolyn Ellis, in favor of analytic autoethnography (e.g., Anderson, 2006; Walford, 2009). Their argument and scholarship restricts the application of autoethnography as part of a larger empirical endeavor by endorsing its usage only on some occasions and under limited conditions in the form that Leon Anderson (2006) introduced as analytic autoethnography in the *Journal of Contemporary Ethnography*.

Walford (2009) and Anderson (2006) intend to protect and preserve the future integrity of ethnography by applying autoethnography through a traditional realist empirical lens that critiques the deliberately evocative and performative applications of autoethnography toward change (Ellis, Adams, & Bochner, 2011) or social justice (Denzin, 2014). Tradition calls for attempts to reduce ambiguity and to exhibit precision in ways that seem to escape much of the autoethnographic work critiqued by opponents of the genre. Still, there is a glimmer of hope among the detractors who uplift the autoethnography work of Chang (2008) as a model for the type of autoethnography that is worthy of association with traditional ethnography. In support of the return of the "simple empiricist," Walford (2009) concedes that storytelling (as applied in autoethnography) is "central to educational ethnography" but asserts that autoethnographers often forget "that the traditional purpose has been to communicate something about others" (p. 280). His acceptance of Chang (2008) is rooted in his interpretation of her work as being restricted to a form of autoethnography that "shares the storytelling features with other genres of self-narrative but transcends mere narration of self to engage in cultural analysis and interpretation" (p. 43). In addition, Walford appreciates that Chang conceptualizes autoethnography as being centrally focused on the concerns of anthropology and argues that it should not be seen as a form of therapy. He notes that 4 out of 10 chapters in Chang's 2008 book are devoted to generating autoethnographic data, starting with the importance of the research focus, then going through personal memory data, self-observation, self-reflective data, and external data (p. 279).

Similar to Walford (2009), Anderson (2006) seeks to legitimize autoethnography by embedding it in realist ontology, symbolic interactionist epistemology, and traditional ethnographic qualitative research. He complicates the notion that empirical evidence can be gathered from evocative autoethnography. For Anderson, only analytic (not evocative) social science research methodology can elicit the type of empirical evidence (or data) that will withstand the tradition of rigor and scrutiny in the academy. He states his hope for the future of autoethnography quite clearly in his concluding thoughts: "[I] hope that other scholars will join me in reclaiming and refining autoethnography as part of the analytic ethnographic tradition" (p. 392). In sum, the scholarship of Delamont (2009), Walford (2009), and Anderson (2006) provides arguments either to remove or to begin reclaiming particularities of autoethnography as an empirical endeavor due to what the authors interpret as epistemological gaps. With pressure from such traditional scholars who have strong international reputations and voices among qualitative methodologists, one can logically surmise that any academic move that autoethnographers make (particularly more evocative autoethnographers) can be perceived as a move with a palpable risk of failure. Yet, the robust evidence we have presented suggests that it is crucial for autoethnographers (evocative, analytic, and everywhere in between) to continue taking that risk in the future to write and disseminate their scholarship if we are all to reap the benefits of the important contributions to critical social research that have been illustrated throughout this textbook.

Taking Healthy Risks: Growth in Autoethnographic Dissertations

University scholars and doctoral students are taking healthy risks with qualitative research and writing in critical social research (Lichtman, 2013, p. 310). One sign of this healthy risk taking is the increase in the numbers of doctoral students willing to write, doctoral advisers willing to advise, and department chairs and university leaders willing to support autoethnographic dissertations. For more than a decade, we have witnessed an increase not only in dissertations that engage autoethnography as a method, tool, or technique within a larger qualitative methodology but also in dissertations that apply autoethnography as the central methodology. For example, as early as August 2003, the Department of Curriculum and Instruction at Louisiana State University approved the dissertation of Pamela K. Autrey, titled *The Trouble with Girls: Autoethnography and the Classroom.* Autrey (2003) states that she engaged autoethnography to study her "experience as girl and woman, student and teacher, in elementary and middle schools and how these informed my pedagogical practices and knowledge as an elementary school teacher" (p. v). One year later, John T. Patten's dissertation, *Navigating Unfamiliar Territory: Autoethnography of a First-Year Elementary School Principal* (2004), was approved by a team of scholars at the University of Utah–Salt Lake City. In 2005, the dissertation of Carl Dethloff, titled *A Principal in Transition: An Autoethnography,* was approved at Texas A&M University. Dethloff (2005) seems particularly impressed with how "the introspection and evaluation provided by the methodology of autoethnography greatly facilitates an understanding of the processes of transition" (p. iii). Ideally, future autoethnographic dissertations will continue to convey critical reflexive accounts of some of the salient encounters, interactions, events, and episodes from the lives of the authors and how those experiences shape and are shaped by the researchers' goals for improving theory, practice, and policy.

Over the course of more than a decade as a tenure-track professor at three research universities, Hughes has served as adviser on a handful of dissertations that have used autoethnography as a method or tool, but only one student has passed the dissertation proposal defense stage with autoethnography at the center of the work: Susan Schatz. A doctoral candidate from Gallaudet University, Schatz (2014) is currently conducting an autoethnographic study that focuses on the change processes that she experiences as she works with a classroom teacher to facilitate the adoption and implementation of a schoolwide reform strategy called *close and critical reading.* This dissertation research is groundbreaking in that autoethnography also allows Schatz to take a critical reflexive look at how being a member of the deaf community influences her positionality, leadership, and biases as well as classroom teachers' responses to her.

Autoethnographic dissertations are available online. Typically a Google search using the keywords "autoethnography" and "dissertation" will return a number of choices to consider. If you are a university scholar or student trying to make an argument for pursuing autoethnography because your university has yet to consider and/or approve an autoethnographic dissertation, then you definitely want to locate those dissertations that have passed from either peer or aspiring peer institutions of higher education.

Determining "Good Enough" Autoethnography

Back in 2008, Hughes pursued the question of determining "good enough" methods for autoethnography as an alternative approach to dilemmas of legitimacy facing the genre (Hughes, 2008c). Drawing on previous inquiry regarding ethnography by Harvard University's Wendy Luttrell (2000), he began to conceptualize good enough methods for autoethnography researchers as being rooted not in mediocrity but in sincere efforts to understand and appreciate difference and accept errors often made because of scholars' blind spots and intense involvement in their fields and in the worlds of social justice, diversity, equity, difference, and resistance. Hughes gathered evidence via autoethnography from cases of his former graduate student practitioners in a course titled Intergroup/Intercultural Education. Moreover, that article added some insight into (a) a connection of autoethnography to research in education, (b) key decisions of a good enough methods approach to autoethnography (redeveloped as five key ideas of autoethnography, or CREPES, as noted in Chapter 1), and (c) how this approach can be applied to expose and address educator biases (Hughes, 2008c). As university scholars and students continue to grapple with legitimizing autoethnographic research, we anticipate that the traditionalists and the postmodernists will continue to move in opposition to what is "good enough" autoethnography.

The future of critical social research may simply follow the trends that are currently opening local, state, and federal funding coffers: causality-driven, evidence-based, traditional validity/reliability-based, replicable studies with interventions that can be scaled up. If that is the case, evocative and analytic autoethnographers would be wise to discuss the practices with the most promise to help legitimize this genre. As mentioned previously, some scholars argue that autoethnography should *not* be considered in light of traditional criteria. Others rely on the validity and reliability argument and compartmentalize autoethnography in the self-study box of qualitative possibilities. Some scholars focus on the construction of autoethnography when applied as self-study as the key to reputable autoethnographic research (Feldman, 2003), rather than the post hoc evaluation of autoethnography proposed by scholars like Hughes, Pennington, and Makris (2012). Moreover, other scholars seem to apply both constructive approaches and evaluative approaches to the validity and reliability of qualitative studies (Holt, 2003, p. 12). For an example of the former, one might consider the work of Feldman (2003), who has developed four criteria on which autoethnographic data collection could be based:

1. Provide clear and detailed description of how we collect data and make explicit what counts as data in our work.

2. Provide clear and detailed descriptions of how we constructed the representation from our data. What specifics about the data led us to make this assumption?

3. Extend triangulation beyond multiple sources of data to include explorations of multiple ways to represent the same self-study.

4. Provide evidence that the research changed or evolved the educator and summarize its value to the profession. This can convince readers of the study's significance and validity. (pp. 27–28)

For an example of the latter (also mentioned earlier in this book), Richardson (2000) doesn't center self-study per se, but instead centers the notion of personal narrative. She then compels readers to begin reviewing personal narrative with at least five criteria and related questions:

1. *Substantive contribution.* Does the piece contribute to our understanding of social life?

2. *Aesthetic merit.* Does this piece succeed aesthetically? Is the text artistically shaped, satisfying, complex, and not boring?

3. *Reflexivity.* How did the author come to write this text? How has the author's subjectivity been both a producer and a product of this text?

4. *Impactfulness.* Does this affect me emotionally and/or intellectually? Does it generate new questions or move me to action?

5. *Expresses a reality.* Does this text embody a fleshed out sense of lived experience? (pp. 15–16)

In addition, autoethnographic manuscripts might include dramatic recall, unusual phrasing, and strong metaphors to invite the reader to "relive" events with the author (Richardson, 2000, pp. 15–16). Although Richardson's criteria and related questions may provide a framework for directing investigators and reviewers, relatively few of them will be familiar with such criteria. Holt (2003) was among the first to use autoethnography to describe how his autoethnography was not accepted by journal editors and reviewers several times before finding a reputable home at the *International Journal of Qualitative Methods*. While laments such as Holt's are still present more than a decade later, as mentioned above, recent years have seen increasing acceptance of both constructive and evaluative tools to assess autoethnography and greater access for autoethnography scholars and scholarship. This increase in acceptance and access, particularly via the Internet, social media, and Web 2.0, brings with it an ethical responsibility on the part of researchers to find reputable journals, books, and associations when they are considering online options for disseminating their autoethnographic work.

The Internet and Other Technologies: Greater Access and Responsibility

Autoethnographic writing, performances, presentations, and professional development at major academic research associations continue to increase with the use of the Internet and social media to disseminate researchers' work. From Twitter, wikis, Facebook, instant messaging, and blogs to iPhones, iPads, e-mail, Listservs, online journals, Wikipedia, and vlogs, autoethnographers are constantly posting new forms and possibilities for the genre.

Autoethnography's relationship with social media influences can be considered both positive and negative. On the positive side, the Internet may offer an avenue for developing autoethnographic narratives via blogs, wikis, Twitter, and so on. In addition to the Internet and social media, new tools have become available for transcribing data and for data analysis. Digital recorders have improved researchers' ability to record conversations, and software such as DragonDictate and Transana can be used for transcription assistance. For analyzing data, there are many computer-assisted qualitative data analysis software (or CAQDAS) products available, including MAXQDA, NVivo, and ATLAS.ti. With such access to the Internet and emergent technologies, autoethnographic researchers also have a great responsibility to take care in how they use these tools.

On the negative tip, the Internet is full of traps—articles that haven't been vetted, false claims, web addresses that are no longer active, and so on—so it is wise to stick to reading dissertations and academic journal articles that adhere to the blind peer-review process. Even with its growing reputation for reliability, Wikipedia, the largest online free encyclopedia, is susceptible to fraud and misinformation. We try to stay current by attending conferences, attending meetings within conferences, and teaching a biannual professional development course in autoethnography for the American Educational Research Association. Moreover, listening to NPR on the commute to and from work provides some needed intellectual stimulation. Still, we are finding after a decade of autoethnography in our lives, and more than three decades of technology in our lives, that we are learning the most about media missteps, miscalculations, and blind spots at the intersection of autoethnography and technology from our students. It was during a critical literature review conducted in a doctoral-level autoethnography course that Hughes once taught at the University of Maryland at College Park (where he worked from 2007 to 2012) that he began identifying additional gaps in autoethnography research—gaps to be addressed for the future of the genre.

Addressing Gaps in Autoethnography for the Future of the Genre

Gaps in Epistemology

Addressing epistemology will be important for the future of autoethnography as critical social research. Studies utilizing autoethnography that are situated within the larger paradigmatic interpretive frames associated with qualitative work represent the ways in which autoethnography is centered on the self, beyond relying on particular data sets. While many qualitative methods, as represented in studies, are not necessarily explicitly bound within paradigmatic frames, autoethnographic work is a dramatic departure from positivist stances as well as most other interpretive frames, such as postpositivism, constructivism, critical theory, and cultural studies. Therefore, failing to convey a clear foundation for autoethnographic study can leave studies open to misunderstandings and misguided critiques. Positioning autoethnographic inquiries as simplistic opportunities to examine the self can lead to questions regarding how such studies contribute to existing work. Tour (2012) offers some promise toward filling this gap as she clearly elucidates her understandings of the nature, status, and production of knowledge. Moreover, she is clear and transparent about her epistemological link to autoethnography, stating, "I discuss the value of autoethnography in the form of a personal narrative in providing an opportunity for reflection on research practice, which may facilitate the development of researchers' professional knowledge" (p. 72).

Gaps in Clarity and Transparency

Addressing gaps in clarity and transparency will also be important for the future of autoethnography as critical social research. Many of the articles referenced in this book name the works as autoethnographies, but beyond the initial statement, they offer little to no evidence of further connection between the methodology and the remainder of the studies. Some authors have written self-studies or action research pieces and linked those to autoethnography, presumably because of the inclusion of "self" in their work, but have not included other aspects of autoethnography. Some of the authors of reviewed articles have used autoethnography as a broad methodology and connected it to their research methods, such as narratives, self-study, or action research. For example, Tsumagari (2010) clearly delineates the research methods used, describing "a qualitative research design that consisted of an interpretive phenomenological analysis of an autoethnography" (p. 294) and a "relational cultural theory framework" (p. 295). Tour (2012) clearly defines autoethnography as the "underlying research method," but she writes in narrative form, bridging the two in order to "construct a critical understanding of the self in relation to research" (p. 71). She also elaborates on the reasons she found using autoethnography in conjunction with narrative form to be the most appropriate approach for her study.

On the other hand, Sander and Williamson (2010) mention autoethnographic methods in their abstract, citing Sparkes (2007), yet the methods they used are not mentioned. The article is a first-person narrative and a dialogue between the two authors, with no research methodology described in the body of the article. These examples illustrate the differences between using autoethnography as a methodology and using it as a method. The gaps in the representations of autoethnography are wide. Yet we do not advocate for prescribing or constraining the presentations of autoethnography. Autoethnography at this point in time resides within the qualitative tradition and is interpretive and subject to wide ranges of expression and methods.

Gaps in Autoethnography

Some autoethnographic work seeks to clarify autoethnography's role in qualitative research relative to the following gaps:

- Epistemology
- Clarity and transparency
- Evaluation

Gaps in Evaluation

Addressing gaps in evaluation is another important consideration for the future of autoethnography as critical social research. If autoethnography is to be applied as empirical research, logic dictates that it must also be valued as a research method(ology) that provides beneficial insight, particularly in the field of education. Evaluation and publication of autoethnography are integral to the genre's longevity and utility both within and outside the academy. Yet evidence from this review suggests a key gap in the literature on evaluation and publication of autoethnography that, if left unaddressed, could undermine the legitimacy of autoethnography as an empirical endeavor. Based on the wide range of published autoethnographies reviewed here, we find a problematic lack of consistency in the evaluation of autoethnography-based articles for publication. A small number of the articles clearly define autoethnography and link it to the theory and methods used in the studies (Hermann-Wilmarth & Bills, 2010; Tour, 2012; Tsumagari, 2010), while many others either loosely connect autoethnography to the studies or merely define autoethnography without connecting it to the remainder of the articles. In order for more top-tier journals to seriously consider autoethnographic pieces for publication, a clear and consistent standard for quality autoethnographies needs to be prevalent.

Challenging and Promising Signs for Addressing the Gaps

During the literature search that contributed to this textbook, we located some autoethnography articles that provide a glimpse of the future of autoethnography that bridges the research gaps of the past. For example, Hermann-Wilmarth and Bills (2010) address each of the widespread gaps discussed above. These authors clearly define autoethnography, citing Reed-Danahay (1997) and Ellis and Bochner (2000), and connect it throughout the article to queer theory, which they utilized in their research study. Hermann-Wilmarth and Bills used autoethnography as both a methodology and a method, and "as an analytical tool [that] became the only way that we could make sense of the work we were doing" (p. 261). They addressed ethical considerations in protecting the identities of the preservice teachers who served as participants in the study, as well as in recognizing their own stance as researchers. Because the authors were working with a group of individuals whose safety could be compromised if their identities were revealed, they found further ethical considerations necessary, and they note that the extra level of protection "required innovation, forethought, and carefulness" (p. 263). Finally, Hermann-Wilmarth and Bills produced a well-written research article with research methods and analysis clearly defined. The study is carefully outlined, and autoethnography is brought back to the reader throughout the article, as the authors continuously explain their reasons for shifts in methods or analysis as related to autoethnography.

Autoethnography provides opportunities for close examination, understanding, and dissemination of the inner world of those engaged in critical social inquiry. The articles reviewed here describe the myriad ways that autoethnographers go about collecting, analyzing, and reporting educational self-study data. Fewer of the articles describe the epistemological and methodological processes involved in autoethnography. For the sake of the future of autoethnography, authors of the genre would be remiss to dismiss the history of legitimizing autoethnography in the academy, including recent efforts to name its "realist" and "empirical" possibilities.

The analysis of the observed articles that contributed to this textbook in one way or another reveals some of the ethical and political elements that have surrounded autoethnography since its initial growth in our field (1990 to the present). The analysis highlights some of the major critiques of autoethnography with regard to relational ethics, legitimacy, rigor, and utility. In addition, this chapter unveils how some authors are working toward problematizing the narcissistic "self" in relation to cultural "others" when attempting to apply autoethnography to social contexts of epiphany, salient encounters, episodes, and other events that influence, challenge, inform, and even transform lived experiences of teaching, learning, schooling, and education.

Through the process of writing this textbook, we found gaps in critical social research that offers tools and techniques for engaging or doing a sound, ethical social science version of autoethnography for publication. Moreover, there is a paucity of research on the criteria that students, reviewers, editors, and authors might use to judge the merit and worth of autoethnographic manuscripts. There is a need for more autoethnographic work that delves into the challenging and yet promising work of detailing the processes of narrative synthesis and crystallization techniques. The American Educational Research Association's call for transparency and clarity in quantitative and qualitative methods is certainly applicable to improving the prospects for the future of the social science form of autoethnography that is highlighted in this review.

Although much of the autoethnographic scholarship discussed in this book treats the explanation of the method and methodology of autoethnography as an ancillary topic, the imagined futures of the genre will include such explanations, albeit in a succinct manner—and such futures are imagined. The imagined futures of autoethnography in critical social research offer more expansive descriptive sections of "how-I" do autoethnography, as opposed to simplistic, stepwise prescriptions for "how-to" do autoethnography. Such sections could be both conceptual and practical as they focus on autoethnography as process and product through the framework of elements that animate the genre (i.e., legitimizing, problematizing, and synthesizing). Despite these recognized challenges and critiques, and those yet to be imagined, and despite the gaps in autoethnography research that have yet to be addressed adequately, the evidence of this book suggests that autoethnography is firmly in place in the academy. Perhaps no sign of this is greater than the increasing acceptance of autoethnography scholarship by highly selective journals of critical social research—the crème de la crème of the academy.

Publishing Autoethnography: Journals and Academic Publishers

We want to call your attention to the following highly selective academic journals and publishers of critical social research that publish autoethnography. These academic journals are labeled as "highly selective" due to their adherence to the blind peer-review process, their Thomson Reuters and SCImago Journal Rank impact factors, and their article acceptance rates, which are less than 25% according to *Cabell's Directory,* which is available through many, if not most, university libraries worldwide (in both print and electronic formats). While many other journals publish articles that apply autoethnography as a method, those listed below have known impact that relates to higher circulation and greater likelihood that the articles will be read by international interdisciplinary audiences. Many highly selective journals that adhere to the blind peer-review process also publish autoethnography as critical social research. Cognizant of Holt's (2003) admonition for the future of autoethnography, most of the journals publish both quantitative and qualitative research. Why Holt? Because he makes the following key statement:

> If autoethnographies are only submitted to purely qualitative journals then autoeth- nographic writers may be reinforcing the dominant practices of verification that emerged here. If autoethnography is to be justified as proper research then publi- cation in broad "mainstream" journals (i.e., that publish qualitative *and* quantitative research) is a necessary step. (p. 18)

Highly Selective Peer-Reviewed Journals

Some brief introductory information about the aims and scope of each journal is presented below. More detailed descriptions of all these journals are available at the web addresses provided and links therein. The journals are listed here in alphabetical order.

- *Anthropology & Education Quarterly* (http://onlinelibrary.wiley.com): Draws on anthro- pological theories and methods to examine educational processes in and out of schools, in U.S. and international contexts. Articles rely primarily on ethnographic research to address immediate problems of practice as well as broad theoretical questions.
- *Educational Studies,* journal of the American Educational Studies Association (http:// www.tandfonline.com): Invites submissions relevant to the association and the dis- ciplines of social and educational foundations. Provides a cross-disciplinary forum for the exchange and debate of ideas generated from the disciplines of anthropology, economics, history, philosophy, politics, and sociology of education, as well as race/ ethnic, gender, queer, cultural, comparative, and transnational studies.

- *Education and Urban Society* (http://online.sagepub.com): Multidisciplinary journal examines the role of education as a social institution in an increasingly urban and multicultural society. Publishes articles exploring the functions of educational institutions, policies, and processes in light of national concerns for improving the environment of urban schools that seek to provide equal educational opportunities for all students.

- *Equity & Excellence in Education* (http://www.tandfonline.com): Publishes articles based on scholarly research utilizing qualitative or quantitative methods, as well as essays that describe and assess practical efforts to achieve educational equity and are contextualized within an appropriate literature review. Considers manuscripts on a range of topics related to equity, equality, and social justice in K–12 or postsecondary schooling, and that focus on social justice issues in school systems, individual schools, and classrooms.

- *Forum Qualitative Sozialforschung/Forum: Qualitative Social Research* (http://www.qualitative-research.net): Multilingual open-access journal publishes empirical studies conducted using qualitative methods and contributions that deal with the theory, methodology, and application of qualitative research. Innovative ways of thinking, writing, researching and presenting are especially welcome.

- *Harvard Educational Review* (http://hepg.org): Committed to featuring the voices of people engaged in various educational activities around the world. Welcomes reflective pieces written by students, teachers, parents, community members, and others involved in education whose perspectives can inform policy, practice, and/or research.

- *International Journal of Mental Health Nursing,* journal of the Australian College of Mental Health Nurses (http://onlinelibrary.wiley.com): Examines current trends and developments in mental health practice and research. Provides a forum for the exchange of ideas on all issues relevant to mental health nursing, including directions in education and training, management approaches, policy, ethical questions, theoretical inquiry, and clinical concerns.

- *International Journal of Qualitative Methods,* journal of the International Institute for Qualitative Methodology, University of Alberta, Canada (http://online.sagepub.com): Eclectic and international forum for papers reporting original methodological insights, study design innovations, and funded-project proposals using qualitative or mixed methods research that are useful to the global research community.

- *International Journal of Qualitative Studies in Education* (http://www.tandfonline.com): Publishes empirical research employing a variety of qualitative methods and approaches, such as ethnographic observation and interviewing, grounded theory, life history, case study, curriculum criticism, policy studies, narrative, ethnomethodology, social and educational critique, phenomenology, deconstruction, genealogy, and autoethnography. Encourages innovative and provocative approaches to qualitative research as well as the ways research is reported.

- *Journal of Advanced Nursing* (http://onlinelibrary.wiley.com): Targets readers who are committed to advancing practice and professional development on the basis of new knowledge and evidence. Contributes to the advancement of evidence-based nursing, midwifery, and health care by disseminating high-quality research and scholarship of contemporary relevance and with potential to advance knowledge for practice, education, management, or policy.

- *Journal of Contemporary Ethnography* (http://online.sagepub.com): International and interdisciplinary forum for research using ethnographic methods to examine human behavior in natural settings. Publishes material that examines a broad spectrum of social interactions and practices—in subcultures, cultures, organizations, and societies—from a variety of academic disciplines, including anthropology, communications, criminal justice, education, health studies, management, marketing, and sociology.

- *Journal of Latinos and Education* (http://www.tandfonline.com): Provides a cross-, multi-, and interdisciplinary forum for scholars and writers from diverse disciplines who share a common interest in the analysis, discussion, critique, and dissemination of educational issues that affect Latinos. Encourages novel ways of thinking about the ongoing and emerging questions around the unifying thread of Latinos and education.

- *Journal of Psychiatric and Mental Health Nursing* (http://onlinelibrary.wiley.com): Publishes research and scholarly papers that advance the development of policy, practice, research, and education in all aspects of mental health nursing. Considers rigorously conducted research, literature reviews, essays and debates, and consumer practitioner narratives.

- *Journal of Research in International Education* (http://online.sagepub.com): Seeks to advance the understanding and significance of international education for schools, examiners, and higher-education institutions around the world. Undertakes a rigorous consideration of the educational implications of the fundamental relationship between human unity and human diversity.

- *Journal of Research in Nursing* (http://online.sagepub.com): Seeks to blend good research with contemporary debates about policy and practice. Contributes knowledge to nursing practice, nursing research, and local, national, and international health and social care policy.

- *Qualitative Health Research* (http://online.sagepub.com): Provides an international, interdisciplinary forum to enhance health care and further the development and understanding of qualitative research in health care settings.

- *Qualitative Inquiry* (http://online.sagepub.com): Provides an interdisciplinary forum for qualitative methodology and related issues in the human sciences. Publishes research articles that experiment with manuscript form and content, focusing on methodological issues raised by qualitative research rather than the content or results of the research.

- *Qualitative Report* (http://nsuworks.nova.edu): Oldest multidisciplinary qualitative research journal in the world, devoted to writing and discussion of and about qualitative, critical, action, and collaborative inquiry and research. Serves as a forum and sounding board for researchers, scholars, practitioners, and other reflective-minded individuals who are passionate about ideas, methods, and analyses permeating qualitative, action, collaborative, and critical study.

- *Qualitative Research* (http://online.sagepub.com): Publishes original research and review articles on the methodological diversity and multidisciplinary focus of qualitative research. Accepts global contributions from within sociology, social anthropology, health and nursing, education, human geography, social and discursive psychology, and discourse studies.
- *Race Ethnicity and Education* (http://www.tandfonline.com): Provides a focal point for international scholarship, research, and debate on racism and race inequality in education. Publishes original and challenging research that explores the dynamics of race, racism, and ethnicity in education policy, theory, and practice.
- *Research in the Teaching of English,* journal of the National Council of Teachers of English (http://www.ncte.org): Multidisciplinary journal publishes original research articles and short scholarly essays on a wide range of topics significant to those concerned with the teaching and learning of languages and literacies around the world, both in and beyond schools and universities.
- *Substance Use & Misuse* (http://www.tandfonline.com): Provides a unique international multidisciplinary venue for the exchange of research, theories, viewpoints, and unresolved issues concerning substance use and misuse (licit and illicit drugs, alcohol, nicotine, caffeine and eating disorders). Features original articles, notes, and book reviews, as well as proceedings and symposia that describe and analyze the latest research and information on clinical prevention, training, law enforcement, and policy efforts.
- *Teachers College Record* (http://www.tcrecord.org): Publishes a variety of scholarly materials in all areas of the fields of education and educational research. All topics related to the field of education broadly conceived are welcomed.
- *Urban Review* (http://www.springer.com): Provides a forum for the presentation of original investigations, reviews, and essays examining the issues basic to the improvement of urban schooling and education. Publishes empirical, interpretive, and critical research studies, as well as theoretical analyses of schooling and education in the contemporary urban setting and reports of original investigations.

Academic Publishers

Some introductory information about the aims and scope of each of these academic publishers is presented below. More detailed descriptions are available at the web addresses provided and links therein. The publishers are listed here in alphabetical order.

- *AltaMira Press (Rowman & Littlefield)* (https://rowman.com): Produces high-quality, peer-reviewed scholarly titles by both established and emerging scholars, making a significant contribution to the scholarship in the humanities and social sciences.
- *Information Age Publishers* (http://www.infoagepub.com): Publishes academic and scholarly book series, monographs, handbooks, encyclopedias, and journals in the social sciences. Seeks to develop a comprehensive collection of materials that break

down and define specific niches that lack high-level research material in the fields of education, psychology, management, leadership, educational technology, mathematics, and Black studies.

- *Left Coast Press (Routledge)* (https://www.routledge.com): Global publisher of academic books, journals, and online resources in the humanities and social sciences. Current publishing program encompasses groundbreaking textbooks and premier, peer-reviewed research in the social sciences, humanities, built environment, education, and behavioral sciences.

- *Palgrave Macmillan* (http://www.palgrave.com): Publishes award-winning research that changes the world across the humanities, social sciences, and business for academics, professionals, and librarians. Offers authors and readers the very best in academic content while also supporting the community with innovative new formats and tools.

- *Peter Lang Publishers* (http://www.peterlang.com): Specializes in the social sciences and humanities and covers the complete spectrum from monographs to student textbooks. Covers the complete range of topics in the social sciences and humanities, including cultural studies, fine arts, religion, sociology, psychology, gender studies, and Black diversity studies.

- *SAGE Publishing* (https://us.sagepub.com): Independent international publisher of journals, books, and electronic media; is the academic and professional publisher of choice. Known for commitment to quality and innovation, a world leader in scholarly, educational, and professional markets.

- *Sense Publishers* (https://www.sensepublishers.com): Fastest-growing publisher of books in educational research and related fields. With offices in Rotterdam, Boston, and Taipei, brings a true global perspective to its publishing efforts.

In the real world of academic publishing, autoethnographers seeking promotion and tenure would do well to select from among the journals and publishers above when looking for potential homes for their research. It has been difficult for researchers to keep track of which journals have stepped up to publish autoethnography. When we began our academic publishing careers more than 15 years ago, very few impact journals published this qualitative genre. Faculty in many universities were either unwilling or unable to accept autoethnography as a legitimate form of ethnographic research, and therefore it was marginalized much more than it is today. If these impact journal editors, publishers, and reviewers who now agree to publish autoethnography are a sign of change, then it is indeed very nice to see that this marginalized status is changing. Yet autoethnography dissertations are still rarely accepted by graduate committees, and there are still plenty of people resisting the possibilities of autoethnography for furthering research. As students and advisers, we are on the front lines of possibility. Our hope is that we will continue to contribute autoethnographic work to the larger body of critical social research.

Toward an Evolving Online Reading List for Autoethnography

Sheryl Shermak (2011) offers the following statement as an introduction to her reading list, which she has posted online: "In qualitative research, there has been a rapid expansion of autoethnographic styles since Carolyn Ellis's early work. The following is a rudimentary reading list. A further place to explore many different styles of autoethnography is in *Qualitative Inquiry* (journal)" (p. 1). Readers of this book are encouraged to enhance Shermak's reading list, an adapted version of which is presented below, and to disseminate their own versions via the Internet. As discussed earlier in this chapter, autoethnography will continue to improve and evolve as critical social research as long as digital technologies continue to enhance opportunities to disseminate it.

AN AUTOETHNOGRAPHY READING LIST (ADAPTED FROM SHERMAK, 2011)

Getting Started: A Few Suggestions

Ellis, C. (2004). *The ethnographic I: A methodological novel about autoethnography.* Walnut Creek, CA: AltaMira Press.

Muncey, T. (2010). *Creating Autoethnographies.* Thousand Oaks, CA: Sage.

Richardson, L., & St. Pierre, E. A. (2005). Writing: A method of inquiry. In N. K. Denzin & Y. S. Lincoln (Eds.), *The SAGE handbook of qualitative research* (3rd ed., pp. 959–978). Thousand Oaks, CA: Sage.

Styles of Autoethnography: A Selection

Evocative Autoethnography

Ellis, C. (1999). Heartful autoethnography. *Qualitative Health Research, 9*(5), 669–683.

Ellis, C., & Bochner, A. (2000). Autoethnography, personal narrative, reflexivity: Researcher as subject. In N. K. Denzin & Y. S. Lincoln (Eds.), *Handbook of qualitative research* (2nd ed., pp. 733–768). Thousand Oaks, CA: Sage.

Analytic Autoethnography

Anderson, L. (2006). Analytic autoethnography. *Journal of Contemporary Ethnography, 35*(4), 373–395.

Critical Autoethnography

Holman Jones, S. (2005). Autoethnography: Making the personal political. In N. K. Denzin & Y. S. Lincoln (Eds.), *The SAGE handbook of qualitative research* (3rd ed., pp. 763–791). Thousand Oaks, CA: Sage.

Kaufmann, J. (2011). An autoethnography of a hacceity: A-wo/man-to-eat-androgen. *Cultural Studies ↔ Critical Methodologies, 11*(1), 38–46.

Spry, T. (2001). Performing autoethnography: An embodied methodological praxis. *Qualitative Inquiry, 7*(6), 706–732.

A Couple of Interesting Examples

Poulos, C. (2010). Spirited accidents: An autoethnography of possibility. *Qualitative Inquiry, 16*(1), 49–56.

Richardson, L. (2011). Hospice 101. *Qualitative Inquiry, 17*(2), 158–165.

• Appendix A •

Autoethnography Data Representation: An Example

Autoethnographic data representation is varied. In this example, we examine an autoethnographic work by Patrick Slattery (2001). His work is grounded in theory and art and encapsulates one way to revise our understandings of what it means to be a student in a school. While Slattery's entire article is an example of autoethnographic work worth analyzing in detail, for our purposes we focus here on how Slattery presents his data.

Data Representation: Artifacts

Before you read the excerpt from Slattery's article below, record how you would define the following items:

- Bouquet
- Wafers
- Calendar

Each of us has some type of notion of what these items mean. Think about how you could represent these items by drawing them, painting them, or describing them in detail. All of us have common knowledge of these items and can state what they are and what purposes they serve. Yet in autoethnography, the responsibility of illustrating how we as individuals assign meaning and significance to artifacts as they relate to our social context is crucial.

Now think about the experiences you have with these items. What do they mean to you? Autoethnographers seek to examine and detail their interpretations of events and artifacts in ways that move the field forward and ask readers to think about the experiences of others.

Data Representation: Artifacts in Context

Now take a look at the art installation in the photo. What do you see? Can you identify the three items? How are they positioned? Why? What is the larger context?

Photograph by Patrick Slattery, Copyright SAGE Publications.

By now you have noticed that the calendar is placed on the floor under a school desk, while the wafers are also on the floor scattered around other items. There is a bouquet of flowers sitting on the seat of the school desk. What other items do you now see? What do you think they mean? Take a moment to record your thoughts about the items in the photo and what they mean.

Data Representation: Critical Interpretation of Artifacts

Now we turn to Slattery's use and interpretation of the same three items: a bouquet, wafers, and a calendar. In his autoethnography, Slattery situates his artifacts from a critical perspective. Relying on Foucault and the work of artist Jackson Pollock, he investigates "the regulation of the human body and human sexuality in a junior high classroom of a Roman Catholic school in the 1960s" (p. 370). Adding Slattery's ideas of regulation and sexuality, we begin to see the items in a new light. From a critical perspective, the notion of demonstrating forms of subjugation and oppression become vivid, and the significance of the items and the context changes. Slattery's work is complex, and we highly recommend that you read the entire article. Here we provide one section of his work that focuses on describing the art installation itself and the artifacts' significance. As you read the excerpt below, keep in mind how you viewed the items and how Slattery defines their meaning in his own life.

THE INSTALLATION: REPRESENTATION OF RESEARCH BY THE EDUCATIONAL ARTIST WORKING WITHIN

In my art installation, I look specifically at the normalization and regulation of sexuality in a Catholic school classroom of the 1960s (Foucault, 1978, 1986a, 1986b). Images from my Catholic catechism are included in the tableau titled *10,000 Ejaculations* and the canvases titled *(De)Evolution of the Marathon Runner* and *Hopelessness*. The

Catholic nuns who taught in my elementary school spent a great deal of time instructing the students to say prayers in Latin and English (e.g., Hail Mary/Ave Maria, Our Father/Pater Noster). One type of prayer was called "the ejaculation." Ejaculations were short and spontaneous prayerful outbursts, such as "Jesus, I love you" or "Jesus, Mary, and Joseph, protect me." Ejaculations were particularly recommended by the nuns in times of temptation. The gravest temptations were impure thoughts, which could lead to the deadly sins of touching one's body, masturbation, orgasm, or sexual intercourse.

> **Reading Note: Context**
>
> Notice how Slattery is setting up the context. He describes the focus of his education and how he was instructed. He is already laying the groundwork for examining regulation and sexuality.

The Catechism displayed in the tableau pictures angelic celibate priests and nuns with the word *best* inscribed under the drawing. A devout and pure married couple is identified as *better*. A single eunuch is labeled *good*. Good, better, and best represented holy lifestyles. However, the unmistakable message was that a sexless celibate life was clearly superior—preferred by God and the nuns. Of course, same-sex relationships and homosexuality were not even options open for discussion. The Baltimore Catechism, still in use today in some Catholic schools, outlines the prescription, "The doctrine of the excellence of virginity and of celibacy, and of their superiority over the married state, was revealed by our Holy Redeemer, so too was it defined as a dogma of divine faith by the holy council of Trent" (Confraternity of Christian Doctrine, 1962, p. 103). (A copy of a 1962 sixth-grade Baltimore Catechism can be seen in the tableau representing not only pre–Vatican II Catholic theology but also the pervasive hidden curriculum and subliminal messages found in all school textbooks.)

Students in Catholic elementary schools in the pre–Vatican II 1950s and 1960s were often required to make "spiritual bouquets." The spiritual bouquet was a decorated greeting card with space provided to list prayer offerings for a special person—often the student's mother. (One such card that I made in school on April 11, 1961, and my mother saved in a scrapbook can be seen in the tableau.) The spiritual bouquet contained a numerical listing of prayers to be offered for the recipient. The greater the quantity of prayers offered, the greater the implied religious fervor of the student. My classmates and I always felt compelled—both in the overt

> **Reading Note: Bouquet**
>
> Think of what a bouquet means to you. How does Slattery's idea fit into your own? How is he showing us as readers how for him bouquets were encased in his spiritual education and how he tied them to his notions of sexuality?

(Continued)

(Continued)

religious instruction and the subliminal suggestions of our conscience—to offer as many prayers as possible. This would not only demonstrate holiness and piety but also our efforts to save the souls in purgatory who needed our prayers to escape to heaven. Each prayer was assigned a numerical indulgence that reduced time spent in purgatory by deceased souls.

The most highly recommended prayers were rosaries and communions at Mass, which provided maximum indulgences for the recipient of the spiritual bouquet and/or the poor souls in purgatory. However, these prayers were time-consuming and laborious. Although I often felt compelled to include a few rosaries and communions on the spiritual bouquet, I usually preferred to pad the prayer offerings with lots of ejaculations. (One of my spiritual bouquets with an offering of 10,000 ejaculations for my mother is seen in front of a replica of the Pieta. I enthusiastically presented a spiritual bouquet to my mother every year along with a ragged bouquet of assorted flowers and weeds from our yard.) Adding thousands of ejaculations to a spiritual bouquet provided an appearance of religious fervor and spiritual gratitude. Offering to recite 10,000 ejaculations for Jesus, Mary, the nuns, and my mother became a passionate religious mantra—although I do not remember actually keeping an exact count of the prayers; I just rattled them off in my head until I got distracted. The ironic juxtaposition of spiritual ejaculations and celibate, heteronormative sexuality are deconstructed in this tableau.

The Religious Sisters of Mercy were my teachers in New Orleans. I was never physically or verbally reprimanded by the nuns—probably because I was a compliant student with an angelic attitude. However, underneath my facade of purity, perfection, and piety was adolescent confusion and guilt, which began during puberty. (There are many interesting parallels to Pollock's inner demons and the manifestation of his complex and at times conflicted sexuality in his sketches and paintings.) Although sexuality was never overtly discussed in my school or home, the hidden message that governed my thinking was that sex was sinful. My Baltimore Catechism again:

> The sixth commandment of God is Thou shalt not commit adultery. The sixth commandment forbids all impurity and immodesty in words, looks, and actions whether alone or with others. Examples of this would he touching one's own body or that of another without necessity simply to satisfy sinful curiosity, impure conversations, dirty jokes, looking at bad pictures, undue familiarity with the opposite sex. (Confraternity, 1962, p. 125)

Along with classmates, I began to privately explore my sexuality as a junior high school student. I wonder today how the catechism lesson about familiarity with the opposite sex may have contributed to the experimental encounters between male classmates. Occasionally in seventh grade, and without my parents' knowledge, I rode the St. Charles streetcar to the French Quarter with friends after school on Fridays to see sexy peep shows at a penny arcade on Bourbon Street. This installation creates a peep show where only a few glimpses into the adolescent experience can be seen, possibly eliciting some of the same emotions: curiosity, discomfort, arousal, guilt, disgust, passion, and so forth. The religious and sexual emotions are juxtaposed to reinforce adolescent confusion. For example, the faces of naked men and women, juxtaposed next to Bernini's *Estasi Di Santa Teresa* (The Ecstasy of St. Theresa), all display similar expressions. With the body of Jesus on their tongues, does this ecstasy portray Christian mysticism or sexual orgasm—or both? The painting of a woman mystic in spiritual ecstasy is remarkably similar to the expressions of sexual ecstasy in the erotica photographs. Juxtaposing sexual and religious symbols invites the viewer to reexperience the confusion and guilt of adolescence.

The impressions that sex was evil and touching the body sinful were reinforced by the fact that the body was always covered in my Catholic school; the nuns only exposed their faces and hands, girls covered their heads with veils, and modest dress was demanded at all times. In the classroom, we were taught to avoid impure thoughts by praying ejaculations. However, I often fantasized about bodies and sex as I sat in my junior high school desk. The images from *Playboy* and *Playgirl* magazines in the tableau foreground my fantasies of the human body as an adolescent student, albeit covered with white hosts—the body of Jesus—to protect me from my impure thoughts. The pubescent male is constantly aware of his body, with spontaneous erections and sexual fantasies. Efforts to control and regulate the body through prayer may have sublimated sexual arousal temporarily, but the religious mantra was seldom successful.

In this tableau installation, I have covered the genitals and explicit eroticism of the photographs with the symbolic body of Jesus: communion wafers. There are layers of meaning: The unconsecrated nonbody of Jesus covers the impure erotic body images in the photographs; the bodiless memory of the student who once sat in this now empty desk remembers suppressed erotic bodily experiences; the bodily remembering is done under the watchful eye of Virgin Mary, who is holding the limp body of Jesus; Mary, whose body was taken into heaven as celebrated on the Assumption, models virginity and purity as she watches over the school desk like the nuns of my 1960s Catholic schooling.

Reading Note: Wafers

How does Slattery define wafers? How do his ideas about wafers connect to your own? Think about his descriptions of not only the artifacts but also how they relate to his life. How does Slattery guide us as readers to understand his experiences in school? How do you see these descriptions connecting to ideas of regulation and sexuality?

In this autoethnography tableau, the viewer enters the bodily experience as voyeur. The viewer may be tempted to move the communion wafers from the photograph of the naked male and female bodies—either physically or in fantasy—to view the genitals.

(Continued)

(Continued)

This may even cause the viewer to experience some level of arousal. However, like the adolescent student, this arousal must be quickly suppressed in the public space of the art gallery. This parallels the experience of students who sit in desks trying to control fantasies for fear that an erection or flush face will be publicly noticed. Many adolescent males hide their uncontrollable erection by covering it with a book, shirttail, or sweater. When I was in school and an unexpected fantasy or erection occurred, I would attempt to regulate my body with the prayerful ejaculations taught by the virgin nuns in an effort to suppress images of sexual ejaculations. If the voyeur attempts to remove the symbolic body of Jesus from the sexual images, he or she will find that the communion hosts are glued to the photographs. The body of Jesus literally suppresses the impure thoughts and prevents them from being manifested.

When I first discovered masturbation in junior high school, I was overcome by guilt. I kept a secret calendar under my mattress—along with any erotica or pornography that my friends at school would share—and I would draw a circle around the date each day that I would masturbate. (A calendar and photograph of a young man masturbating are placed under my desk, hidden in a sense like my calendar and pornography under my mattress.) The calendar served several functions. First, it recorded the number of times that I masturbated so that I would have an accurate count for Friday confession before Mass. Communion was not allowed unless the soul had first been washed clean by the priest's absolution. Because a missed communion was a public admission of mortal sin and because my catechism and religion lessons had convinced me that the worst mortal sin was sex or touching one's body, the calendar protected me from a public admission of masturbation—or worse, the suspicion of sexual intercourse. Second, I thought that by keeping a count of my evil transgressions, I could gradually wean myself off this sinful act. Third, the calendar provided me with hope that during the next month, I could reduce the number of times that I would masturbate and thus minimize the risk of a scolding from the priest at the next Friday confession.

Reading Note: Calendar

As you learn about Slattery's use of the calendar, what connections can you make about how his life in school shaped his understandings and use of these three items?

The final element of the installation is a cardboard artwork in the bottom corner of the desk, an art therapy project completed by my father in a psychiatric hospital on the morning of his death by suicide. After finishing the art project, my father left the hospital with a 24-hour pass, bought a pistol, called me in Santa Fe, and told me that he was going to shoot himself. I tried to dissuade him and asked if he had seen a priest, said his prayers, or gone to communion to eat the body of Jesus. As I listened frantically and helplessly on the other end of the phone, his final words to me were "Only God can help me now." He shot himself in the heart and died 2 hours later. My active imagining of these dramatic events creates a parallel between my father's limp body, the limp body of Jesus in the Pieta in the tableau, and the limp body of those who were taught to recite 10,000 ejaculations to suppress impure thoughts, erections, and orgasms. Thus, my desk and the floor beneath the desk are littered with 10,000 white communion hosts—reminiscent of Jesus' body as well as globs of white semen staining my linen and the floor beneath my seat. My elementary education was regulated by thousands of ejaculations, literally and spiritually. A complex curriculum of governmentality is exposed in the tableau.

This installation is a construction and reconstruction of memories of my body in junior high classrooms. I collected artifacts from scrapbooks, yearbooks, and family closets. I also imagined furniture and icons, which I searched for in antique stores and junkyards. I worked within to reconstruct images from my unconscious while remembering Pollock's admonition that the creative process also involves consciousness of the overall effect of the piece. Although the symbols are particular to my Catholic school experience, I believe that the issues I raise in this installation are applicable to many students. Repression of the body,

Reading Note: Interpretation

Notice how Slattery brings all of his artifacts together. He connects his life to how other students might experience school. Here his unique experience is transformed into a larger area of inquiry. How do students in schools relate to types of regulation? How can Slattery's work assist others in education to see the impact of school structures and doctrines?

sexual fantasies, uncontrollable sexual responses, and guilt and anxiety about sexuality are all a part of the educational experience of students who sit in school desks. Because there is no student seated in the desk in this installation—only the reminder of my presence with the plaster casts of my hands and my actual handprints from a first grade art project—the viewer is reminded of the absence of the body and the attempt to repress sexuality in the school curriculum.

The hidden curriculum of the body has a powerful impact on the lived experience of students. These early life experiences, according to Jungian and other psychologies, emerge from the unconscious and affect our relationships and our education in multiple ways for our entire life. I have worked as an adult to (re)member my body with my spirit, my sexuality with my spirituality, and my fantasies with my imagination. I have concluded that the only way to avoid the hopelessness of my father's suicide and Pollock's alcoholism and depression is to remember holistically, to live with my whole body, and to take the power of my body back from those who regulated it—including the governmentality by my own conscious and unconscious actions (Foucault, 1978, 1986a, 1986b). This autoethnographic arts-based research tableau is an ongoing project to (re)member teaching and learning with the whole body. Autoethnography has the power to evoke memories and elicit insights that contribute to our understanding of students and classrooms. I believe that the educational researcher as artist working within makes an important contribution to this process.

(Continued)

(Continued)

References

Confraternity of Christian Doctrine. (1962). *The new St. Joseph Baltimore catechism* (2nd rev. ed.). New York: Catholic Book Publishing.

Foucault, M. (1978). *The history of sexuality: Vol. 1. An introduction* (R. Hurley, Trans.). New York: Vintage.

Foucault, M. (1986a). *The history of sexuality: Vol. 2. The use of pleasure* (R. Hurley, Trans.). New York: Pantheon.

Foucault, M. (1986b). *The history of sexuality: Vol. 3. The care of the self* (R. Hurley, Trans.). New York: Pantheon.

Source: Slattery, P. (2001). The educational researcher as artist working within. *Qualitative Inquiry,* 7(3), 370–398.

Data Representation: Critical Interpretation of Artifacts and Connections to Other

Now that you have read through Slattery's description and interpretation of artifacts, consider how this brief excerpt guides your understanding of three simple items, a bouquet, wafers, and a calendar. These items may have new meaning to you now because of Slattery's interpretive representation of each artifact and how it fits into the context of his school experiences. The power of autoethnographic work is in its ability to translate individual understandings of contexts, events, and practices in ways that relate to and resonate with readers who may never have those same experiences but can begin to comprehend the lives of others in order to transform them. We do not all have to attend Roman Catholic school in New Orleans to begin to see how regulation of student bodies could occur in other education contexts.

• Appendix B •

Sample Undergraduate
Mini-Autoethnography Student Work

Hannah Fischler

Education 508

October 21, 2014

Mini-Autoethnography Midterm

Morehead City is known as a small, quiet beach town in eastern North Carolina. It is a town consisting of predominantly white, Christian people with very conservative points of view. While it was a great place to grow up, Morehead City ultimately caused a lack of cultural competence in my life. After arriving at the University of North Carolina at Chapel Hill and being exposed to all of the various groups of socially and ethnically diverse people on campus, I became alarmingly aware that I am not sufficiently competent with cultures other than my own. Although at different points in my life my parents, friends, and groups on campus have specifically addressed homosexuality and the lesbian, gay, bisexual, and transgender (LGBT) society, I still sit at the cultural precompetence level of the cultural competence continuum with this lived experience that is most different from my own.

My first experience with homosexuality was during the spring break trip of my 7th grade year. My family and I were on vacation in Arizona and decided to take a break from the heat by visiting one of the nation's only indoor amusement parks. While standing in line for one of the attractions, I noticed a couple in the line holding each other closely and kissing continuously. This couple was unlike any other couple I had ever encountered. Instead of a male and female publicly displaying their affection, it was two males. I, along with my ten-year-old brother Daniel, immediately pointed out this phenomenon, a same-sex couple, to my parents. My dad's body immediately stiffened with irritation and my mom suggested that it was time that we leave the park. I remember feeling confused because we hadn't had a chance to ride all of the rides yet. After this event at the amusement park, my parents acted as if nothing significant had just occurred and we continued on with the remainder of our trip. I later realized my parents' views on homosexuality. My parents, along with a majority of my hometown, believe that a couple should only consist of one man and one woman. I found that my dad's cultural destructiveness and my mom's cultural blindness standpoints on the cultural competence continuum would ultimately conflict with my own views on the lived experiences of homosexuality.

Before coming to Carolina, I was never aware of the privileges and penalties of different individuals in my town. Growing up in Morehead City, I experienced privilege as a Caucasian, Christian daughter of a conservative family that had resided there for several generations. My culture mainly consisted of interactions between Caucasian, Christian heterosexuals so it was therefore easy to fit in with the majority of the residents. I discovered the penalty issues of my experiences in Morehead City after arriving at Carolina. The penalty of being a white, Christian daughter of a conservative family in Morehead City was the fact that I had not been exposed to any cultures other than my own. I found this lack of cultural competence to be a huge penalty against my intercultural experiences because it caused a sense of cultural blindness along the cultural competence continuum. Although I would run into situations involving cultures other than my own, I often avoided the interaction by pretending it was not there in fear that I would not know how to properly interact. Although I had no control over the fact, my first experience with homosexuality cast a negative light, and it greatly affected my views on the lived experiences of LGBT individuals that I ran into on campus, even individuals whom I considered very close friends.

Midway through my first year at Carolina, my best friend Tyler unintentionally helped me confront the cultural blindness I had with homosexuality. Also from Morehead City, Tyler had been my best friend since the third grade. Because we were two of the only people our age from our town to come to Carolina, we became even closer friends during our first year at school. One day during one of our frequent lunch outings at Chipotle Mexican Grill, Tyler got very quiet before saying, "Hannah, there's something I've been meaning to talk to you about." I immediately stopped eating and looked up to see Tyler's suddenly serious expression. My best friend of, then, ten years proceeded to confide in me that he was gay and had known he had been gay for several years. He explained to me that the reason for him not coming out sooner was the different levels of acceptance between our hometown and Carolina. I remember feeling honored that I was the first person Tyler had decided to share this part of his life with. However, I wish I had known how to respond better than how I had responded to Tyler back then. If I had been more culturally competent, I would've understood his situation more comprehensively. Tyler is an example of someone who used the diversity of Carolina's campus to become culturally proficient despite growing up in a culturally restrictive hometown.

With the help from Tyler and many other new friends at Carolina, I have been able to improve my position on the cultural competence continuum in regard to the lived experiences of homosexuality on campus. Thanks to these friends, I was able to have the opportunity to walk in a pride parade in Durham, North Carolina. Seeing all kinds of people from all kinds of cultural backgrounds come together to support the equality of other individuals positively affected my views on homosexuality. Although I honestly would have felt uncomfortable if I had gone to this event alone, being with a group allowed me to have the confidence that I could one day expand my horizons and eventually adapt to diversity. However, there are still many obstacles I have to face in order to achieve this cultural competence, and ultimately cultural proficiency. In relation to the rest of campus, I am aware of my limitations when interacting with these other cultural groups. The penalty I experienced by growing up in a town that was not culturally diverse affects my ability to respond adequately to the LGBT culture that I feel is most different from my own.

Thanks to the Campus Y organization at UNC–Chapel Hill, I was able to have an in-group experience in relation to the rest of the campus in regard to homosexuality. The Campus Y is a group on Carolina's campus that focuses on the pursuit of social justice and gaining social and human rights not just locally, but across the world. During my first year at UNC, I had the unique opportunity to participate in their "Carolina Kickoff" event where several diverse groups from campus came and talked about their missions and what they represented. This was one of the first campus events I attended after moving away from Morehead City. I was amazed at all the diversity that existed just a few hours from my hometown. In their own way, UNC's Campus Y strives for cultural competence amongst groups on campus and eventually throughout the world. This mission inspired me to expand my views of cultures different than my own and adopt a more intercultural mind-set.

In reflection, I currently see myself at the cultural precompetence level on the cultural competence continuum with regard to the LGBT students and culture on campus. However, I certainly did not start at this position when I came to Carolina. After spending the first 18 years of my life in a town where Caucasian, Christian conservatives were culturally superior, I struggled mainly with the process of changing my perspective of other cultures. Because a majority of my life was spent in a place where there was no such thing as an intercultural society, I used to find myself subconsciously feeling superior to minority cultures and lived experiences. This has been my most significant personal problem when it comes to trying to improve my placement on the cultural competence continuum. Basing off of my struggles, I eventually hope to become culturally competent with LGBT cultural groups and ultimately, I hope to become culturally proficient. I hope to one day be culturally competent enough that I could stand up to my parents if we were ever in another situation similar to the situation I experienced in Arizona. I believe it is possible for me to become culturally competent enough to be comfortable attending a pride parade on my own instead of with a group. Ultimately, I hope to be comfortable enough with this culture one day so that when someone like my friend Tyler comes to me in confidence, I will be able to respond appropriately and help them embrace and value the diversity in their life.

Although I admittedly have not reached cultural competence when it comes to the LGBT community, I do believe that I sit at the precompetence level on the cultural competence continuum. I am capable of seeing the difference between my dominant cultural experiences of heterosexuality and LGBT lived experiences, as well as understanding that one cultural group is not superior to the other. However, I am also aware that I still have difficulty responding adequately during interactions within this group. I recognize that currently at the precompetence level, I am limited when it comes to knowledge of certain LGBT customs and practices.

Eventually, with the help of this diverse campus and the multitude of organizations that are continuously promoting culture competence on campus, I do not doubt my ability to ultimately reach the level of cultural proficiency when it comes to lesbian, gay, bisexual, and transgender lived experiences.

Megan Stanley

Education 508

October 21, 2014

Mini-Autoethnography Midterm

Whether it was climbing across the monkey bars to avoid falling into the lava-covered mulch or searching for treasure in the jungle, which was more commonly known as the playground, it seemed as though my friends and I always had an adventure during recess. While usually fun and carefree, there was one day in particular that changed my young and naive four-year-old mind due to its congruency with the black and white racial binary. As my best friend and I embarked on a mission to find our friends in hide-and-seek, we split up amongst the playground to cover more ground. Ironically, while I searched for my companions, someone found me rather than me finding them; pulling me aside, the new African American girl at my preschool asked, "Why are you playing with them? They're white." Undoubtedly being my first introduction to race and ethnic relations, this instance essentially served as the catalyst for my internal struggle and social dilemma in relation to racial categorization.

Assuming color classifications were similar to those in a Crayola box, I told my mom about the incident at school and expected her to say a uniform color to describe me. Instead, I got two in addition to a word I had never heard before: black, white, and Puerto Rican. In an attempt to understand my interracial background, my child-self became more confused with the specific labels that no one seemed to identify with. Adopting the simple descriptor "mixed" because it was not only easy to say but made more sense, I thought back to the girl at my preschool. She assumed I could not play with my white friends because I was black, but I am part white so is that why it's okay? Or is that not enough? She also assumed we could play together, but I am only part black—does this change things? There is this random Hispanic component as well, so what does that mean for me? Am I just unable to play with everyone? Luckily, my newfound knowledge did not affect my childhood friendships or playground experiences, and although I went to a predominantly white elementary school, race never seemed to be an impeding factor either; however, I was always prepared to recite my racial makeup just in case another encounter occurred, and the situation has allowed me to identify monoracial individuals as the group that differs most from myself.

My awareness of race became heightened in middle school when my peers continuously asked what I was; having to ponder the philosophical question of my existence, I realized that there seemed to be a curious fascination with the idea that a person can hold more than one racial identity. Being just black was not enough—one had to be black plus a slew of other identities in order to be cool or "exotic." This discovery was made when I tiredly said I was just black to a classmate who asked what I was one day. The disappointment that fell over their face is forever engrained in my memory and their response was, "Are you sure you're nothing else?" which was then followed by random "ethnic" guesses. This instance allows me to see that simply being mixed is seen as a privilege in the eyes of certain racial groups; to go a step further, being mixed is seen as a privilege in the eyes of a lot of people, regardless of their racial identification. Aside from the attention and attraction that comes with having an ambiguous identity, I have racial components that can take away from and even overshadow pure blackness. While I believe the remnants of slavery's "one drop rule," in which you were deemed a Negro if you had Negro blood, as well as the harsh stereotypes and associations that were placed on the African American race as a whole are still prevalent in today's society, my multiracial identity pulls me in a way that I am not solely restricted to the black race. To offer a clearer explanation, Jared Ball's "The Multiracial Sheep IS the White Supremacist Fox" states that the multiracial label and census box "offers 'freedom' from Blackness" which creates an opportunity to leave the "black baggage" behind.

Reading this initially made me uncomfortable because while I acknowledge I am mixed and bubble in multiple boxes on application forms if the "Mixed" category isn't there, I personally identify as black because that is what I happen to be closer to; in order to think critically though, I had to ignore the discomfort that the article caused me (partly due to its phrasing and title) and realized I somewhat agree. As a mixed person, I have the privilege of choice—I can self-identify myself. Despite the tint in my skin, I have the ability to completely dissociate from my blackness if I wanted to; while I cannot pass for white, I know that I have the choice to downplay the blackness that runs through my veins. In comparison to monoracial people, they cannot simply choose what they are. They have a single racial or ethnic identifier that they are expected to accept and embrace; a minority that is stuck in a structural and oppressive system due to their race typically didn't choose the race they are in—I theoretically can however. Aside from feeling closer to my oppressed groups, this was a hard concept for me to grapple with because you tend to only hear about white privilege; while I knew that I would never have the privileges that a white person has, I didn't want to be associated with racial privileges in general because I believed I would be seen in the same light by minority monoracial individuals. I cannot be color-blind to myself and my own heritage however, so I must and can accept that I was born with a set of privileges for simply having a mixed race background.

Along with this acknowledgment, I personally feel as though a mixed race identity is simultaneously a penalty. The fascination and constant questioning makes me become an object rather than a person and there are countless times when I have felt and still feel as though who I am is a trend rather than an actual identity. Consequently, while the "what are you" questioning has always bothered me, it took me a while to realize and accept that these were in fact daily micro-aggressions. Defining part of my marginalized experience, I have been unable to explain or communicate this experience with a person who has a singular racial identifier and because of this, I am just now realizing that I have unfortunately normalized numerous micro-aggressions. "What are you" has become so engrained in my everyday life that I have an automatic answer for it; I memorized black, white, and Puerto Rican at the age of four and since that time I have always said my racial makeup in that exact order with no second thought. Rather than reciting a list of identities or giving a sassy, sarcastic response when approached with these questions, I intend to be more mindful and essentially voice why this common experience is not okay. In order for education and possible change to occur, I recognize that I must voice and share my own personal discomfort.

"Complimentary othering," an idea from Jessica M. Vasquez's *Blurred Borders for Some but Not "Others,"* was another privileged yet unfortunate experience that I tended to take pride in. Being a form of racial alienation, complimentary othering occurs when individuals are complimented for not being like others with their heritage; they are ascribed and thus possess a sense of superiority because they are not like the stereotypically negative aspects normally attributed to their race. From a young age, I was always referred to as the Oreo, and I naively wore that badge with pride. Being black on the outside and white on the inside, I assumed it to be the closest description of my racial makeup. However when involved in situations where the term Oreo was obviously referring to the way I acted or talked (implication of acting white despite having a black outer appearance), I still went along with the backhanded compliment rather than accepting it was a phrase to demean my African American roots and in turn reacting to the insult. In addition, I tended to go along with other racial "jokes" and innuendos that spoke directly to my heritage in regard to the singular minority identities (black, Hispanic). While I can confidently say that I have never been ashamed of my multiracial identity, I feel my young decisions to mock and not speak up show the inner conflict that existed in me, although I was completely unaware of its presence. Along with this, I was unintentionally reinforcing the oppressive implications that are placed on my people.

Unable to describe with a singular phrase, the associated penalty that I identified can result in an unsettling view of your internal self. While everyone shares the common experience of walking into a room and having an automatic perception placed on them, I believe the multiracial experience of perceptual attributions creates a more potent and exhausting identity crisis. Not only am I perceived immediately based on sole perceptions, my actions or speech sometimes clashes with the initial perception (seen through complimentary othering), and who I truly am does not match that either so I'm further depersonalized by the curiosity and assumptions of others.

Using the experiences that I have shared with the identified monoracial group, I believe that many strides can be made in regard to building intercultural relations on our campus. My main hope is that alternative storytelling, a major tenet of Greg Tanaka's framework that works to build an intercultural society, is integrated within our school systems. Although difficult because of the strict guidelines that teachers must follow, I am optimistic that storytelling activities will one day be included in curriculum and coursework. Enabling each individual with the power to share their own history, the embracement of vulnerability coupled with idealistic and positive hopes allows each person to take ownership of their life, feel comfortable with their own identity, and be more open and receptive to those with differing identities.

In relation to multiracial groups and monoracial groups, I feel alternative storytelling will be incredibly beneficial for both parties. There is a common archetype known as the "tragic mulatto" which refers to the common identity crisis that a mixed person faces. Through alternative storytelling, I believe an individual with multiple backgrounds can talk through their confusions and differing experiences to fully embrace all of who they are; I view this self-reflexive process as a written form of alternative storytelling for example, because I was able to not only share the things I've gone through but actually think about and interpret what was happening in my life.

With regard to monoracial groups, I feel as though they will equally benefit. Aside from positioning themselves in a supportive role to hear the differing side's perspective, they also have the opportunity to share their own experiences. It is amazing, because alternative storytelling gives everyone the ability to glimpse into the true reality of the opposite side. Because this hope is a long-term anticipation, I can utilize the alternative storytelling method in little conversations with people. For example, if faced with a situation where I cannot determine if the event was a hit or false alarm, I can engage in conversation to better build an understanding. Keeping the "assume best intentions" phrase in mind, I cannot assume that everyone knows how I interpreted a statement made; similarly, I cannot assume that everything I say to a person has the true intent that I mean to make.

While alternative storytelling ensures that I along with other participants don't compromise our being, personally being mindful of my own identity will also allow me to stay true to myself and not get lost when working with the identified differing group. As stated previously, I cannot be color-blind to my own identity. I cannot ignore the different aspects that make me up racially due to a fear of being further marginalized. Reflecting on my life thus far, there have been periods where I have been conflicted with my black and Hispanic side and/or apologetic with my white side. While I love talking about race and racial experiences and social justice, when it came to a personal event or interaction related to my own race, I struggled to find a balance between my differing identities. While I do believe that I have experienced a lot of growth in regard to my identity development, this assignment has shown me that there is a lot more to still uncover. I believe true understanding of yourself will not only allow for others to better understand you and your story but also put you in a better position to understand someone else, so my final hope is to continue working on my acceptance and introspective understanding in order to better recognize the viewpoints of others and foster an open dialogue with them as well.

In order to fully triangulate narratives and perspectives, I used the following sources:

Ball, J. A. (2010, March 16). The multiracial sheep IS the White supremacist fox. Black Agenda Report. Retrieved from http://www.blackagendareport.com/content/multiracial-sheep-white-supremacist-fox

Vasquez, J. M. (2010). Blurred borders for some but not "others": Racialization, "flexible ethnicity," gender and third-generation Mexican American identity. *Sociological Perspectives, 53*(1), 45–72.

• Appendix C •

Sample Mini-Autoethnography Midterm Assignment—Undergraduate Level

Education 508

TAKE-HOME MIDTERM EXAM: 5–7 double-spaced pages of AUTOETHNOGRAPHY (20 points): "Mini-autoethnography" is a form of self-study and action research that is designed to be a catalyst for individual growth along the cultural competence continuum. You will receive handouts and substantial practice prior to the distribution of your Take-Home Midterm Exam.

You may recall from chapter 1 that mini-autoethnography involves a clear and sustained focus upon at least three salient experiences, episodes, moments, or events from one's life.

Sample Mini-Autoethnography Midterm Questions

Select one of the questions below, and write a 5- to 7-double-spaced-page mini-autoethnography. You should use a story from your own lived experience as a springboard, and please be sure to respond to the question completely.

1. Where do I sit along the cultural competence continuum with regard to the cultural group on campus that I feel is most different from my own?

2. How might I participate in gaining the cultural competence to validate that intercultural group on campus?

3. How might I work to build cultural competence with that group by challenging the major tenets of my own cultural values?

4. How might I have misused the language that comprises "the cultural competence continuum," as a way to avoid rather than engage the naming of equity issues related specifically to structural racism, sexism, classism, homophobia, Islamophobia, etc.?

The points along the cultural continuum are listed below.

Cultural destructiveness: See the difference, stomp it out. The elimination of other people's cultures.

Cultural incapacity: See the difference, make it wrong. Belief in the superiority of one's own culture and behavior that disempowers another's culture.

Cultural blindness: See the difference, act like you don't. Acting as if the cultural differences you see do not matter, or not recognizing that there are differences among and between cultures.

Cultural precompetence: See the difference, respond inadequately. Awareness of the limitations of one's skills or an organization's practices when interacting with other cultural groups.

Cultural competence: See the difference, understand the difference that difference makes. Interacting with other cultural groups using the five essential elements of cultural competence:

- Name the differences: Assess cultural nuances.
- Claim the differences: Value diversity and equity.
- Reframe the differences: Manage the dynamics of difference and inequity.
- Train about differences: Adapt to diversity and equity.
- Change for differences: Institutionalize cultural knowledge of equity and inequity.

Cultural proficiency: See the difference, respond positively and affirmingly. Esteeming culture, knowing how to learn about individual and organizational culture, and interacting effectively in a variety of cultural environments toward equity and justice.

Midterm Tips, Based on Undergraduate Student–Faculty Correspondence

- *Tip 1:* Maintain the Language of "I" and "my."
- *Tip 2:* CHOOSE ONLY 3 salient events, episodes, or experiences to make your main point (e.g., a course, a camp, an annual event, an argument, a fight).
- *Tip 3:* Remember the cultural competence continuum (CCC) is cyclical, dynamic, and ongoing. One can't move, for example, from precompetence to competence with regard to ALL religious, race-ethnic, gender, or other cultural groups. The gerund, *-ing,* is crucial, as in "I am thinking, working, learning," and so on, for steering one's thinking and writing toward the main tenets of CCC. One could argue more strongly via autoethnography, for example: "I am working toward applying a cultural competence approach when considering the _____ religion." One could precede that comment with a statement about one's perspective; for example, "My precollege thoughts and actions regarding the idea of the _____ religion seem most aligned with cultural destructiveness on the cultural competence continuum, but I have been working and learning to apply more of a cultural competence approach to _____ religion."
- *Tip 4:* Begin answering the midterm question(s) you select by reframing the question(s) to personalize them. For example: Begin your response to Midterm Question 1 with one or more reflexive/complicit questions:

  1. "How does my precollege background seem to influence the religious/race-ethnic/gender/sexuality element of my cultural identity?" (CHOOSE ONE)

  2. If I choose religion: "What am I learning about my thoughts/actions toward ONE group on campus whose religious cultural identity seems most different from my own?"

  This type of reframing of the question will provide a stronger base for your autoethnography for yourself and your readers.

Autoethnography Midterm

EDCI 508—Dr. Hughes—Tues/Thurs 11:00–12:15pm—PE 206

Student Name _____

MIDTERM: Mini-Autoethnography Demonstration	4.00–3.65	3.64–3.00	2.99–2.40	Below 2.40
Triangulation of narratives (self-narrative; standpoint of at least one person who may agree with your narrative; and standpoint of at least one person who may disagree with your narrative)	**Exceeds Expected** application of triangulation concepts and processes discussed in class	**Meets Expected** application of triangulation concepts and processes discussed in class	**Below Expected** application of triangulation concepts and processes discussed in class	**Well Below Expected** application of triangulation concepts and processes discussed in class
Consideration of privilege and penalty	**Exceeds Expected** signs of sincerely wrestling with some of the privilege and penalty issues of your intercultural experiences	**Meets Expected** signs of sincerely wrestling with some of the privilege and penalty issues of your intercultural experiences	**Below Expected** signs of sincerely wrestling with some of the privilege and penalty issues of your intercultural experiences	**Well Below Expected** signs of sincerely wrestling with some of the privilege and penalty issues of your intercultural experiences
Reflexive thinking	**Exceeds Expected** ways of being explicit about assumptions, positions, self-critical of taken-for-granted knowledge and how it influences your cultural competence	**Meets Expected** ways of being explicit about assumptions, positions, self-critical of taken-for-granted knowledge and how it influences your cultural competence	**Below Expected** ways of being explicit about assumptions, positions, self-critical of taken-for-granted knowledge and how it influences your cultural competence	**Well Below Expected** ways of being explicit about assumptions, positions, self-critical of taken-for-granted knowledge and how it influences your cultural competence

(Continued)

(Continued)

MIDTERM: Mini-Autoethnography Demonstration	4.00–3.65	3.64–3.00	2.99–2.40	Below 2.40
Consideration of multiple levels of experiences; i.e., personal level (experiences alone), group level (your within-group experiences), and institutional level (your in-group experience in relation to the rest of the campus)	**Exceeds Expected** narratives that include multiple levels of your intercultural experiences	**Meets Expected** narratives that include multiple levels of your intercultural experiences	**Below Expected** narratives that include multiple levels of your intercultural experiences	**Well Below Expected** narratives that include multiple levels of your intercultural experiences
Consideration of struggles (problems) and hopes (possibilities)	**Exceeds Expected** clarity of expression and logical connections to struggles (problems) and hopes (possibilities) in narratives about intercultural experiences	**Meets Expected** clarity of expression and logical connections to struggles (problems) and hopes (possibilities) in narratives about intercultural experiences	**Below Expected** clarity of expression and logical connections to struggles (problems) and hopes (possibilities) in narratives about intercultural experiences	**Well Below Expected** clarity of expression and logical connections to struggles (problems) and hopes (possibilities) in narratives about intercultural experiences
	Clarity of expression also includes neat and complete work with few grammatical/spelling errors)	Clarity of expression also includes neat and complete work with few grammatical/spelling errors	Clarity of expression also includes neat and complete work with few grammatical/spelling errors	Clarity of expression also includes neat and complete work with few grammatical/spelling errors

Triangulation   _____   _____   _____   _____

Privilege/pen.   _____   _____   _____   _____

Reflexive   _____   _____   _____   _____

Multiple levels   _____   _____   _____   _____

Struggle/hope   _____   _____   _____   _____

SCORE   =   GRADE

_____   _____

• Appendix D •

Sample Syllabus for an Autoethnography Course—Graduate Level

The University of North Carolina at Chapel Hill School of Education EDUC 977-001: Autoethnography in/as Educational Research

Spring 2014 (Wednesdays, 1:00pm–3:50pm)
(Location: Peabody Hall, Room 010)

Professor:	Dr. Sherick A. Hughes
	Associate Professor
	Graduate Program Coordinator
	Cultural Studies and Literacies Program
School of Education Office:	212b Peabody Hall (PE)
Office phone:	919-XXX-XXXX
	office hours by appointment
Cell phone (confidential):	419-XXX-XXXX
E-mail:	shughes@email.unc.edu

A few key assignments (within the standard academic copyright guidelines) will come from the pioneering work of Ellis noted below; however, you don't need to purchase the book. The remaining readings for the course will come primarily from peer-reviewed academic journals.

Ellis, C. (2004). *The ethnographic I: A methodological novel about autoethnography.* Walnut Creek, CA: AltaMira Press.

General Information

Course Description and Objectives

Ethnography has a long tradition in the social sciences, practiced by scholars in anthropology, sociology, communication studies, education, social work, and other fields. In the past 20 years, autoethnography has emerged as a significant challenge to traditional social scientific research methods, including traditional ethnography.

Autoethnography is both process and product, both art and science, a reflexive research practice that uses the lens of the self (auto) to describe and write (graphy) about people and cultures (ethno). This course will introduce students to the methodological and theoretical roots of autoethnography and then guide them in becoming autoethnographic researchers.

This course will focus on the theory and practice of autoethnography, or "reading" significant patterns in everyday experience and connecting those patterns to the self and to broader social concerns. Because it would be impossible to teach everything about the theoretical underpinnings and method of autoethnography before having students start their own independent research, most of the semester will include a combination of reading models of autoethnography, reading methodological "how-to" works, doing writing exercises, and creating independent autoethnographic projects. At the end of this course, students will be able to do the following:

- Summarize the emergence of autoethnography from its epistemological and methodological roots.
- Critically analyze contemporary examples of autoethnography.
- Conduct observations and construct field notes.
- Evaluate the scholarly and artistic merits of autoethnographic writing.
- Write an autoethnographic manuscript.

Course Policies

Classroom Community

I am committed to providing an atmosphere of learning that is representative of diversity. I operate under the assumption that all of us have important insights to offer, but that each of our perspectives is limited. Students are asked to take a post-critical literacy approach to education autoethnographies, which involves negotiating the critique of self and others with a no-fault, collaboration, and consensus objective for learning. This approach relies on validation, commitment, and, to some degree, confidentiality within the class. It also relies heavily on the hits (perceived identity threats with triangulated evidence to support that perception), misses (no initial perceived identity threats with later triangulated evidence to reject that initial perception), and false alarms (perceived identity threats without triangulated evidence to support that perception) communicative approach. With the hits, misses, and false alarms approach, we may become more open to having our assumptions challenged in dyadic and larger group spaces within the classroom and to letting ourselves and others be correct and incorrect en route to transforming our understandings of self in relation to others. Students will be expected to play their part in creating a classroom environment where people are free to learn by challenging and being challenged by others' contributions. They will also be asked to remain respectful and sensitive to others while working to make our classroom environment productive and welcoming to everyone. This class will "succeed" if all of us embrace the challenge to read and think and talk in ways that challenge our taken-for-granted knowledge, ideologies, and habits of thought about education and schooling.

Attendance and Participation

The University of North Carolina attendance and participation goals are in effect in this course. All assignments are due in class on the assigned date for full credit. Papers not turned in during class may receive a penalty, unless arrangements are made with me ahead of time. If you know that you will miss an assignment due to a university-sponsored event, you must make arrangements with me to make up the work in advance.

Additional Accommodations

It is my honor and duty to provide you the accommodations to help you reach your highest potential in this course. So, if necessary, please take the following steps as soon as possible:

- Please bring a copy of our UNC letter verifying the accommodations needed.
- Make an appointment with me to go over the letter and discuss reasonable accommodations.

Academic Integrity

Students are expected to abide by the rules and regulations outlined by The Graduate School and the UNC Student Honor Code. Any form of academic dishonesty will result in a grade of "F" for the course. The UNC Student Honor Code exists to remind you of your responsibilities: (1) to work as hard as you can, (2) to learn as much as you can, and (3) to ensure always that the work you submit is your own (or that those portions of it that are based on outside sources are appropriately acknowledged via internal citation and references/bibliographies).

Assignments

In Class Work/Participation

This is not a lecture course. I will come each day prepared to facilitate discussion and in-class activities, and I ask that you come having read the entire assignment and reflected on it well enough to discuss it thoroughly in class. Reading is just the first step, however; often we come to really understand something only after we discuss it and/or practice it. Therefore, we will spend class time discussing the material in a seminar-style format, as well as doing activities and writing exercises designed to help you deepen your understanding and connect theory to practice. Quality class participation does not mean that you dominate every class period, but that you offer meaningful contributions on a regular basis throughout the semester. Individual students and student teams will take turns initiating/leading class discussions; to be negotiated on Day 1.

Writing Assignments

Particularly because this is a doctoral course, I am assuming that you have already mastered the basics of academic writing and can take this opportunity to hone your basic skills and stretch them by learning a new form of writing. Attention to grammar, style, clarity, organization, and proofreading are all basic expectations. ***Details for each of these assignments will be discussed further in class, but here are some general descriptions to let you know what you can expect.*** The writing assignments are as follows:

Critical Self-Reflexive Journaling

This assignment involves a record of careful reading/writing practice in the form of critical self-reflexive responses. At the ends of several designated class periods, you will have time to write at least briefly in your journal to connect the discussions of the day with your own emerging thoughts toward your own autoethnography. While most of this will be done in class, some *may* be done on your own outside of class time. You should keep your journal in a notebook of some sort and bring it to class each day. I will periodically check your journal. Overall, the journal will be worth 20% of your course grade.

Autoethnography Part 1: Research

Your major projects for this course will all revolve around writing your own autoethnography, with the potential for submitting it for conference presentation and publication. The project will involve the following processes: (a) locating a phenomenon of interest; (b) constructing an autoethnographic research question; (c) finding a relevant and current cultural group experience in relation to your own autobiography to study in depth; (d) reading the current literature that is linked to that experience; (e) observing and writing field notes, triangulating, and translating across narratives; and (f) in some cases, member checking (20% of your course grade). **Due February 19, 2014**

Autoethnography Part 2: Midterm—Writing

Getting down the results of your research into a preliminary draft (20% of your course grade). **Due March 5, 2014**

Autoethnography Part 3: Revising

Getting and giving feedback to peers on their projects using Hughes, Pennington, and Makris's (2012) rubric for autoethnography published in *Educational Researcher* and then using feedback to begin revising your autoethnography into a final publishable format (20% of your course grade).
Due March 26, 2014

Autoethnography Part 4: Presenting Your Work

Presenting your work to the class (conference style, 10–15 minutes) (20% of your course grade). **April 16, 2014**

Publishable Version Along With Journal (Part of Your Participation)

Due: April 23, 2014

Evaluation

Assignments

Journaling	20/100
Autoethnography Part 1	20/100
Autoethnography Part 2	20/100
Autoethnography Part 3	20/100
Autoethnography Part 4	20/100
TOTAL	100/100

Grading Scale

Consistent with The Graduate School of UNC–Chapel Hill: H (93–100), P (92–80), L (79–60), and F (< 60).

Course Schedule

This schedule is subject to change, so please bring your syllabus to class and note any announced deviations from the initial plan. While the major assignments will not change, I reserve the right to alter the course activities if necessary to promote student learning. Please do the assigned reading before class and keep up.

Date	Unit	Assignments and Reading
Week 1 Jan. 8	Introduction to Autoethnography in/as Educational Research	No assignment due—Hughes PowerPoint and interactive session
Week 2 Jan. 15	Getting into a culture and looking around	**Applying the Rubric to Autoethnographies** Evans, K. D. (2007). Welcome to Ruth's world: An autoethnography concerning the interview of an elderly woman. *Qualitative Inquiry, 13*(2), 282–291. Meghan and Nitasha Laubscher, L., & Powell, S. (2003). Skinning the drum: Teaching about diversity as "other." *Harvard Educational Review, 73*(2), 203–224. Derrick and Sharon **In-class journaling**
Week 3 Jan. 22	Historical perspective on ethnography	**Applying the Rubric for Readings About Autoethnography** Walford, G. (2009). For ethnography. *Ethnography and Education, 4*(3), 271–282. Sharon and Esmeralda
		Mitra, R. (2010). Doing ethnography, being an ethnographer: The autoethnographic research process and I. *Journal of Research Practice, 6*(1). http://jrp.icaap.org/index.php/jrp/article/view/184/182 Nitasha and Meghan
Week 4 Jan. 29	Historical perspective and emergence of autoethnography	*The Ethnographic I* (Ellis—writing prompt week 1) **Sherick A. Hughes** **In-class journaling**
Week 5 Feb. 5	Nuts and bolts of observing, taking field notes, and reflecting	**Autoethnography Part 1: Research** Hughes, S. A., Pennington, J. L., & Makris, S. (2012). Translating autoethnography across the AERA standards: Toward understanding autoethnographic scholarship as empirical research. *Educational Researcher, 41*(6), 209–219. Meghan and Esmeralda

Date	Unit	Assignments and Reading
		Hughes, S. A. (2008). Teaching theory as "other" to White urban practitioners: Mining and priming Freirean critical pedagogy in resistant bodies. In J. Diem & R. J. Helfenbein (Eds.), *Unsettling beliefs: Teaching theory to teachers* (pp. 245–272). Greenwich, CT: Information Age. Nitasha and Sharon
Week 6	Observing and writing critically	***The Ethnographic I* (Ellis—writing prompt week 2)** Pearson, H. (2010). Complicating intersectionality through the identities of a hard of hearing Korean adoptee: An autoethnography. *Equity & Excellence in Education, 43*(3), 341–356. Meghan and Sharon Hairston, K. R., & Strickland, M. J. (2011). Contrapuntal orchestration: An exploration of an interaction between researchers' and teachers' stories around the concept of culture. *Race Ethnicity and Education, 14*(5), 631–653. Esmeralda and Nitasha
Feb. 12		**In-class journaling**
Week 7	Theory and method **Berry (2005) to Skype in (TBA)** **Part 1: DUE!**	***The Ethnographic I* (Ellis—writing prompt week 3)** Hughes, S. A. (2008). Toward "good enough methods" for autoethnography in a graduate education course: Trying to resist the matrix with another promising red pill. *Educational Studies, 43*(2), 125–143. Esmeralda and Sharon
		Berry, T. R. (2005). Black on Black education: Personally engaged pedagogy for/by African American pre-service teachers. *Urban Review, 37*(1), 31–48. Meghan and Nitasha
Feb. 19		**In-class journaling**
Week 8	Theory and method AND a critique of the method	**MIDTERM WORKSHOP** Delamont, S. (2009). The only honest thing: Autoethnography, reflexivity and small crises in fieldwork. *Ethnography and Education, 4*(1), 51–63. Esmeralda and Sharon

(Continued)

(Continued)

Date	Unit	Assignments and Reading
Feb. 26		Delamont, S. (2007, February). Arguments against auto-ethnography. *Qualitative Researcher, 4*, 2–4. http://www.cardiff.ac.uk/socsi/qualiti/QualitativeResearcher/QR_Issue4_Feb07.pdf Nitasha and Meghan
Week 9	Getting it down/writing it up	***The Ethnographic I* (Ellis—writing prompt week 4)** Chatham-Carpenter, A. (2010). "Do thyself no harm": Protecting ourselves as autoethnographers. *Journal of Research Practice, 6*(1). http://jrp.icaap.org/index.php/jrp/article/view/213 Sharon and Meghan
		Chavez, M. S. (2012). Autoethnography, a Chicana's methodological research tool: The role of storytelling for those who have no choice but to do critical race theory. *Equity & Excellence in Education, 45*(2), 334–348. Esmeralda and Nitasha
Mar. 5	**Part 2: MIDTERM DUE**	**In-class journaling**
Mar. 12	**Spring Break**	**NO CLASS**
Week 10	Performative autoethnography (Conquergood video)	**Assignment Part 3 Workshop** Correa, E., & Lovegrove, D. (2012). Making the rice: Latina performance *testimonios* of hybridity, assimilation, and resistance. *Equity & Excellence in Education, 45*(2), 349–361. Esmeralda and Sharon Moreira, C. (2008). Life in so many acts. *Qualitative Inquiry, 14*(4), 590–612. Nitasha and Meghan
Mar. 19		**In-class journaling**
Week 11	Analyzing recent exemplars **Cozart (2010) to Skype in (TBA)**	**(Choose 1 to read and analyze for the class)** Hughes, S. A. (2008). Maggie and me: A Black professor and a White urban school teacher connect autoethnography to critical race pedagogy. *Educational Foundations, 22*(3/4), 73–95. Meghan

Date	Unit	Assignments and Reading
		Theoharis, G. (2007). Social justice educational leaders and resistance: Toward a theory of social justice leadership. *Educational Administration Quarterly, 43*(2), 221–258. Sharon
		Garza, E., Jr. (2008). Autoethnography of a first-time superintendent: Challenges to leadership for social justice. *Journal of Latinos and Education, 7*(2), 163–176. Nitasha
		Cozart, S. C. (2010). When the spirit shows up: An autoethnography of spiritual reconciliation with the academy. *Educational Studies, 46*(2), 250–269. Esmeralda
Mar. 26		**In-class journaling**
Week 12	**Part 3: Revisions Due!**	**Preliminary draft due** (bring 3 copies—1 to turn in and 2 to exchange with classmates for feedback)
   Apr. 2	**No Class** Assignment: Revise autoethnographies toward the goal of being publishable	**AERA-2014 in Philadelphia, PA** Hughes presentations
Week 13	Analyzing recent exemplars **Pennington (2007) to Skype in (TBA)**	Supplementary readings (samples of autoethnography) **(Choose 1 to read and analyze for the class)** Pennington, J. L. (2007). Silence in the classroom/whispers in the halls: Autoethnography as pedagogy in White pre-service teacher education. *Race Ethnicity and Education, 10,* 93–113. Nitasha Smagorinsky, P. (2011). Confessions of a mad professor: An autoethnographic consideration of neuroatypicality, extranormativity, and education. *Teachers College Record, 113*(8), 1700–1732. Meghan McClellan, P. (2012). Race, gender, and leadership identity: An autoethnography of reconciliation. *International Journal of Qualitative Studies in Education, 25*(1), 89–100. Esmeralda

(Continued)

(Continued)

Date	Unit	Assignments and Reading
Apr. 9		DeLeon, A. P. (2010). How do I begin to tell a story that has not been told? Anarchism, autoethnography, and the middle ground. *Equity & Excellence in Education, 43*(4), 398–413. Sharon **Future Reading to Consider After Semester Ends** Murray, L., Pushor, D., & Renihan, P. (2012). Reflections on the ethics-approval process. *Qualitative Inquiry, 18*(1), 43–54. White, C. J., Sakiestewa, N., & Shelley, C. (1998). TRIO: The unwritten legacy. *Journal of Negro Education, 67*(4), 444–454.
Week 14 Apr. 16	**Final Presentations**	**Presentations**
Week 15 Apr. 23	Final Exam Week	**Final Autoethnography Paper Due: Publishable Version**

• Glossary •

action research: A type of applied critical social research that aims to address perceived problematic situations in given cultural contexts through a process in which researchers initiate and evaluate interventions.

assemblage: Data collection method designed to represent a multilayered moment; relies on literature, items, and accounts assembled in order to respond to the central research question(s).

autoethnography: The study of the self; related to autobiography, narrative, and ethnography, but unique from a research perspective in that the researcher is the subject of study.

candidate studies: Studies with the potential to be selected for meta-synthesis.

commensurate: Similar, able to fit together.

critical social research: Research that focuses on the use of critical theory; encompasses a broad range of approaches and disciplines.

critical social theory: Theorizing that intends to move beyond understanding or explaining social phenomena to critiquing them and toward influencing social change.

empirical: Based on or validated by observational or experiential data in addition to or instead of traditional theory or logic.

epistemology: Theory of knowledge, ways of knowing, or ways of thinking about how one knows what one knows; asks, "What is the relationship between the knower and the known?"

ethnography: The study of individuals within their communities; name is derived from two Greek words— *graphein* (to write) and *ethnoi* (the nations, or the others).

legitimizing (legitimation): The process of making something "legitimate." In the context of scholarly research, this involves the existence and prevalence of habitual social acts, positions, structures, and practices that become taken-for-granted (legitimated) objects with established rules and norms for participation.

meta-autoethnography: A systematic process of critical reflexive thinking and synthesis of one's own previous autoethnography work in order to learn from it and through it.

meta-synthesis of individualized and coauthored autoethnography (MICA): A systematic approach to conducting meta-synthesis that maintains the integrity of individual studies; a method through which qualitative researchers can synthesize two or more autoethnographies of interest by other authors and thereby gain emerging insights from considering how the pieces work in relation to each other.

methodology: The established and evolving approach to and foundation of a research study.

methods: The actual techniques, tools, or means used for data collection and analysis.

ontology: Theory concerned with ways of being, or ways of thinking about being.

paradigms: Various perspectives in research methodology, or sets of assumptions about how the world operates and what influences human actions and activities.

postmodernism: Paradigm in research methodology that asserts that there are many ways to see the world and that reality is fluid and changing.

postpositivism: Paradigm in research methodology that views research as a limited way to try to find the truth about a topic.

poststructuralism: Movement asserting that each individual is able to make new and unique meanings of texts—there are no authoritative interpretations and meanings.

problematizing: The act of considering or treating something as a problem; may involve a teaching and learning project intended to introduce counterevidence that challenges what individuals think they know about particular subjects.

qualitative research: Research methodology that relies on multiple types of data and analysis that can respond to the "how" and "why" questions of a study.

realist ontology: Theory concerning questions about the nature of reality and of being. Asserts that if something can be qualified and quantified, then it must be real, and that a cultural reality exists that can be at least partially captured.

reflexivity: A qualitative researcher's in-depth awareness of her or his social biases and other human flaws. Involves a process of constant critical reflection upon oneself and the theoretical framing, data collection, and interpretation processes that one engages throughout the research process.

rigor: Adherence to strict standards of implementation in research.

social theory: Theory related to the study of humans as social beings.

subalterns: Excluded, oppressed, or marginalized persons.

subjectivity: Personal views and perspectives related to understanding research.

symbolic interactionism: Sociological theory for explaining human communication as a pattern of symbols developed, shared, and resisted by human interlocutors.

theoretical frameworks: Specific perspectives that researchers use to explore, interpret, understand, or explain lived experiences and the communicative behavior of participants and events within the larger cultural contexts they are studying.

triangulation: The gathering of evidence from at least three sources to examine a topic or phenomenon of interest.

tropes: Commonly repeated words, phrases, and images that may be used as rhetorical devices to provide clarity and for informative and persuasive purposes.

• References •

Adams, T. E. (2008). A review of narrative ethics. *Qualitative Inquiry, 14*(2), 175–194.

Adams, T. E., & Holman Jones, S. (2008). Autoethnography is queer. In N. K. Denzin, Y. S. Lincoln, & L. T. Smith (Eds.), *Handbook of critical and indigenous methodologies* (pp. 373–390). Thousand Oaks, CA: Sage.

Akintoye, A. (2015, July 3). *Developing theoretical and conceptual frameworks.* PowerPoint presentation delivered at the EDMIC 2015 Research Workshop, Obafemi Awolowo University, Ile-Ife, Nigeria. Retrieved from http://jedm.oauife.edu.ng/wp-content/uploads/2015/03/Akintola-Akintoye_Developing-Theoretical-and-Conceptual-Frameworks.pdf

Alexander, M. (2010). *The new Jim Crow: Mass incarceration in the age of colorblindness.* New York: New Press.

Anderson, L. (2006). Analytic autoethnography. *Journal of Contemporary Ethnography, 35*(4), 373–395.

Anderson, N. (1923). *The hobo: The sociology of the homeless man.* Chicago: University of Chicago Press.

Anfara, V. A. Jr., & Mertz, N. T. (Eds.). (2006). *Theoretical frameworks in qualitative research.* Thousand Oaks, CA: Sage.

Anzaldúa, G. (1987). *Borderlands/la frontera: The new mestiza.* San Francisco: Aunt Lute Books.

Atkinson, P., Coffey, A., Delamont, S., Lofland, J., & Lofland, L. (Eds.). (2001). *Handbook of ethnography.* Thousand Oaks, CA: Sage.

Attard, K., & Armour, K. M. (2005). Learning to become a learning professional: Reflections on one year of teaching. *European Journal of Teacher Education, 28*(2), 195–207.

Austin, J., & Hickey, A. (2007). Autoethnography and teacher development. *International Journal of Interdisciplinary Social Sciences, 2*, 1–8.

Autrey, P. K. (2003). *The trouble with girls: Autoethnography and the classroom* (Doctoral dissertation, Louisiana State University).

Avalos-C'deBaca, F. (2002). We do not want you to be human, we want you to be right: Dilemmas of legitimacy in environments of privilege. In L. Vargas (Ed.), *Women faculty of color in the White classroom: Narratives on the pedagogical implications of teacher diversity.* New York: Peter Lang.

Bacchi, C. (2012). Why study problematizations? Making politics visible. *Open Journal of Political Science, 2*(1), 1–8. doi:10.4236/ojps.2012.21001

Banks, S. P., & Banks, A. (2000). Reading the critical life: Autoethnography as pedagogy. *Communication Education, 49*(3), 233–238.

Bartleet, B., & Ellis, C. (Eds.). (2009). *Music autoethnographies.* Queensland: Australian Academic Press.

Behar, R. (1993). *Translated woman: Crossing the border with Esperanza's story.* Boston: Beacon Press.

Behar, R. (1996). *The vulnerable observer: Anthropology that breaks your heart.* Boston: Beacon Press.

Bell, L. A. (2002). Sincere fictions: The pedagogical challenges of preparing White teachers for multicultural classrooms. *Equity & Excellence in Education, 35*(3), 236–244.

Benson, T. (1981). Another shootout in cowtown. *Quarterly Journal of Speech, 67*, 347–406.

Berger, P. L., & Luckmann, T. (1967). *The social construction of reality: A treatise in the sociology of knowledge.* New York: Anchor Books.

Berliner, D. C. (2014). Effects of inequality and poverty vs. teachers and schooling on America's youth. *Teachers College Record, 116*(1). Retrieved from http://www.tcrecord.org/content.asp?contentid=16889

Berry, K. (2007). Embracing the catastrophe: Gay body seeks acceptance. *Qualitative Inquiry, 13*(2), 259–281.

Berry, T. R. (2005). Black on Black education: Personally engaged pedagogy for/by African American pre-service teachers. *Urban Review, 37*(1), 31–48.

Bochner, A. P., & Ellis, C. (1995). Telling and living: Narrative co-construction and the practices of interpersonal relationships.

In W. Leeds-Hurwitz (Ed.), *Social approaches to communication* (pp. 201–213). New York: Guilford Press.

Boote, D. N., & Beile, P. (2005). Scholars before researchers: On the centrality of the dissertation literature review in research preparation. *Educational Researcher, 34*(3), 3–15.

Boufoy-Bastick, B. (2004). Auto-interviewing, auto-ethnography and critical incident methodology for eliciting a self-conceptualised worldview. *Forum Qualitative Sozialforschung/Forum: Qualitative Social Research, 5*(1). Retrieved from http://www.qualitative-research.net/index.php/fqs/article/view/651/1410

Bowers, C. A. (1984). *The promise of theory: Education and the politics of cultural change.* New York: Longman.

Boyd, D. (2008). Autoethnography as a tool for transformative learning about White privilege. *Journal of Transformative Studies, 6*(3), 212–225.

Briskin, L. (1990). *Feminist pedagogy: Teaching and learning liberation.* Ottawa: Canadian Research Institute for the Advancement of Women/ICREF.

Bryant, A., & Charmaz, K. (Eds.). (2007). *The SAGE handbook of grounded theory.* Thousand Oaks, CA: Sage.

Bryman, A. (2004). Triangulation. In M. S. Lewis-Beck, A. Bryman, & T. F. Liao (Eds.), *The SAGE encyclopedia of social science research methods.* Thousand Oaks, CA: Sage. Retrieved from http://srmo.sagepub.com/view/the-sage-encyclopedia-of-social-science-research-methods/n1031.xml

Bullough, R. V., & Pinnegar, S. (2001). Guidelines for quality in autobiographical forms of self-study research. *Educational Researcher, 30*(3), 13–21.

Camangian, P. (2010). Starting with self: Teaching autoethnography to foster critically caring literacies. *Research in the Teaching of English, 45*(2), 179–204.

Cann, C. N., & DeMeulenaere, E. J. (2012). Critical co-constructed autoethnography. *Cultural Studies ↔ Critical Methodologies, 12*(2), 146–158. doi:10.1177/1532708611435214

Carless, D. (2012). Negotiating sexuality and masculinity in school sport: An autoethnography. *Sport, Education and Society, 17*(5), 607–625.

Chang, H. (2008). *Autoethnography as method.* Walnut Creek, CA: Left Coast Press.

Charmaz, K. (1983). The grounded theory method: An explication and interpretation. In R. M. Emerson (Ed.), *Contemporary field research: A collection of readings* (pp. 109–125). Prospect Heights, IL: Waveland.

Chatham-Carpenter, A. (2010). "Do thyself no harm": Protecting ourselves as autoethnographers. *Journal of Research Practice, 6*(1). Retrieved from http://jrp.icaap.org/index.php/jrp/article/view/213

Chavez, M. S. (2012). Autoethnography, a Chicana's methodological research tool: The role of storytelling for those who have no choice but to do critical race theory. *Equity & Excellence in Education, 45*(2), 334–348.

Chinn, P. L., & Kramer, M. K. (1999). *Theory and nursing: A systematic approach* (5th ed.). St. Louis: Mosby.

Cleveland, D. (2005). Creating productive space: Approaching diversity and social justice from a privilege perspective in teacher education. In S. A. Hughes (Ed.), *What we still don't know about teaching race: How to talk about it in the classroom.* Lewiston, NY: Edwin Mellen Press.

Clough, P. (2009). Finding God in Wellworth High School: More legitimations of story-making as research. *Ethnography and Education, 4*(3), 347–356.

Coffey, A., & Atkinson, P. (1996). *Making sense of qualitative data: Complementary research strategies.* Thousand Oaks, CA: Sage.

Coia, L., & Taylor, M. (2013). Uncovering our feminist pedagogy: A co/autoethnography. *Studying Teacher Education, 9*(1), 3–17.

Collins, P. H. (1990). *Black feminist thought: Knowledge, consciousness, and the politics of empowerment.* Boston: Unwin Hyman.

Collins, P. H. (2000). *Black feminist thought: Knowledge, consciousness, and the politics of empowerment* (2nd ed.). New York: Routledge.

Corey, S. (1953). *Action research to improve school practices.* New York: Teachers College, Columbia University.

Corradetti, C. (n.d.). The Frankfurt School and critical theory. In *Internet Encyclopedia of Philosophy.* Retrieved from http://www.iep.utm.edu/frankfur

Correa, E., & Lovegrove, D. (2012). Making the rice: Latina performance *testimonios* of hybridity, assimilation, and resistance. *Equity & Excellence in Education, 45*(2), 349–361.

Cozart, S. C. (2010). When the spirit shows up: An autoethnography of spiritual reconciliation with the academy. *Educational Studies, 46*(2), 250–269.

Crotty, M. J. (1998). *The foundations of social research: Meaning and perspective in the research process.* London: Sage.

Dalton, M. (2003). Media studies and emancipatory praxis: An autoethnographic essay on critical pedagogy. *Journal of Film and Video, 55*(2/3), 88–97.

Deacon, R. (2000). Theory as practice: Foucault's concept of problematization. *Telos, 118,* 127–142.

Delamont, S. (2007, February). Arguments against auto-ethnography. *Qualitative Researcher, 4,* 2–4. Retrieved from http://www.cardiff.ac.uk/socsi/qualiti/QualitativeResearcher/QR_Issue4_Feb07.pdf

Delamont, S. (2009). The only honest thing: Autoethnography, reflexivity and small crises in fieldwork. *Ethnography and Education, 4*(1), 51–63.

DeLeon, A. P. (2010). How do I begin to tell a story that has not been told? Anarchism, autoethnography, and the middle ground. *Equity & Excellence in Education, 43*(4), 398–413.

Denshire, S., & Lee, A. (2013). Conceptualizing autoethnography as assemblage: Accounts of occupational therapy practice. *International Journal of Qualitative Methods, 12,* 221–236.

Denshire, S., & Lee, A. (2014). *Conceptualising autoethnography as assemblage: Accounts of occupational therapy practice.* PowerPoint presentation, University of Technology, Sydney.

Denzin, N. K. (1978). *The research act: A theoretical introduction to*

sociological methods. New York: McGraw-Hill.

Denzin, N. K. (1989). *Interpretive biography.* Newbury Park, CA: Sage.

Denzin, N. K. (1995). *The alcoholic society: Addiction and recovery of the self.* New Brunswick, NJ: Transaction.

Denzin, N. K. (1997). *Interpretive ethnography: Ethnographic practices for the twenty-first century.* Thousand Oaks, CA: Sage.

Denzin, N. K. (2001). *Interpretive interactionism.* Thousand Oaks, CA: Sage.

Denzin, N. K. (2003). *Performance ethnography: Critical pedagogy and the politics of culture.* Thousand Oaks, CA: Sage.

Denzin, N. K. (2014). *Interpretive autoethnography* (2nd ed.). Thousand Oaks, CA: Sage.

Denzin, N. K., & Lincoln, Y. S. (Eds.). (1994). *Handbook of qualitative research.* Thousand Oaks, CA: Sage.

Denzin, N. K., & Lincoln, Y. S. (Eds.). (2000). *Handbook of qualitative research* (2nd ed.). Thousand Oaks, CA: Sage.

Denzin, N. K., & Lincoln, Y. S. (Eds.). (2005). *The SAGE handbook of qualitative research* (3rd ed.). Thousand Oaks, CA: Sage.

Denzin, N. K., & Lincoln, Y. S. (2008a). Introduction: The discipline and practice of qualitative research. In N. K. Denzin & Y. S. Lincoln (Eds.), *Collecting and interpreting qualitative materials* (3rd ed., pp. 1–43). Thousand Oaks, CA: Sage.

Denzin, N. K., & Lincoln, Y. S. (Eds.). (2008b). *Strategies of qualitative*

inquiry (3rd ed.). Thousand Oaks, CA: Sage.

Denzin, N. K., & Lincoln, Y. S. (2011). Introduction: The discipline and practice of qualitative research. In N. K. Denzin & Y. S. Lincoln (Eds.), *The SAGE handbook of qualitative research* (4th ed., pp. 1–20). Thousand Oaks, CA: Sage.

Denzin, N. K., Lincoln, Y. S., & Smith, L. T. (Eds.). (2008). *Handbook of critical and indigenous methodologies.* Thousand Oaks, CA: Sage.

Dethloff, C. (2005). *A principal in transition: An autoethnography* (Doctoral dissertation, Texas A&M University).

Diem, J., & Helfenbein, R. J. (Eds.). (2008). *Unsettling beliefs: Teaching theory to teachers.* Greenwich, CT: Information Age.

Diversi, M., & Moreira, C. (2009). *Betweener talk: Decolonizing knowledge production, pedagogy, and praxis.* Walnut Creek, CA: Left Coast Press.

Dowling, M. (2006). Approaches to reflexivity in qualitative research. *Nurse Researcher, 13*(3), 7–21.

Dowling, M. (2008). Reflexivity. In L. M. Given (Ed.), *The SAGE encyclopedia of qualitative research methods.* Thousand Oaks, CA: Sage.

Duarte, F. P. (2007). Using autoethnography in the scholarship of teaching and learning: Reflective practice from "the other side of the mirror." *International Journal for the Scholarship of Teaching and Learning, 1*(2), 1–11.

Duncan, M. (2004). Autoethnography: Critical appreciation of an emerging art. *International Journal of Qualitative Methods, 3*(4). Retrieved from

http://www.ualberta.ca/~iiqm/
backissues/3_4/pdf/duncan.pdf

Duran, R. P., Eisenhart, M. A.,
Erickson, F. D., Grant, C. A., Green,
J. L., Hedges, L. V., & Schneider, B.
L. (2006). Standards for reporting
on empirical social science
research in AERA publications:
American Educational Research
Association. *Educational Researcher,
35*(6), 33–40.

Elder, J., Bremser, P., & Sheridan, M.
(2007). *Assigning personal narratives
across the disciplines: Exploring
pedagogies and tools.* Middlebury
College. Retrieved from https://
segueuserfiles.middlebury.edu/
ctlrworkshops07/Assigning%20
Personal%20Narratives%20
across%20the%20Disciplines.doc

Eldridge, L. (2012). A collaged
reflection on my art teaching: A visual
autoethnography. *Journal of Social
Theory in Art Education, 32,* 70–79.

Ellis, C. (1991). Sociological
introspection and emotional
experience. *Symbolic Interaction,
14*(1), 23–50.

Ellis, C. (1999). Heartfelt
autoethnography. *Qualitative Health
Research, 9*(5), 669–683.

Ellis, C. (2004). *The ethnographic
I: A methodological novel about
autoethnography.* Walnut Creek, CA:
AltaMira Press.

Ellis, C. (2007). Telling secrets,
revealing lives: Relational ethics
in research with intimate others.
Qualitative Inquiry, 13(1), 3–29.
doi:10.1177/1077800406294947

Ellis, C. (2008). Do we need to know?
Qualitative Inquiry, 14(7), 1314–1320.

Ellis, C. (2009). *Revision:
Autoethnographic reflections of life

and work.* Walnut Creek, CA: Left
Coast Press.

Ellis, C., Adams, T. E., & Bochner,
A. P. (2011). Autoethnography:
An overview. *Forum Qualitative
Sozialforschung/Forum: Qualitative
Social Research, 12*(1). Retrieved
from http://nbn-resolving.de/
urn:nbn:de:0114-fqs1101108

Ellis, C., & Bochner, A. P. (2000).
Autoethnography, personal narrative,
reflexivity: Researcher as subject.
In N. K. Denzin & Y. S. Lincoln (Eds.),
Handbook of qualitative research (2nd
ed., pp. 733–768). Thousand Oaks,
CA: Sage.

Ellis, C., Kiesinger, C. E., & Tillmann-
Healy, L. M. (1997). Interactive
interviewing: Talking about emotional
experience. In R. Hertz (Ed.),
Reflexivity and voice (pp. 119–149).
Thousand Oaks, CA: Sage.

Epictetus. (1920). *The golden
sayings of Epictetus: With the Hymn
of Cleanthes* (H. Crossley, Trans.).
London: Macmillan.

Erickson, F. (2011). A history of
qualitative inquiry in social and
educational research. In N. K. Denzin
& Y. S. Lincoln (Eds.), *The SAGE
handbook of qualitative research* (4th
ed., pp. 43–60). Thousand Oaks, CA:
Sage.

Ettorre, E. (2013). Drug user
researchers as autoethnographers:
"Doing reflexivity" with women drug
users. *Substance Use & Misuse, 48*(13),
1377–1385.

Evans, K. D. (2007). Welcome to
Ruth's world: An autoethnography
concerning the interview of an elderly
woman. *Qualitative Inquiry, 13*(2),
282–291.

Fals Borda, O. (2006). Participatory
(action) research in social theory:

Origins and challenges. In P. Reason
& H. Bradbury (Eds.), *Handbook of
action research: Participative inquiry
and practice* (pp. 27–37). London:
SAGE.

Feldman, A. (2003). Validity and
quality in self-study. *Educational
Researcher, 32,* 26–28.

Fine, M. (1994). Working the hyphens:
Reinventing self and other in
qualitative research. In N. K. Denzin
& Y. S. Lincoln (Eds.), *Handbook
of qualitative research* (pp. 70–82).
Thousand Oaks, CA: Sage.

Flores Carmona, J., & Luschen, K. V.
(Eds.). (2014). *Crafting critical stories:
Toward pedagogies and methodologies
of collaboration, inclusion, and voice.*
New York: Peter Lang.

Foster, K., McAllister, M., & O'Brien,
L. (2006). Extending the boundaries:
Autoethnography as an emergent
method in mental health nursing
research. *International Journal of
Mental Health Nursing, 15*(1), 44–53.

Foucault, M. (1977). *Language,
counter-memory, practice: Selected
essays and interviews* (D. F. Bouchard,
Ed.; S. Simon, Trans.). Ithaca, NY:
Cornell University Press.

Foucault, M. (1985). *Discourse
and truth: The problematization of
parrhesia* (J. Pearson, Ed.). Evanston,
IL: Northwestern University Press.

Fox, K. (2008). Rethinking experience:
What do we mean by this word
"experience"? *Journal of Experiential
Education, 31*(1), 36–54.

Frank, A. W. (1995). *The wounded
storyteller: Body, illness, and ethics.*
Chicago: University of Chicago Press.

Freire, P. (1972). *Pedagogy of the
oppressed.* Harmondsworth: Penguin
Books. (Original work published 1968)

Freire, P. (1974). *Education for critical consciousness.* London: Sheed and Ward.

Freund, A. M., & Ritter, J. O. (2009). Midlife crisis: A debate. *Gerontology, 55*(5), 582–591.

Gadotti, M. (1994). *Reading Paulo Freire: His life and work.* Albany: State University of New York Press.

Gale, K., & Wyatt, J. (2009). *Between the two: A nomadic inquiry into collaborative writing and subjectivity.* Newcastle upon Tyne: Cambridge Scholars.

Gale, K., Pelias, R., Russell, L., Spry, T., & Wyatt, J. (2013). Intensity: A collaborative autoethnography. *International Review of Qualitative Research, 6*(1), 165–180.

Gannon, S. (2006). The (im) possibilities of writing the self-writing: French poststructural theory and autoethnography. *Cultural Studies ↔ Critical Methodologies, 6*(4), 474–495.

Garza, E., Jr. (2008). Autoethnography of a first-time superintendent: Challenges to leadership for social justice. *Journal of Latinos and Education, 7*(2), 163–176.

Giroux, H. A. (1983). *Theory and resistance in education: A pedagogy for the opposition.* Westport, CT: Bergin & Garvey.

Giroux, H. A. (1996). Is there a place for cultural studies in colleges of education? In H. Giroux, C. Lankshear, P. McLaren, & M. Peters (Eds.), *Counternarratives: Cultural studies and critical pedagogies in postmodern spaces* (pp. 41–58). New York: Routledge.

Goffman E. (1963). *Stigma: Notes on the management of spoiled identity.* Englewood Cliffs, NJ: Prentice Hall.

Goodall, H. L., Jr. (1989). *Casing a promised land: The autobiography of an organizational detective as cultural ethnographer.* Carbondale, IL: Southern Illinois University Press.

Goodall, H. L., Jr. (2000). *Writing the new ethnography.* Walnut Creek, CA: AltaMira Press.

Goodall, H. L., Jr. (2006). *A need to know: The clandestine history of a CIA family.* Walnut Creek, CA: AltaMira Press.

Gordon, V. (1987). *Black women, feminism, and Black liberation: Which way?* Chicago: Third World Press.

Grant, A. (2010). Writing the reflexive self: An autoethnography of alcoholism and the impact of psychotherapy culture. *Journal of Psychiatric and Mental Health Nursing, 17*(7), 577–582.

Guba, E. G. (1990). The alternative paradigm dialog. In E. G. Guba (Ed.), *The paradigm dialog* (pp. 17–30). Newbury Park, CA: Sage.

Guba, E. G., & Lincoln, Y. S. (1989). *Fourth generation evaluation.* Newbury Park, CA: Sage.

Gurin, P., & Nagda, B. A. (2006). Getting to the what, how and why of diversity on campus. *Educational Researcher, 35*(1), 20–24.

Hairston, K. R., & Strickland, M. J. (2011). Contrapuntal orchestration: An exploration of an interaction between researchers' and teachers' stories around the concept of culture. *Race Ethnicity and Education, 14*(5), 631–653.

Hamann, E. T., & Harklau, L. (2010). Education in the new Latino diaspora. In E. G. Murillo Jr., S. A. Villenas, R. T. Galván, J. S. Muñoz, C. Martínez, & M. Machado-Casas (Eds.), *Handbook of Latinos and education: Theory, research, and practice* (pp. 157–169). New York: Routledge.

Hamilton, M., Smith, L., & Worthington, K. (2008). Fitting the methodology with the research: An exploration of narrative, self-study and auto-ethnography. *Studying Teacher Education, 4*(1), 17–28.

Hancock, S. D., Allen, A., & Lewis, C. W. (Eds.). (2015). *Autoethnography as a lighthouse: Illuminating race, research, and the politics of schooling.* Charlotte, NC: Information Age.

Hanisch, C. (1969). *The personal is political.* Retrieved from http://www.carolhanisch.org/CHwritings/PIP.html

Harvey, L. (1990). *Critical social research.* New York: Routledge.

Hayano, D. M. (1979). Auto-ethnography: Paradigms, problems, and prospects. *Human Organization, 38*, 99–104.

Henning, T. (2012). Writing professor as adult learner: An autoethnography of online professional development. *Journal of Asynchronous Learning Networks, 16*(2), 9–26.

Hermann-Wilmarth, J. M., & Bills, P. (2010). Identity shifts: Queering teacher education research. *Teacher Educator, 45*, 257–272.

Herr, K. G., & Anderson, G. L. (2005). *The action research dissertation: A guide for students and faculty.* Thousand Oaks, CA: Sage.

Herrmann, A. F., & DiFate, K. (2014). The new ethnography: Goodall, Trujillo, and the necessity of storytelling. *Storytelling, Self, Society: An Interdisciplinary Journal of Storytelling Studies, 10*, 299–306.

Hill, D. C. (2014). A vulnerable disclosure: Dangerous negotiations of race and identity in the classroom. *Journal of Pedagogy, 5*(2), 161–181. doi:10.2478/jped-2014-0008

Holman Jones, S. (2005). Autoethnography: Making the personal political. In N. K. Denzin & Y. S. Lincoln (Eds.), *The SAGE handbook of qualitative research* (3rd ed., pp. 763–791). Thousand Oaks, CA: Sage.

Holman Jones, S., Adams, T. E., & Ellis, C. (Eds.). (2013a). *Handbook of autoethnography.* Walnut Creek, CA: Left Coast Press.

Holman Jones, S., Adams, T. E., & Ellis, C. (2013b). Introduction: Coming to know autoethnography as more than a method. In S. Holman Jones, T. E. Adams, & C. Ellis (Eds.), *Handbook of autoethnography* (pp. 17–48). Walnut Creek, CA: Left Coast Press.

Holt, N. L. (2003). Representation, legitimation, and autoethnography: An autoethnographic writing story. *International Journal of Qualitative Methods, 2*(1). Retrieved from http://www.ualberta.ca/~iiqm/backissues/2_1/pdf/holt.pdf

Hoodfar, H. (1992). Feminist anthropology and critical pedagogy: The anthropology of classrooms' excluded voices. *Canadian Journal of Education, 17*(3), 303–320.

Houston, J. (2007). Indigenous autoethnography: Formulating our knowledge our way. *Australian Journal of Indigenous Education, 36,* 45–50.

Hughes, S. A. (Ed.). (2005). *What we still don't know about teaching race: How to talk about it in the classroom.* Lewiston, NY: Edwin Mellen Press.

Hughes, S. A. (2006). *Black hands in the biscuits not in the classrooms:*

Unveiling hope in a struggle for Brown's promise. New York: Peter Lang.

Hughes, S. A. (2008a). Maggie and me: A Black professor and a White urban school teacher connect autoethnography to critical race pedagogy. *Educational Foundations, 22*(3/4), 73–95.

Hughes, S. A. (2008b). Teaching theory as "other" to White urban practitioners: Mining and priming Freirean critical pedagogy in resistant bodies. In J. Diem & R. J. Helfenbein (Eds.), *Unsettling beliefs: Teaching theory to teachers* (pp. 245–272). Greenwich, CT: Information Age.

Hughes, S. A. (2008c). Toward "good enough methods" for autoethnography in a graduate education course: Trying to resist the matrix with another promising red pill. *Educational Studies, 43*(2), 125–143.

Hughes, S. A. (2013, May 20). Troubling Jim Crow: A guest editorial. Dr. Christine Sleeter's Family and History Blog. Retrieved from http://historyandfamily.blogspot.com

Hughes, S. A., & Berry, T. R. (Eds.). (2012). *The evolving significance of race: Living, learning and teaching.* New York: Peter Lang.

Hughes, S. A., Morant, T., Lawrence, A., Jacobs, D., & Smith, D. (2010). *Exploring cases of critically reflexive action research: A review of autoethnography in education.* Retrieved from http://www.education.umd.edu/TLPL/aboutTLPL/faculty.html

Hughes, S. A., Pennington, J. L., & Makris, S. (2012). Translating autoethnography across the AERA standards: Toward understanding autoethnographic scholarship as

empirical research. *Educational Researcher, 41*(6), 209–219.

Hughes, S. A., & Willink, K. (2014). Engaging co-reflexive critical dialogues when entering and leaving the "field": Toward informing collaborative research methods at the color line and beyond. In J. Flores Carmona & K. V. Luschen (Eds.), *Crafting critical stories: Toward pedagogies and methodologies of collaboration, inclusion, and voice* (pp. 95–114). New York: Peter Lang.

Hughes, S. A., & Willink, K. (2015). Going native/being native: The promise of critical co-constructed autoethnography for checking "race," class, and gender in/out of the "field." In S. D. Hancock, A. Allen, & C. W. Lewis (Eds.), *Autoethnography as a lighthouse: Illuminating race, research, and the politics of schooling* (pp. 25–45). Charlotte, NC: Information Age.

Imenda, S. (2014). Is there a conceptual difference between theoretical and conceptual frameworks? *Journal of Social Sciences, 38*(2), 185–195.

Jackson, A. Y., & Mazzei, L. A. (Eds.). (2009). *Voice in qualitative inquiry: Challenging conventional, interpretive, and critical conceptions in qualitative research.* New York: Routledge.

Jacobs, W. R. (2005). *Speaking the lower frequencies: Students and media literacy.* Albany: State University of New York Press.

Jennings, M., & Lynn, M. (2005). The house that race built: Critical pedagogy, African-American education, and the re-conceptualization of a critical race pedagogy. *Educational Foundations, 19*(3/4), 15–32.

Johnson, C. (2010). Legitimizing. In J. M. Levine & M. A. Hogg (Eds.),

Encyclopedia of group processes and intergroup relations. Thousand Oaks, CA: Sage.

Jones, R. L. (2009). Coaching as caring (the smiling gallery): Accessing hidden knowledge. *Physical Education and Sport Pedagogy, 14*(4), 377–390.

Jupp, V. (1993). Unit 21: Critical analysis of text. In *Principles of social research* (Open University course DEH313). Milton Keynes: Open University.

Kahl, D. R. (2010). Connecting autoethnography with service learning: A critical communication pedagogical approach. *Communication Teacher, 24*(4), 221–228.

Kaufmann, J. (2011). An autoethnography of a hacceity: A-wo/man-to-eat-androgen. *Cultural Studies ↔ Critical Methodologies, 11*(1), 38–46.

Keenan, J., & Evans, A. (2014a). "I am a Starbucks worker . . . my life no longer belongs to me": The performance of estrangement as a learning tool. *Teaching in Higher Education, 19*(2),101–112

Keenan, J., & Evans, A. (2014b). The use of estrangement autoethnography in higher education teaching. *Worcester Journal of Learning and Teaching, 9*, 118–127.

Kenyatta, J. (1965). *Facing Mount Kenya.* New York: Random House. (Original work published 1938)

Khosravi, S. (2010). *"Illegal" traveller: An auto-ethnography of borders.* New York: Palgrave Macmillan.

Kincheloe, J. L., McLaren, P., & Steinberg, S. R. (2011). Critical pedagogy and qualitative research:

Moving to the bricolage. In N. K. Denzin & Y. S. Lincoln (Eds.), *The SAGE handbook of qualitative research* (4th ed., pp. 163–178). Thousand Oaks, CA: Sage.

Kochanek, K. D., Arias, E., & Anderson, R. N. (2013, July). *How did cause of death contribute to racial differences in life expectancy in the United States in 2010?* (NCHS Data Brief, No. 125). Hyattsville, MD: National Center for Health Statistics. Retrieved from http://www.cdc.gov/nchs/data/databriefs/db125.pdf

Kuhn, T. S. (1996). *The structure of scientific revolutions* (3rd ed.). Chicago: University of Chicago Press.

Ladson-Billings, G. (1995). Toward a theory of culturally relevant pedagogy. *American Educational Research Journal, 32*(3), 465–491.

Lakoff, G., & Johnson, M. (1980). *Metaphors we live by.* Chicago: University of Chicago Press.

Lather, P. (1991). *Getting smart: Feminist research and pedagogy with/in the postmodern.* New York: Routledge.

Laubscher, L., & Powell, S. (2003). Skinning the drum: Teaching about diversity as "other." *Harvard Educational Review, 73*(2), 203–224.

LeFrançois, B. A. (2013). The psychiatrization of our children, or, an autoethnographic narrative of perpetuating First Nations genocide through "benevolent" institutions. *Decolonization: Indigeneity, Education & Society, 2*(1), 108–123.

Lerum, K. (2001). Subjects of desire: Academic armor, intimate ethnography, and the production of critical knowledge. *Qualitative Inquiry, 7*(4), 466–483.

Lichtman, M. (2013). *Qualitative research in education: A user's guide* (3rd ed.). Thousand Oaks, CA: Sage.

Long, L. (2008). Narrative autoethnography and the promotion of spiritual well-being in teacher research and practice. *Pastoral Care in Education, 26*(3), 187–196.

Lorde, A. (1983). The master's tools will never dismantle the master's house. In C. Moraga & G. Anzaldúa (Eds.), *This bridge called my back: Writings by radical women of color* (pp. 94–101). New York: Kitchen Table Press.

Luttrell, W. (2000). "Good enough" methods for ethnographic research. *Harvard Educational Review, 70*(4), 499–523.

Madison, D. S. (2005). *Critical ethnography: Method, ethics, and performance.* Thousand Oaks, CA: Sage.

Madison, D. S. (2012). *Critical ethnography: Method, ethics, and performance* (2nd ed.). Thousand Oaks, CA: Sage.

Martin, A. J. (2011). The dramaturgy approach to education in nature: Reflections of a decade of International Vacation School Lipnice courses, Czech Republic, 1997–2007. *Journal of Adventure Education and Outdoor Learning, 11*(1), 67–82.

Martinez, E. (1993). Beyond Black/White: The racisms of our time. *Social Justice, 20*(1/2), 22–34.

Maxwell, J. A. (1992). Understanding and validity in qualitative research. *Harvard Educational Review, 62*(3), 279–301.

Maxwell, J. A. (2006). Literature reviews of, and for, educational research: A commentary on Boote and Beile's "Scholars before researchers." *Educational Researcher, 35*(9), 28–31.

Mayuzumi, K. (2009). Unfolding possibilities through a decolonizing project: Indigenous knowledges and rural Japanese women. *International Journal of Qualitative Studies in Education, 22*(5), 507–546.

McClellan, P. (2012). Race, gender, and leadership identity: An autoethnography of reconciliation. *International Journal of Qualitative Studies in Education, 25*(1), 89–100.

McIlveen, P. (2008). Autoethnography as a method for reflexive research and practice in vocational psychology. *Australian Journal of Career Development, 17*(2), 13–20.

McMahon, J., & Dinan-Thompson, M. (2011). "Body work—Regulation of a swimmer body": An autoethnography from an Australian elite swimmer. *Sport, Education and Society, 16*(1), 35–50.

Merriam, S. (2009). *Qualitative research: A guide to design and implementation.* San Francisco: Jossey-Bass.

Merwin, W. S. (1988). *The rain in the trees.* New York: Alfred A. Knopf.

Mezirow, J. (1997). Transformative learning: Theory to practice. *New Directions for Adult and Continuing Education, 74*, 5–12.

Milner, H. R. (2003). Reflection, racial competence, and critical pedagogy: How do we prepare pre-service teachers to pose tough questions? *Race Ethnicity and Education, 6*(2), 193–208.

Milner, H. R., & Tenore, F. B. (2010). Classroom management in diverse

classrooms. *Urban Education, 45*(5), 560–603.

Mitra, R. (2010). Doing ethnography, being an ethnographer: The autoethnographic research process and I. *Journal of Research Practice, 6*(1). Retrieved from http://jrp.icaap.org/index.php/jrp/article/view/184/182

Moreira, C. (2008). Life in so many acts. *Qualitative Inquiry, 14*(4), 590–612.

Muncey, T. (2010). *Creating autoethnographies.* Thousand Oaks, CA: Sage.

Murray, L., Pushor, D., & Renihan, P. (2012). Reflections on the ethics-approval process. *Qualitative Inquiry, 18*(1), 43–54.

Nethsinghe, R. (2012). The influence of informal music education in teacher formation: An autoethnography. *Qualitative Report, 17*(49), 1–16. Retrieved from http://www.nova.edu/ssss/QR/QR17/nethsinghe.pdf

Newton, J. (2006). Action research. In V. Jupp (Ed.), *The SAGE dictionary of social research methods.* Thousand Oaks, CA: Sage. doi:10.4135/9780857020116

Nice, P. (2007). Autoethnography exercise. In S. E. Spencer & K. Tuma (Eds.), *The guide to successful short-term programs* (2nd ed.). Washington, DC: NAFSA, Association of International Educators.

Noblit, G. W. (1999). *Particularities: Collected essays on ethnography and education.* New York: Peter Lang.

Noblit, G. W., Flores, S. Y., & Murillo, E. G., Jr. (2004). Postcritical ethnography: An introduction.

In G. W. Noblit, S. Y. Flores, & E. G. Murillo Jr. (Eds.), *Postcritical ethnography: Reinscribing critique* (pp. 1–52). Cresskill, NJ: Hampton Press.

Noblit, G. W., & Hare, R. D. (1988). *Meta-ethnography: Synthesizing qualitative studies.* Newbury Park, CA: Sage.

Noddings, N. (1992). *The challenge to care in schools: An alternative approach to education.* New York: Teachers College Press.

Norris, J., & Sawyer, R. D. (2012). Toward a dialogic methodology. In J. Norris, R. D. Sawyer, & D. E. Lund (Eds.), *Duoethnography: Dialogic methods for social health and educational research* (pp. 9–39). Walnut Creek, CA: Left Coast Press.

Nutbrown, C. (2011). A box of childhood: Small stories at the roots of a career. *International Journal of Early Years Education, 19*(3/4), 233–248.

Pacanowsky, M. (1988). Slouching towards Chicago. *Quarterly Journal of Speech, 74*, 453–467.

Patten, J. (2004). *Navigating unfamiliar territory: Autoethnography of a first-year elementary school principal* (Doctoral dissertation, University of Utah–Salt Lake City).

Pearson, H. (2010). Complicating intersectionality through the identities of a hard of hearing Korean adoptee: An autoethnography. *Equity & Excellence in Education, 43*(3), 341–356.

Pelias, R. J. (2011). *Leaning: A poetics of personal relations.* Walnut Creek, CA: Left Coast Press.

Pennington, J. L. (2004). *The colonization of literacy education: A* story of reading in one elementary school. New York: Peter Lang.

Pennington, J. L. (2006). The mission of disposition: A White teacher educator's press for race consciousness. *International Journal of Learning, 12*(4), 299–308.

Pennington, J. L. (2007). Silence in the classroom/whispers in the halls: Autoethnography as pedagogy in White pre-service teacher education. *Race Ethnicity and Education, 10*, 93–113.

Pennington, J. L., & Brock, C. H. (2012). Constructing critical autoethnographic self-studies with White educators. *International Journal of Qualitative Studies in Education, 25*(3), 225–250. doi:10.1080/09518398.2010.529843

Pennington, J. L., & Prater, K. (2014, March 11). The veil of professionalism: An autoethnographic critique of White positional identities in the figured worlds of White research performance. *Race Ethnicity and Education.* Published online. doi:10.1080/13613324.2014.885431

Peterson, A. L. (2015). A case for the use of autoethnography in nursing research. *Journal of Advanced Nursing, 71*(1), 226–233.

Peterson, E. (1990). Helping TAs teach holistically. *Anthropology and Education Quarterly, 12*, 179–185.

Piechowski, M. M. (1999). Overexcitabilities. In M. Runco & S. Pritzker (Eds.), *Encyclopedia of creativity* (Vol. 2, pp. 325–334). New York: Academic Press.

Piirto, J. (2010). 21 years with the Dabrowski theory: An autoethnography. *Advanced Development Journal, 12*, 68–90.

Pillow, W. (2003). Confession, catharsis, or cure? Rethinking the uses of reflexivity as methodological power in qualitative research. *International Journal of Qualitative Studies in Education, 16*(2), 175–196.

Poulos, C. (2008). Narrative conscience and the autoethnographic adventure: Probing memories, secrets, shadows, and possibilities. *Qualitative Inquiry, 14*(1), 46–66.

Poulos, C. (2010). Spirited accidents: An autoethnography of possibility. *Qualitative Inquiry, 16*(1), 49–56.

Preston, A. (2011). Using autoethnography to explore and critically reflect upon changing identity. *Adult Learner: The Irish Journal of Adult and Community Education, 2011*, 110–125.

Problematize. (n.d.). In *Merriam-Webster's online dictionary* (11th ed.). Retrieved from http://www.merriam-webster.com/dictionary/problematize

Quicke, J. (2010). Narrative strategies in educational research: Reflections on a critical autoethnography. *Educational Action Research, 18*(2), 239–254.

Raab, D. (2013). Transpersonal approaches to autoethnographic research and writing. *Qualitative Report, 18*, 1–18. Retrieved from http://www.nova.edu/ssss/QR/QR18/raab42.pdf

Rambo, C. (2005). Impressions of grandmother: An autoethnographic portrait. *Journal of Contemporary Ethnography, 34*(5), 560–585.

Reed-Danahay, D. (Ed.). (1997). *Auto/ethnography: Rewriting the self and the social.* Oxford: Berg.

Reta, M. (2010). Border crossing knowledge systems: A PNG teacher's autoethnography. *Australian Journal of Indigenous Education, 39*, 128–137.

Richardson, L. (2000). New writing practices in qualitative research. *Sociology of Sport Journal, 17*, 5–20.

Richardson, L. (2011). Hospice 101. *Qualitative Inquiry, 17*(2), 158–165.

Richardson, L., & St. Pierre, E. A. (2005). Writing: A method of inquiry. In N. K. Denzin & Y. S. Lincoln (Eds.), *The SAGE handbook of qualitative research* (3rd ed., pp. 959–978). Thousand Oaks, CA: Sage.

Rocco, T. S., & Plakhotnik, M. S. (2009). Literature reviews, conceptual frameworks, and theoretical frameworks: Terms, functions, and distinctions. *Human Resource Development Review, 8*(1), 120–130. doi:10.1177/1534484309332617

Rodriguez, D. (2009). The usual suspect: Negotiating White student resistance and teacher authority in a predominantly White classroom. *Cultural Studies ↔ Critical Methodologies, 9*(4), 483–508. doi:10.1177/1532708608321504

Rogers, D. L., Noblit, G. W., & Ferrell, P. (1990). Action research as an agent for developing teachers' communicative competence. *Theory Into Practice, 29*(3), 179–184.

Romo, J. J. (2005). Border pedagogy from the inside out: An autoethnographic study. *Journal of Latinos and Education, 4*(3), 193–210.

Ronai, C. R. (1992). The reflexive self through narrative: A night in the life of an erotic dancer/researcher. In C. Ellis & M. G. Flaherty (Eds.), *Investigating subjectivity: Research on lived experience* (pp. 102–124). Newbury Park, CA: Sage.

Ronai, C. R. (1995). Multiple reflections of child sex abuse. *Journal of Contemporary Ethnography, 23*(4), 395–426.

Ronai, C. R. (1996). My mother is mentally retarded. In C. Ellis & A. P. Bochner (Eds.), *Composing ethnography: Alternative forms of qualitative writing* (pp. 109–131). Walnut Creek, CA: AltaMira Press.

Rorty, R. (1982). *Consequences of pragmatism (essays 1972–1980).* Minneapolis: University of Minnesota Press.

Rossman, G. B., & Rallis, S. F. (2012). *Learning in the field: An introduction to qualitative research* (3rd ed.). Thousand Oaks, CA: Sage.

Sandelowski, M., & Barroso, J. (2003). Toward a metasynthesis of qualitative findings on motherhood in HIV-positive women. *Research in Nursing & Health, 26,* 153–170.

Sandelowski, M., Docherty, S., & Emden, C. (1997). Qualitative metasynthesis: Issues and techniques. *Research in Nursing & Health, 20*(4), 365–371.

Sander, P., & Williamson, S. (2010). Our teachers and what we have learnt from them. *Psychology Teaching Review, 16*(1), 61–69.

Schatz, S. J. (2014). *An instructional leader's account of change process in teaching and learning: In search of the meaning of change an autoethnographic study* (Doctoral dissertation proposal, Gallaudet University).

Schatzki, T. (2002). *The site of the social: A philosophical account of the constitution of social life and change.* University Park: Pennsylvania State University Press.

Schulz, S. (2007). Inside the contract zone: White teachers in the Anangu Pitjantjatjara Yankunytjatjara lands. *International Education Journal, 8*(2), 270–283.

Scott, J. C. (1990). *Domination and the arts of resistance: Hidden transcripts.* New Haven, CT: Yale University Press.

Sealy, P. A. (2012). Autoethnography: Reflective journaling and meditation to cope with life-threatening breast cancer. *Clinical Journal of Oncology Nursing, 16*(1), 38–41.

Shermak, S. (2011, December 3). *An autoethnography reading list.* Retrieved from http://www.uvic.ca/hsd/nursing/assets/docs/current/tutor/autoethno_readings.pdf

Short, N. P., Grant, A., & Clarke L. (2007). Living in the borderlands; writing in the margins: An autoethnographic tale. *Journal of Psychiatric and Mental Health Nursing, 14*(8), 771–782.

Shrewsbury, C. M. (1987). What is feminist pedagogy? *Women's Studies Quarterly, 15,* 6–14.

Shudak, N. J. (2015). Resonance-based inquiry: An epistemological approach to Indian studies. In P. Blessinger & J. M. Carfora (Eds.), *Inquiry-based learning for multidisciplinary programs: A conceptual and practical resource for educators* (pp. 83–99). Bingley, England: Emerald Group.

Sieber, J. E., & Tolich, M. B. (2013). *Planning ethically responsible research* (2nd ed.). Thousand Oaks, CA: Sage.

Slattery, P. (2001). The educational researcher as artist working within. *Qualitative Inquiry, 7*(3), 370–398.

Smagorinsky, P. (2011). Confessions of a mad professor: An autoethnographic consideration of neuroatypicality, extranormativity, and education. *Teachers College Record, 113*(8), 1700–1732.

Smith-Shank, D., & Keifer-Boyd, K. (2007). Editorial: Autoethnography and arts-based research. *Visual Culture & Gender, 2,* 1–5).

Sparkes, A. C. (2000). Autoethnography and narratives of self: Reflections on criteria in action. *Sociology of Sport Journal, 17,* 21–41.

Sparkes, A. C. (2007). Embodiment, academics, and the audit culture: A story seeking consideration. *Qualitative Research, 7*(4), 521–550.

Spenceley, L. (2011). Breaking the wall? Autoethnography and the transition from subject specialist to professional educator in FE. *Journal of Further and Higher Education, 35*(3), 409–421.

Spry, T. (2001). Performing autoethnography: An embodied methodological praxis. *Qualitative Inquiry, 7*(6), 706–732.

Starr, L. J. (2010). The use of autoethnography in educational research: Locating who we are in what we do. *Canadian Journal for New Scholars in Education, 3*(1), 1–9.

Stewart, J. (2013). Digital literacies assignment. Retrieved from http://www.scribd.com/doc/168753294/Literacy-Autoethnography

Sudnow, D. (1978). *Ways of the hand: The organization of improvised conduct.* Cambridge, MA: Harvard University Press.

Sumner, M. (2006). Epistemology. In V. Jupp (Ed.), *The SAGE dictionary* of social research methods. Thousand Oaks, CA: Sage. doi:10.4135/9780857020116

Sutton-Brown, C. (2010). Review of Carolyn Ellis' book, *Revision: Autoethnographic reflections of life and work. Qualitative Report, 15*(5), 1306–1308. Retrieved from http://www.nova.edu/ssss/QR/QR15–5/ellis.pdf

Swim, J. K., & Stangor, C. (Eds.). (1998). *Prejudice: The target's perspective.* San Diego, CA: Academic Press.

Sykes, B. E. (2014). Transformative autoethnography: An examination of cultural identity and its implications for learners. *Adult Learning, 25*(1), 3–10.

Tax, S. (1964). The uses of anthropology. In S. Tax (Ed.), *Horizons of anthropology* (pp. 248–258). Chicago: Aldine.

Taylor, J. Y., Mackin, M. A. L., & Oldenburg, A. M. (2008). Engaging racial autoethnography as a teaching tool for womanist inquiry. *Advances in Nursing Science, 31*(4), 342–355.

Tedlock, B. (1991). From participant observation to the observation of participation: The emergence of narrative ethnography. *Journal of Anthropological Research, 47*(1), 69–94.

Theoharis, G. (2007). Social justice educational leaders and resistance: Toward a theory of social justice leadership. *Educational Administration Quarterly, 43*(2), 221–258.

Theoharis, G. (2008). Woven in deeply: Identity and leadership of urban social justice principals. *Education and Urban Society, 41*(1), 3–25.

Thorne, S., Jensen, L., Kearney, M. H., Noblit, G., & Sandelowski, M.

(2004). Qualitative metasynthesis: Reflections on methodological orientation and ideological agenda. *Qualitative Health Research, 14*(10), 1342–1365.

Tillmann, L. M. (2009). Body and bulimia revisited: Reflections on "A secret life." *Journal of Applied Communication Research, 37*(1), 98–112.

Tobin, K. (2011). Global reproduction and transformation of science education. *Cultural Studies of Science Education, 6*(1), 127–142.

Tour, E. (2012). A cross-cultural journey into literacy research. *English Teaching: Practice and Critique, 11*(2), 70–80.

Toyosaki, S., & Pensoneau, S. (2005). Yaezakura—Interpersonal culture analysis. *International Journal of Communication, 15*(1/2), 51–88.

Toyosaki, S., Pensoneau-Conway, S. L.; Wendt, N. A., & Leathers, K. (2009). Community autoethnography: Compiling the personal and resituating Whiteness. *Cultural Studies ↔ Critical Methodologies, 9*(1), 56–83.

Tozer, S. E., Violas, P. C., & Senese, G. (2008). *School and society: Historical and contemporary perspectives* (6th ed.). Boston: McGraw-Hill.

Trahar, S. (2009). Beyond the story itself: Narrative inquiry and autoethnography in intercultural research in higher education. *Forum Qualitative Sozialforschung/Forum: Qualitative Social Research, 10*(1). Retrieved from http://nbn-resolving.de/urn:nbn:de:0114-fqs0901308

Tsumagari, M. (2010). The enduring effects of a United World College education as seen through a

graduate's eyes. *Journal of Research in International Education, 9*(3), 289–305.

Turner S. (1980). *Sociological explanation as translation.* New York: Cambridge University Press.

U.S. Department of Education. (2008). Coordinated Early Intervening Services (CEIS) guidance. Retrieved from http://www2.ed.gov/policy/speced/guid/idea/ceis_pg3.html

Valenzuela, A. (1999). *Subtractive schooling: U.S.-Mexican youth and the politics of caring.* Albany: State University of New York Press.

Vande Berg, L., & Trujillo, N. (2008). *Cancer and death: A love story in two voices.* Cresskill, NJ: Hampton Press.

Van Maanen, J. (1988). *Tales of the field: On writing ethnography.* Chicago: University of Chicago Press.

Walford, G. (2009). For ethnography. *Ethnography and Education, 4*(3), 271–282.

Wallace, A. F. C. (1965). Driving to work. In M. E. Spiro (Ed.), *Context and meaning in cultural anthropology: In honor of A. Irving Hallowell* (pp. 277–292). New York: Free Press.

Wallace, D. L. (2002). Out in the academy: Heterosexism, invisibility, and double consciousness. *College English, 65*(1), 53–66.

Warren, J. T., & Hytten, K. (2004). The faces of Whiteness: Pitfalls and the critical Democrat. *Communication Education, 53*(4), 321–339.

Weber, M. (1958). The three types of legitimate rule (H. Gerth, Trans.). *Berkeley Publications in Society and Institutions, 4*(1), 1–11.

Weil, S. (1998). Rhetorics and realities in public service organizations: Systemic practice and organizational learning as critically reflexive action research (CRAR). *Systemic Practice and Action Research, 11*(1), 37–62.

White, C. J., Sakiestewa, N., & Shelley, C. (1998). TRIO: The unwritten legacy. *Journal of Negro Education, 67*(4), 444–454.

Whyte, W. F. (1943). *Street corner society: The social structure of an Italian slum.* Chicago: University of Chicago Press.

Wildemeersch, D., & Jansen, T. (Eds.). (1992). *Adult education, experiential learning, and social change: The postmodern challenge.* The Hague: VUGA.

Wink, J. (2005). *Critical pedagogy: Notes from the real world* (3rd ed.). Boston: Pearson.

Winograd, K. (2002). The negotiative dimension of teaching: Teachers sharing power with the less powerful. *Teaching and Teacher Education, 18*(3), 343–362.

Winograd, K. (2003). The functions of teacher emotions: The good, the bad, and the ugly. *Teachers College Record, 105*(9), 1641–1673.

Woods, C. (2010). Reflections on pedagogy: A journey of collaboration. *Journal of Management Education, 35*(1), 154–167.

Wright, J. (2008). Searching one's self: The autoethnography of a nurse teacher. *Journal of Research in Nursing, 13*(4), 338–347.

Wright, S. (2006). Teacher as public art. *Journal of Aesthetic Education, 40*(2), 83–104.

Wyatt, J., Gale, K., Gannon, S., & Davies, B. (2011). *Deleuze and collaborative writing: An immanent plane of composition.* New York: Peter Lang.

Zurcher, L. A. (1983). *Social roles: Conformity, conflict, and creativity.* Beverly Hills, CA: Sage.

• Index •

Milton Keynes UK
Ingram Content Group UK Ltd.
UKHW051117231223
434801UK00019B/136

9 781483 306766